POLITICAL THEOLOGY

ALSO BY MICHAEL KIRWAN

Discovering Girard

POLITICAL THEOLOGY

An Introduction

Michael Kirwan

Fortress Press
Minneapolis

POLITICAL THEOLOGY
An Introduction
First Fortress Press edition 2009

Published in collaboration with Darton, Longman, and Todd. Copyright

Cover image: William Blake (1757-1827), "The Angel Michael Binding
Satan" (`He Cast him into the Bottomless Pit, and Shut him up') c.1805
(w/c, ink & graphite on paper). Fogg Art Museum, Harvard University,
gift of W. A. White. The Bridgeman Art Library.

Cover design: Judy Linard

Library of Congress Cataloging-in-Publication data available

ISBN 978- 0-8006-6367-4
Manufactured in Great Britain

13 12 11 10 09 1 2 3 4 5 6 7 8 9 10

CONTENTS

Part 4: The Gift

PREFACE

Man must & will have some religion; if he has not the
Religion of Jesus, he will have the Religion of Satan, &
will erect the Synagogue of Satan, calling the Prince of this
world, God; and destroying all who do not worship Satan
under the name of God.

William Blake, *Jerusalem*, ch. 3: 'To the Deists'

I am minding my own business, travelling on the London
Underground. I pick up a copy of the free newspaper, the *Metro*,
which features a '60 second interview' with a well-known film
actor, Jason Isaacs. He begins by telling us of his involvement
with the Holocaust commemoration in Liverpool (January
2008); how remembrance is important, not least in the face of
Holocaust deniers and the like. At the end of the interview, he is
asked what he would do if he ruled the world. His answer?
First, get everyone using Macintosh computers. Then 'abolish
religion'.

Where to begin? As I am typing this on an iMac I suppose I
am happy enough with the first sentiment. It is the casual illogi-
cality of the second that causes dismay and needs attention.
What I would call the John Lennon syndrome – 'and no religion
too' – has become such a commonplace that it is hardly worth
noting: a throwaway comment in a free commuter newspaper.
And it certainly blends into the current intellectual and cultural
climate, shaped not least by the prodigious output from writers
who have been dubbed the 'new atheists'.[1]

A vast, apparently unbridgeable gulf seems to be opening up
between belief and unbelief, and it is not pretty. The splenetic

tenor of onslaughts such as *The God Delusion* by Dawkins and *God Is Not Great* (Hitchens) cannot, surely, be at the service of clear-sighted thinking, any more than religious belief is served by those who choose to respond in acerbic kind. The Germans have words for these things: the term *Kulturkampf*, or 'culture struggle', describes the conflict between Chancellor Otto von Bismarck and the Roman Catholic Church in Germany between 1871 and 1878 (for the record, Bismarck's anticlerical policies largely failed). What we seem to have, in Britain and the USA, in the first decade of the twenty-first century, is another bitter *Kulturkampf*, this time between secular science and religious belief: in fact the term 'culture war' has already been in used in recent decades in the United States to describe the battle between secular liberals and religious social conservatives.

The present book is not specifically intended as a contribution to this current debate, though it is not easy to ignore the fireworks. My modest aim is to provide an introduction – for students of theology and religious studies, but also for a more general discerning readership – to the fascinating and contentious discipline of 'political theology'. No subject is more *aktuell*, again as the Germans say: more 'relevant'. Yet genuinely useful resources for thinking sensibly about the relation between religion and politics are surprisingly scarce. I will go further, and suggest that much of the literature is useless, because it starts with an inadequate and unhelpful understanding of religion. In saying this I have no wish to take on Dawkins, Hitchens, or even Jason Isaacs, but in the case of the latter simply to point out the glaring discrepancy of commemorating the Holocaust, while at the same time wishing to exterminate religion.

To put this very simply, if the term 'religion' refers to a set of (probably mistaken) ideas, such as believing in Santa Claus or the tooth fairy, then desiring its abolition makes perfect sense. If the term 'religion' refers to an unhealthy but contingent socio-economic or medical condition, like urban deprivation or breast cancer, then, once again, desiring its abolition makes perfect sense. If, however, the word 'religion' is held to refer to complexes of belief, worship and action which are deeply embedded in practices and traditions, and which are felt to be crucial to both individual and communal self-understanding and identity, then 'abolishing religion' is more like getting rid of sexuality or imagination. And it is very hard to see how this end can be achieved without 'abolishing' religious believers.

Here is the rub: believers themselves, of whatever epoch or faith tradition, cannot but regard themselves in this third category. Some, perhaps many people, may fervently wish that this was not the case: but to raise the question of religion in any other way, to simply *not see* that there is a chilling disconnect between wishing to commemorate the Holocaust and wanting rid of religion, is to embark on a strategy that is not only offensive but irresponsible. And too many of the current polemicists generate more heat than light because they work with one or both of the dubious premises: religion as a set of ideas, or religion as an external state of affairs, which can be surgically separated from the religious person like a dangerous tumour.

This medical image occurs in one of the more thoughtful, if still problematic analyses, Mark Lilla's *The Stillborn God*.[2] Lilla defines 'political theology' as 'discourse about political authority based on a revealed divine nexus', which he regards as a malignant growth in the body politic. In seventeenth-century Western Europe this growth required drastic surgery, what Lilla calls the 'Great Separation'. He regards Thomas Hobbes's *Leviathan* (1651) as the first attempt at a formal disentanglement of theological ideas from political concerns. A tradition of political philosophy that Lilla locates in the 'children of Hobbes' (John Locke and David Hume) developed and consolidated this innovative separation. Unfortunately, another line of thinkers, the 'children of Rousseau', meaning Immanuel Kant and G. W. F. Hegel, did not perform the necessary operation with the same rigour. Though these thinkers agreed in principle with the Great Separation, the cancer of political theology remained latent in their work – only to break out as the terrible tumours of twentieth-century messianic politics, Hitlerism and Stalinist Marxism.

It is curious how persistently the challenge of the 'theologico-political' (to use one of the jargon phrases) has been presented in binary, oppositional terms. A famous formulation by Pope Gelasius in the fifth century declares: 'two there are, by which this world is governed'. Yes, but two *what*? Two Cities (Augustine)? Two Swords (medieval political theology)? The King's 'Two Bodies' (ditto)? Two Kingdoms (Luther)? Church and State? Jesus or Satan (Blake)? Christ or Caesar – or Hitler, for that matter? For Lilla, it is a straight choice: political theology or political philosophy.

Is he right? Wikipedia thinks not, since its entry on 'political theology' intriguingly describes 'a branch of both political philosophy and theology that investigates the ways in which theological concepts or ways of thinking underlie political, social, economic and cultural discourses'. If this is so, we have a curious hybrid discipline, one which, it is hoped, can stimulate believer and non-believer alike to the kind of reconsideration which Mark Lilla calls for, when he says we need to 'revisit the tension between political theology and modern political philosophy' (9) – even if we may have reservations about the way he has set up the discussion. Suffice to note here that the principal weakness of *The Stillborn God* has to be the one mentioned above: the ingrained habit of Lilla, who is after all a historian of ideas, to see 'religion', and therefore political theology, as almost exclusively an intellectual concern. As he admits himself, understanding political theology is hard for us, because we are on the 'other shore' of the Great Separation. Lilla's contribution to the *Kulturkampf* runs as follows:

> The story reconstructed here should remind us that the actual choice contemporary societies face is not between past and present, or between the west and 'the rest.' It is between two grand traditions of thought, two ways of envisaging the human condition. We must be clear about those alternatives, choose between them, and live with the consequences of our choice. That is the human condition.
>
> (Lilla, 2007:13)

Contemporary political theologians will dispute Lilla's account, as we shall see: for example, William T. Cavanaugh reads differently the history that preceded the Great Separation. To speak of the horrendous conflicts between 1550 and 1648 as 'Wars of Religion' is an anachronism, says Cavanaugh, one which serves to bolster a useful myth about the nation state as our 'saviour' from religious fanaticism. If Cavanaugh is correct, then Lilla's ineluctable 'choice' between political theology and political philosophy is false. Yet another perspective, set out in John Gray's *Black Mass*,[3] draws a line of continuity (not rupture) between the apocalyptic dimensions of historical Christianity and those modern political projects that have aimed at radical, and inevitably violent, transformations of the human. Gray lists the French Revolution; Nazism; Soviet and Maoist communism; and most recently the attempt, in the name of American 'exceptionalism', to impose democracy in Iraq:

> Modern politics is a chapter in the history of religion. ... The greatest of the revolutionary upheavals that have shaped so much of the history of the last two centuries were episodes in the history of faith – moments in the long dissolution of Christianity and the rise of modern political religion. The world in which we find ourselves at the start of the new millennium is littered with the debris of utopian projects, which though they were framed in secular terms that denied the truth of religion were in fact vehicles for religious myths. (Gray, 2007:1)

Gray insists that 'the political violence of the modern West can only be understood as an eschatological phenomenon'; that the dominant (though not exclusive) strands of Western thought have looked to alter the very nature of human life, an aspiration which has always tended to violence (35). He offers a devastating critique of the 'faith-based' ideology that led the USA and Britain into the disastrous war in Iraq, but there is much else of importance in this short book, not least a withering counterblast to the 'new atheists'. The militant Darwinism of Richard Dawkins and Daniel Dennett is a pale imitation of the relatively nuanced critiques of Marx and the French Positivists: '[c]ontemporary atheism is a Christian heresy that differs from earlier heresies chiefly in its intellectual crudity' (189). One consequence of this view is the need to re-think the secularist agenda:

> Those who demand that religion be exorcized from politics

think this can be achieved by excluding traditional faiths from public institutions; but secular creeds are formed from religious concepts, and suppressing religion does not mean it ceases to control thinking and behaviour. Like repressed sexual desire, faith returns, often in grotesque forms, to govern the lives of those who deny it. ... Human beings will no more cease to be religious than they will stop being sexual, playful or violent. If religion is a primary human need it should not be suppressed or relegated to a netherworld of private life. It ought to be fully integrated into the public realm, but that does not mean establishing any one religion as public doctrine. (190, 209)

Gray reminds us that 'at its best religion has been an attempt to deal with mystery rather than the hope that mystery will be unveiled'. But it is precisely this reticence, this 'civilising perception', which has been lost in the clash of fundamentalisms, leaving little prospect of a future that is not shaped by violent faith (210).

In all of this it is hard not to be reminded of the theology of the *wager*. Blaise Pascal famously posed the question of belief in these terms: he argued that theism is the rationally correct option for every individual, since betting my life on the assumption that there is no God cannot benefit me if I 'win', and could be disastrous if I 'lose'. Not everyone finds this argument convincing! As we shall see, contemporary Christian political and liberation theologians posit another argument from belief, this time a *mutual wager* between the poor and God. The poor trust in God as their champion, the one who will liberate them from their suffering, while God 'wagers' on humanity, by daring to enter, repeatedly, into political partnership (covenant) with human beings, and by handing over his Son (Bell, 2001; Kirwan, 2006).

Still we await the outcome of these wagers, the first especially. Are the 'losers' of history, all those mutilated and forgotten victims, really losers – or will God vindicate them, as wonderfully and spectacularly as he vindicated his dead Son?

But it is not just the religious believer whose life is at hazard. For John Gray, the future of humanity depends on the choice of non-utopian over utopian forms of politics. For Mark Lilla, we are faced with the claims of political philosophy and political theology: '[w]e must be clear about those alternatives, choose between them, and live with the consequences of our choice'. It seems we have no option but to stake our claim: on God, on humanity, on some understanding of divine and human inter-action. The parameters of Enlightenment hope itself, as set out by Immanuel Kant, are strictly demarcated by Kant's own version of the 'divine wager', to which he gave the name 'postu-lates of practical reason'. Kant claimed that to live ethically – and by extension politically – we must either trust in God, or run the risk of a terrible moral despair; like the liberation and political theologians who came after him, Kant turned his eyes to the biblical figure of Job.[4]

The twentieth-century heirs of Kant's Enlightenment, writing 'in dark times', found themselves suspended over the same abyss: our noble aspirations for conviviality, drowned out in a 'land of screams'. For Lilla and Gray it is the temptation of 'utopian' political religion, recurrent like a cancer, which leads to Auschwitz. Contemporary political theologians like Jürgen Moltmann and Johann Baptist Metz argue the opposite: the Nazi catastrophe, above all, demonstrates the absolute indispensability of religious hope.

The consequences of getting the wager 'wrong' will be all too apparent – in this world, not the 'next'. Can a *polis* exist, be sustained, without God? The advocates of the Great Separation say that it can and must: we must rely on ourselves alone. But how, then, does such a polity and its leaders avoid placing themselves on the Messiah's throne – how do we prevent an Enlightenment which 'radiates disaster triumphant'?

My ambition is for this book to be a straightforward, largely unpolemical introduction to this fascinating and sometimes bewildering area of theology. To this extent the treatment is mainly expository, and I do my best to avoid technical theo-logical terms. This book was written during a sabbatical term in the summer and autumn of 2007, which enabled me to spend time with my brother Jesuits in Guyana, South America, and with the seminarians and staff at the regional seminary of St John Vianney and the Ugandan Martyrs, Trinidad. My thanks to all, for their wonderful hospitality and superb witness.

And my sincerest gratitude goes once again to the students and colleagues of Heythrop College, London, who have helped me over the years with their insights and suggestions; above all to the undergraduates and postgraduate classes of 2006–7, whose insights I enlisted specially when planning this work (a special thanks, with much love, to Sarz and Muttley). My apologies to those students – few, I hope – who were not able to follow my ramblings, and my regrets to all, because we did not move closer to the abyss, nor were our memories dangerous enough.

MICHAEL KIRWAN
Trinidad and London

Part 1

THE PARAMETERS

Chapter 1

WHAT IS POLITICAL THEOLOGY?

Mark Lilla in *The Stillborn God* has put a health warning on 'political theology'. He sees it as a poisonous hangover from pre-modernity, and insists that we should turn instead to its alternative, 'political philosophy', for articulating our vision of conviviality. The reader has been warned.

As soon becomes apparent, however, there are plenty of other answers to the question, 'what is political theology?' A British theologian, Charles Davis, put the matter trenchantly:

> Nothing could be more absurdly untrue to Christian history than the contention that the Christian religion as embodied institutionally in the Church is apolitical or above politics … The Christian religion has always been thoroughly political, with social and political action the major vehicle of the distinctively Christian religious experience. Briefly, Christians find God in their neighbour rather than in their consciousness or in the cosmos. (Davis, 1994:58)

But how do we move from this kind of principled conviction to specific decisions and commitments – what we normally understand by the word 'politics'? Another British theologian Nicholas Lash reminds us that '[t]he gospel does not itself provide the program for the politics that it stimulates and engenders', giving us a clue to why this peculiar hybrid discipline called 'political theology' generates so much anguish. Christians who take their faith seriously know that it has political implications – that the gospel calls us to imagine and work for a transformed world. However – here is the anguish – the Bible leaves no blueprint or manifesto for this transformation; only lots of options (some more feasible than others) about what kind of society Christians should be struggling for, and by what means. So perhaps political theology is meant to bridge this gap, between gospel inspiration and specific political commitments. Yet another theologian, Oliver O'Donovan, would seem to agree:

> The passage from what God said to Abraham to what we are now to do about Iraq, is one which the intuition of faith may accomplish in a moment, and a preacher's exhortation in twenty minutes. An intellectual account of it, however, can be the work of decades! (O'Donovan, 1996:ix)

Three Versions of Political Theology (Scott and Cavanaugh)

'Political theology', then, consists of prolonged and painstaking explication of insights which, in themselves, may seem obvious. What else might it involve? We have seen that one intriguing description holds political theology to be 'a branch of both political philosophy and theology', and we will need to keep this in mind. A good place to begin is the splendid and yet in some ways frustrating *Blackwell Companion to Political Theology*[1], a collection of thirty-five essays on a considerable range of political theological themes edited by Peter Scott and the North American theologian William T. Cavanaugh. The frustration lies in the editors' decision, for reasons of space, to shy away from any programmatic essay that would tell us what political theology is. The *Companion*'s introduction, though only five pages long, is suggestive. First, the editors assert the discrediting of Fukuyama's thesis of the 'end of history' as a result of the 1989 triumph of liberal capitalist democracy. Osama bin Laden has ensured that 'history has not finished with us yet'! The editors have an expansive understanding of 'political theology':

> Theology is broadly understood as discourse about God, and human persons as they relate to God. The political is

broadly understood as the use of structural power to organize a society or community of people ... Political theology is, then, the analysis and criticism of political arrangements (including cultural-psychological, social and economic aspects) from the perspective of differing interpretations of God's way with the world.

(Scott and Cavanaugh, eds, 2004:1)

Cavanaugh and Scott explore three different conceptions of the task of political theology. First, *politics is seen as a 'given', with its own secular autonomy.* 'Politics and theology are therefore two essentially distinct activities ... the task of political theology might be to relate religious belief to larger societal issues while not confusing the proper autonomy of each.' Secondly, *theology is critical reflection on the political. Theology is related as superstructure to the materialist politico-economic base, and therefore reflects and reinforces just or unjust political arrangements.* The task of political theology might then be 'to expose the ways in which theological discourse reproduces inequalities of class, gender and race' and to seek to reconstruct theology to serve the cause of justice. Thirdly, *theology and politics are essentially similar activities: both are constituted in the production of metaphysical images around which communities are organised.* All politics has theology embedded in it, and particular forms of organisation are implicit in doctrines of, for example, the Trinity, the church, eschatology. There is no essential separation of material base and cultural superstructure. The task then might be one of 'exposing the false theologies underlying supposedly "secular" politics and promoting the true politics implicit in a true theology'. (2)

The first of these three positions sounds familiar from Christ's injunction to 'give unto Caesar'. These words of Jesus are usually read to mean that the secular power has legitimate claims that must be recognised alongside the religious claims of the Church. Each has their 'proper autonomy'; if this autonomy is infringed then both sides suffer.[2] One small problem here is that this is precisely what the command of Jesus does not and cannot mean! Such a division of sacred and secular would have

been inconceivable in his time and culture, and certainly incompatible with the Kingdom that Jesus was proclaiming. If
Charles Davis is correct, that 'Christianity has always been
thoroughly political', then this *cordon sanitaire* (O'Donovan) is
a distortion of the Gospel. Whether such a separation is even
coherent is another matter; theologians have become increasingly vocal about its inadequacy. To mention two: Johann
Baptist Metz, one of the key figures in European political
theology, has consistently protested against the 'privatised' or
'bourgeois' version of European Christianity, which has pre-
vailed in the modern period, but at an unacceptably high cost:
the negation of any kind of prophetic (what Metz calls 'messianic') power to challenge and oppose injustice. This emasculation
of Christianity is evidenced for Metz in a triple difficulty for
contemporary Christianity: firstly, its domestication by the
Enlightenment; secondly, the inability of theology to respond
adequately to the questions posed by the Holocaust; thirdly, the
plight of the suffering in the Third World.

Cavanaugh is a more recent critic of the modern insistence on
keeping religion in 'quarantine'. He stresses that the implicit
judgement of this insistence on separation – that religion must
be kept private because it leads to violence, while the power of
secular authorities is justified because it is directed towards the
maintenance of peace and harmony – is false. The alleged
volatility of religious belief is a highly serviceable myth, which
the secular powers can use to reinforce the legitimacy of their
own violence. He argues this through a re-reading of the so-
called 'Wars of Religion': this term is anachronistic, he maintains, because on closer inspection these conflicts are more
truthfully described as the birth-pangs of the modern state, out
of which our contemporary notion of 'religion' comes into
being, rather than wars fought on denominational lines
(Cavanaugh, 1995; see discussion in chapter 5). As we have
already seen, Cavanaugh's view conflicts with that of Mark
Lilla, champion of modernity's Great Separation.

What about the second approach suggested by Scott and
Cavanaugh, theology as *critical reflection on the political?* This
is inspired by the critique of religion that we associate with
Ludwig Feuerbach and Karl Marx: here, religion is part of the

cultural 'superstructure' that mirrors the socio-economic base. As such, the religious beliefs of the rich and powerful will serve to maintain their interests, by masking the conditions of alienation and injustice on which their privilege rests. As the notorious verse from *All Things Bright and Beautiful* puts it:

> The rich man in his castle,
> the poor man at his gate,
> he made them, high or lowly,
> and ordered their estate.[3]

On this account, religion functions as an 'opiate' for the victims of oppression, offering some degree of anaesthetic comfort, but without possibility of emancipation. Such a bleak view of religion seems to be an unpromising basis for political theology – except that theologians would want to draw attention to the positive elements within biblical and church traditions. The strands of subversion and prophecy within Israel's political traditions, as well as the assertion of God's preferential option for the poor, can offer as incisive a critique as Marxist analysis. Theologians within this tradition, such as Metz and Jürgen Moltmann, have sought to engage in dialogue with secular theorists of the left (notably the critical theorists associated with the so-called Frankfurt School). They accept the validity of the claim that religion can be alienating and oppressive, but insist that it need not be. They go further in claiming that a purely secular emancipation is impossible, and that without recognition of the religious dimension the Enlightenment dream will forever end in disappointment, even disaster. These claims derive from some critical theorists themselves, such as Ernst Bloch, who theorised about hope, and Walter Benjamin, whose thought is laced with Jewish messianic speculations.

The dialogue between theology and the different strands of Critical Theory has given shape to post-war European political theology. The 'unmasking' of alienating forms of religious belief is crucial to the method of the theologians of liberation in Latin America, and that of Johann Baptist Metz, who criticised 'bourgeois' religion, as we have seen. The most important recent conversation partner for the Europeans has been Jürgen

Habermas, who has increasingly come to acknowledge the religious implications which others see in his work. As the title of
Habermas' important book, *Knowledge and Human Interest*
implies, one question is key: *cui bono*?: 'for whose benefit'?
Who *profits* from theology being done this way rather than that,
in whose interest is it to make such and such a claim about God?
But the theologians, of course, do not end with this critique, as
a secular critic would; rather it is the prelude to a more positive
expression of liberative or 'messianic' faith.

The third approach to political theology suggested by Scott
and Cavanaugh is the one best suited to a post-Marxist context,
and it is the one they themselves would seem to espouse:

> Theology and Politics are essentially similar activities:
> both are constituted in the production of metaphysical
> images around which communities are organised. All poli-
> tics has theology embedded in it, and particular forms of
> organization are implicit in doctrines of e.g. the Trinity, the
> church, eschatology. There is no essential separation of
> material base and cultural superstructure. The task then
> might be one of 'exposing the false theologies underlying
> supposedly "secular" politics and promoting the true
> politics implicit in a true theology'. (2)

Hence Cavanaugh's analysis of the modern State as a 'rival' to
the true political community, the Church, graphically expressed
in his contrast in *Torture and Eucharist* (1998) of the Chilean
state's 'anti-liturgy' of torture and the Church's practice of
Eucharist. Cavanaugh draws our attention to the curious fact of
the State's transcendent hold on us, even to the point at which
we are willing to kill and die for it. And just as apparently
secular realities (monarchs and presidents, flags and constitu-
tions) are in fact imbued with transcendence, so religious
concepts, doctrines and institutions, such as God and Church,
have political implications.

So, thanks to Scott and Cavanaugh, we have three possible
ways of understanding political theology. Political theology is
concerned with:

- the maintenance of a *cordon sanitaire* between politics and religion;
- or with reflection on unjust and alienating political structures;
- or with the production of metaphysical images around which communities are organised.

Divine and Political Authority (O'Donovan)

Our second resource for delineating political theology is *The Desire of the Nations,*[4] in which Oliver O'Donovan posits an 'analogy (grounded in reality)' between the political vocabulary of salvation which we find in the Bible, and secular use of these same political terms, 'between the acts of God and human acts, both of them taking place within the one public history which is the theatre of God's saving purposes and mankind's social undertakings' (1996:2). O'Donovan calls for an *expansion* of the horizon of commonplace politics, opening it up to the activity of God. Earthly events of liberation provide us with partial indications of what God is doing in history, but 'theology needs more than scattered political images; it needs a full political conceptuality'.

Such a strategy will also seek to enable political theology to break out of the quarantine that has in our time kept religious and political discourses distinct from one another, so as to avoid mutual contamination. By contrast, 'theology is political simply by responding to the dynamics of its own proper themes': Christ, salvation, church, Trinity. We see how this coheres with the scheme of Scott and Cavanaugh, reinforcing the inadequacy of the first of their three models, and affirming the value of the third. This is a matter of allowing theology to be true to its task: 'theology must be political if it is to be evangelical' (3). O'Donovan indicates how political theology of the Southern school (which includes, but is broader than, South American liberation theology) has proved its seriousness by bringing neglected theological themes back into circulation. However, while the Southern school is barely thirty years old, O'Donovan wants to investigate a much longer history of political theology. He discerns a 'High Tradition' which he dates roughly speaking from 1100 to 1650: at the beginning, the conflicts between

papacy and secular authority occasioned by the reforms of Pope
Gregory the Great, at the other end, the early Enlightenment
seeing the development of a political theory (Moral Science)
which is independent of theology. For the most part, contemporary political theology is ignorant of this tradition – hence
O'Donovan's desire to retrieve it.

O'Donovan charges contemporary political theologians with
a twofold neglect: as well as this High Tradition, we need to
recover the biblical roots of political authority, specifically conveyed in the proclamation *Yahweh malek*, 'God rules'. It is from
this acknowledgement that both the Christian political vocation
and secular political systems are 'authorised'. O'Donovan also
calls for more nuanced attention to the positive ways in which
'Christendom' has nurtured the early liberal traditions of politics
and the secular.

We have seen that O'Donovan challenges the quarantining of
religion and politics from each other. This separation, he suggests, arises from two opposed suspicions, a fear of contamination which works both ways. On the one hand, Augustine and
Kant each assert that a 'political theology' can only be a corruption of theology (or morality) by something baser, namely
politics. On the other hand, there is a widespread fear that the
rightful autonomy of politics is under threat by religious revelation. 'In the popular imagination of late-modern liberalism these
twin suspicions have broadened and fused together' and this
division has become internalised: 'Each of us has a mind parti-
tioned by a frontier, and accepts responsibility for policing it'
(8–9).

Once again he commends the Southern school's attempts to
challenge this late-modern liberal consensus regarding the separation of politics and theology. What is often lacking from their
approaches, however, is an account of theological *authority*. The
only reason, ultimately, for taking up the cause of the poor is
because it is a theologically given mandate; the alternative is to
be caught in a never-ending game, of 'allegations of sectional
interest volleyed to and fro across the net, never to be ruled out
of court, never to land beyond reach of return'. This highlights
the limitation of criticism as a 'total' stance, what is sometimes
referred to as the 'hermeneutic of suspicion': 'Totalised

criticism is the modern form of intellectual innocence ... by elevating suspicion to the dignity of a philosophical principle, it destroys trust and makes it impossible to learn' (11). God commissions his prophets, but they cannot speak only of the errors of false prophets: they are also to speak positively, of God's purposes of renewal and mercy towards weak and fragmentary societies like the people of Israel.

Public Religions in a Post-Secular World

A third source for reviewing the 'theologico-political', though a more challenging one than the first two, is a collection of essays entitled *Political Theologies*.[5] In his long Introduction to this volume, Hent de Vries offers the kind of programmatic essay that Scott and Cavanaugh shy away from in the *Blackwell Companion*. His concern is to re-open the enquiry concerning religion's engagement with the political (*le politique*) as well as with politics (*la politique*) under the conditions of post-secularity. In particular, the globalisation of markets and information media has had a 'post-Westphalian effect' of 'loosening or largely suspending the link that once tied theological-political authority to a social body determined by a certain geographic territory and national sovereignty'.[6] This raises the possibility or desirability of a disembodied (virtual, transcendental) substitute for the 'theologico-political body'. De Vries recognises that 'religions contain both an integrative and a potentially disintegrating or even violent aspect of modern societies'; this ambivalence needs to be factored into any account of religion's relationship to the political, a relationship 'which is no longer obvious, let alone direct'. Our current problems are more elusive and delocalised than those of the past, placing great demand on our theoretical skill, and leaving us in need of new concepts and new research practices. 'No unified theory is currently available to hold these trends together in a compelling explanatory account or historical narrative' (8), hence the insistence on 'political theologies' as a plural noun.

In attempting to define 'political theologies' (pp. 25 ff) de Vries begins with Jan Assmann's definition of 'the ever-changing relationships between political community and religious order, in short, between power [or authority: *Herrschaft*] and salvation [*Heil*]'. He then traces the actual term 'political theology' through a number of authors,[7] though rather mysteriously he makes no reference to the post-war political theology of Metz and others, whom we cited above.

But throughout these traditions, one question remains (de Vries, 2006:26, citing Lagrée). How are we to understand the co-ordination of these two adjectives, *political* and *theological*:

• as juxtaposition;
• strict separation;
• subordination of the political to the theological;
• subordination of the theological to the political;
• or interdependence?

The questions opened up by de Vries are a prelude to a daunting collection of thirty-four essays, in four sections: 'What are Political Theologies?'; 'Beyond Tolerance: Pluralism and Agonistic Reason'; 'Democratic Republicanism, Secularism and Beyond'; and 'Opening Societies and the Rights of the Human'. This includes classic texts by Jürgen Habermas and Pope Benedict XVI, Jean-Luc Nancy, Claude Lefort and Judith Butler. Hardly a book for beginners, *Political Theologies* is nevertheless an important resource, both for the breadth of its scholarship and its attempt (implied in the section titles) to look 'Before, Around, and Beyond the Theologico-Political'. This volume augments the interest of de Vries in previous writings; arguing, for example in *Minimal Theologies*, for the continued and extraordinary relevance of theology to contemporary thought: 'I would suggest that we could conceive of philosophical theology as the touchstone and guardian of universality, truth, veracity, intersubjective validity, even authentic expressivity in all matters concerning (the study of) religion and, perhaps, not religion alone.'[8]

An even more impenetrable collection of essays appeared in 2005 as *Theology and the Political: the New Debate*,[9] and is certainly not for faint hearts. The Introduction from Rowan Williams sets out what he sees as the common conviction of these essays, that:

the fundamental requirement of a politics worth the name is that we have an account of human action that decisively marks its distance from assumptions about action as the successful assertion of will. If there is no hinterland to human acting except the contest of private and momentary desire, meaningful action is successful action, an event in which a particular will has imprinted its agenda on the 'external' world. Or, in plainer terms, meaning is power; Thrasymachus in the *Republic* was right, and any discourse of justice is illusory. (Creston Davis et al, eds, 2005:1)

In place of the 'barbarism' that is being rejected here – namely, the notion of meaningful action in terms of assertion, which raises 'the spectre of the purest fascism' – Rowan Williams sees these essays appealing to an understanding of action as *testimony*. For the Christian, the category of martyrdom is the most distinctive instance of this, rooted in the self-exposure of Jesus Christ to death 'at the hands of political and religious meaning makers'. So a dialogue between politics and theology opens up, with theology understood as 'the discipline that follows what is claimed as the supreme act of testimony, and thus the supremely generative and revisionary act of all human history: the Cross for Christians, the gift of Torah and communal identity for Judaism' (3). This is all well and good, though it is not clear exactly how this wide range of interdisciplinary contributions (Terry Eagleton, Zizek, Milbank, Daniel Bell Jr., Catherine Pickstock, Antonio Negri and others) constitutes a 'new debate'; while the horrendous opacity of too many of these essays renders the category of 'testimony' highly optimistic.

Setting the Stage: the Parameters, the History, the Crisis, the Gift

I attempt in the present book to provide an introductory overview of this vibrant and important area of Christian theological reflection, not least as it is being delineated in the three examples cited above: Scott/Cavanaugh, O'Donovan and de Vries/Sullivan, as well as other commentators. I will introduce themes and authors who are less familiar to a general English readership: for this reason, I have for the most part steered clear of discussing Latin American Liberation Theology, which continues to inspire a wealth of literature and interest, despite its alleged demise, and whose significance as a 'cousin' of European political theology has been noted (see Petrella, 2006). There is a similar lack of attention to other theologies which could be gathered under the rubric 'political', such as feminist/womanist, black, queer, and so on, while the challenges posed by Islamic political theology will be addressed only indirectly.

The book is divided into four sections. The first two chapters after this introduction attempt to set out the parameters for political theology. This involves working with a rough and ready distinction in chapter 2 between 'political theology' and 'political mythology', which leads us to an understanding of politics as '*katēchon*', or 'Leviathan', or restraining force. In chapter 3, entitled 'Love of the World', I will invoke the contribution of Hannah Arendt, an important if idiosyncratic political philosopher. Arendt offers a strident critique of Christianity, arguing for its incompatibility with the sphere of politics, because Christians are incapable of nurturing a 'love of the world', and because the Christian virtue of humility 'separates' the agent from his or her deed. Though Arendt's take on Christianity is quirky, it is one which political theology needs to take seriously, not least because Arendt's own proposals have been influential for political philosophy.

The second section (chapters 4–6) offers a breathless historical overview of the patristic, medieval, reformation and early modern roots of political theology, taking up O'Donovan's specification of a 'High Tradition'. Important figures such as Augustine, Aquinas, Luther and Calvin will feature, as well as the challenge for political theology posed by William T. Cavanaugh's 'revisioning' of the early modern 'Wars of Religion'. The roots of this theology in the Enlightenment hope of Immanuel Kant will also be explored.

Twentieth-century European political theology is a theology of crisis, above all with the challenge of National Socialism, the collapse into barbarism of the Second World War, and the *Shoah*, the attempted systematic extermination of the Jewish people. Out of these disasters there arose a desperate need to reconceive our understanding of God, the relationship between Christians and Jews, and the nature of theology. Section 3 looks at some themes in this history (chapter 7), as well as the main figures in post-war political theology: Johann Baptist Metz, Dorothee Sölle and Jürgen Moltmann (chapters 8–9). In general, these thinkers are united by their insistence on keeping faith with the project of Enlightenment, despite its catastrophes, and therefore by a shared quest with Critical Theory (Frankfurt School) for the grounds of hope on which the task of Enlightenment may be carried forward.

By contrast, theorists associated with Radical Orthodoxy, such as John Milbank and William T. Cavanaugh, see in our post-modern condition an irreversible collapse of the project of modernity. They seek instead to resource theology from pre-modern thinkers, notably Augustine, offering a concept of political theology as ecclesiology, or doctrine of the Church, which we examine in the concluding chapter 11, together with public theologies in North America. Both this and the penultimate chapter (which explores the scriptural resources for political theology), draw attention to how questions of 'eschatology', or the 'end time', are crucial.

The respective section headings are straightforward, I think: 'the parameters', 'the history', 'the crisis'. For the fourth section, which treats of the resources for political theology in ecclesiology, scripture, and eschatology, I chose the heading 'the gift'. Somewhere I felt there should be a more explicit recognition of the ambivalence of religion in the public sphere. The word '*Gift*' in German means 'poison'.

Chapter 2

WITNESS AGAINST THE BEAST[1]

Leviathan versus Covenant Theologies

We will further explore the subject matter of 'political theology' in two investigations. The present chapter attempts a distinction between 'political theology' and 'political mythology'; and between two conceptions of politics, summed up by the German theologian Jürgen Moltmann as 'Covenant or Leviathan'. These alternatives offer an optimistic and pessimistic opinion respectively, of the capacity of human beings to co-operate socially – two different conceptions, therefore of politics and of political theology.

Chapter 3 will examine a strident critique made against Christianity by Hannah Arendt. She alleges that the Christian ideal is unsuited to political life, that there is an inbuilt hostility between the gospel and politics: the opposite claim, in other words, to that made by theologians such as Lash and Davis in the opening chapter. Christianity, she claims, endorses a retreat or withdrawal from the world, rather than an engagement with it – hence the title of the chapter, 'Is Political Theology Possible?' It is by examining Arendt's critique, and by looking at some of the historical evidence which might support or refute it, that we will arrive at a clearer understanding of the issues involved.

Violent Beginnings

Scott and Cavanaugh asserted the similarity of 'Theology and Politics' insofar as 'both are constituted in the production of metaphysical images around which communities are organised.' What 'metaphysical images' are we talking about?

An investigation into the sources and origins of political thought soon brings us to what some commentators believe is the distinguishing mark of the ancient *polis,* namely the *paradox of violence.* Whether we look at the world of the gods of the *polis*, or at the philosophical reflection of antiquity, we find the paradox of a 'harmony of opposites' that holds the antique city-state together. In Plato's *Politics* we have the image of the Watchers: these should be like good watchdogs, friendly to the inhabitants of the city, but aggressive when they meet the enemies of the state. The citizenry as a whole needs to be in readiness for violence towards their enemies. The pre-Socratic philosopher Heraclitus makes the paradox even more explicit, since he goes beyond the idea of a harmony of opposites and emphasises the *fatherhood* of war. Strife is not simply the destroyer that brings an end to all peace, but, also the life-spending power at the source of culture: 'War is the father of all things, the King of all things. One recognises him as god, the other as men – he makes some slaves, he sets others free.'

Marcel Detienne (2006:91–101) discusses the founding of early Greek cities, and how 'a number of aspects of action, decision, and the strategies of politics took shape and were analysed with reference to the divine powers'. He gives a roll call, as it were, of the deities involved: first of all, Apollo, known as a founder, *Archēgetēs*, who marked out the territory, including the space for the *agora*, then Hesta who brought the sacrificial fire. 'There could be no city without an *agora*, no city without altars and sacrificial fire'. Hesta in particular represents the unity of the multiplicity of individual domestic hearths and altars, and 'political' authority effectively came from her. As well as these two, however, Detienne asserts 'that the Aphrodite–Ares pair, which is of major importance and represents the relationship between the rituals of warfare, on the one hand, and harmony and concord, on the other, introduces a set of major tensions that must be taken into account in any analysis of the political field.' (101) We can put this more strongly with the aid of René Girard, who urges an intimate link between violence, political origins and the sacred.[2] Girard would posit a thematic connection between the four deities mentioned by Detienne. The pairing of the god of war and the goddess of love hints at the problem of violence, but the activities associated with Apollo and Hesta (demarcation of space, preservation of a sacrificial flame) are themselves not free of violent overtones, if we see them as related to the practice of foundational sacrifice.

Antigone and the *Eumenides*

We can see how the ambiguity of violence in social formation is played out by examining two Greek tragedies. Shortly we will look at *Antigone*, by Sophocles; but we begin with the tragedy by Aeschylus, *The Eumenides*. In this play, Orestes, at the instigation of Apollo, kills his mother, out of rage for the murder of his father. He is attacked by the goddesses of wrath, the Furies, who are the ministers of justice, and the goddess Athena, patroness of the city of Athens, seeks to adjudicate. Divine forces, ranged against each other: this seems to be the fundamental paradox of the *polis*, where the feuds of the gods are played out: 'one recognises [strife] as god, the other as men'. The central problem of the play is: how is civil strife to be overcome? The Chorus of the now beneficient Eumenides (formerly the goddesses of wrath) promises an end to the civil war:

> CHORUS (chanting):
> And nevermore these walls within
> shall echo fierce sedition's din,
> unslaked with blood and crime;
> the thirsty dust shall nevermore
> suck up the darkly streaming gore
> of civic broils, shed out in wrath
> and vengeance, crying death for death!
> But man with man and state with state
> shall vow the pledge of common hate
> and common friendship, that for man
> hath oft made blessing, out of ban,
> be ours unto all time.
>
> (*Eumenides*, 978–87)

The play ends with songs of praise and joy over 'these alien Powers that thus are made Athenian evermore', and over their promise of protection for Athens. The overcoming of civil strife is partially attributed to the collective *hatred*, or readiness to channel warfare from within the state to outside its walls: now the citizens are united by a 'pledge of common hate and common friendship'.[3]

So the *Eumenides* gives us one account of 'the political'. In the second play, *Antigone*, we are presented with another dilemma, similar to the first in some respects but markedly different in others. Antigone is the daughter of Oedipus, and the brother of Polynices, who has been killed in a civil war. Creon (king of Thebes), gives orders that the body of Polynices is to remain unburied because he is a traitor; Antigone disobeys this order and buries him secretly at night. Creon in turn commands that Antigone should be buried alive (later she commits suicide before this sentence is carried out). We should be clear that the play presents a conflict between two *religious* obligations: the need to preserve and protect the city state, and the duty to honour the dead. Both Creon and Antigone appeal to Zeus; and while we are more inclined to see justice on the side of Antigone, spiritedly resisting a cruel tyrant's edict, the original audience would have been much more in sympathy with the king. Creon gives his reason for the maltreatment of Polynices, and of anyone who places friendship before the good of the country:

> Remember this:
> our country is our safety.
> Only while she voyages true on course
> can we establish friendships, truer than blood itself.
> Such are my standards. They make our city great.
> *(Antigone, ll. 231–235)*

It is because of this imperative to that Polynices, 'who thirsted to drink his kinsmen's blood and sell the rest to slavery', should remain unburied. The common good demands that the dead traitor and the dead patriot be treated differently, and it is this 'common good' that Antigone has violated by burying her brother. When Antigone is captured and brought before Creon, however, she insists that she broke Creon's law in the name of a higher law: the justice of Zeus himself:

It wasn't Zeus, not in the least,
who made this proclamation – not to me.
Nor did that Justice, dwelling with the gods
beneath the earth, ordain such laws for men.
Nor did I think your edict has such force
that you, a mere mortal, could override the gods,
their great unwritten, unshakeable traditions.

(ll. 499–505)

Antigone's spirited self-defence marks a rift in the ancient alliance of religion and the state. Although he calls on Zeus as witness, Creon's inhumane proclamation cannot be truly from God, and she challenges it in the name of a more ancient, more 'authentic' divine justice. This makes Antigone a heroic resistance figure, like Socrates, a martyr who dies at the hands of the state for witnessing to a higher truth. This sympathy (to repeat, not shared by the original audience of Sophocles' play) fascinated the Western philosophical tradition, with Hegel, Kierkegaard and others writing at length and with great enthusiasm about her (Steiner, 1984).

Incidentally, we find a moving and important parallel to Antigone's plight in the *City of God*, where Augustine retells Livy's account of Horatius killing his sister, Horatia, because she shed tears for her fiancé, whom he has just killed in combat in order to save Rome. The hero is put on trial: Livy's sympathy (and Rome's) is with Horatius – even the father speaks out in his defence – but for Augustine '[t]he feelings of this woman seem to me more humane than that of the entire Roman people.'[4]

Political Mythology versus Political Theology

If we take these two passages: firstly, the mysterious and disturbing transformation of the Furies into the Eumenides, secondly, the inspiring, heroic figure of Antigone, we have distinctive pictures of what political theology is. Antigone appeals to religious tradition in a way which challenges and negates the claim of political authority to some kind of legitimising religious transcendence. This appeal 'desacralises' the political; it protests against the tendency of political leaders and authorities to declare themselves divine. What is happening with *The Eumenides* is more sinister, and perhaps harder to accept. Implicit in this play is a definition of 'the political' as the successful containment of a society's aggression. If the tensions within a group are not managed successfully they will bring about the violent destruction of the group through civil war. In such an event, the destructive aspect of these energies – the Furies – is evident. However, if this aggression is harnessed and channelled outwards, it becomes a beneficial force (the Eumenides). Not only do the Eumenides provide protection for the society, but they allow the group to define itself over against outsiders, and thus find its own identity. Terry Eagleton's essay on 'Tragedy and Revolution'[5] comments as follows:

> Only if our imaginary social bonds are founded upon the Real, upon a certain horror at the heart of the social itself, will they prove sufficiently durable. Only if the Furies are installed within the city-state itself will it be secure – which is to say that only if the terrorism of the law is turned inward as well as outward, to become domesticated as hegemony as well as armed and helmeted as military might, will the social contract stand.
>
> (Eagleton, 2005:8)

I propose that a political ideology which attempts, like Creon's, to claim religious legitimacy for itself may be more properly understood as 'political mythology' – with 'myth' understood here as something untrue, a made-up story which nevertheless enables a community to achieve some kind of coherence. 'Myth' here means a kind of useful lie. By contrast, where religious authority is invoked as a challenge to a regime or ideology – as with Antigone, Socrates, Christ – then we are talking about 'political theology' in a normative sense. The phrase from R. A. Markus describing Augustine's *City of God* as a 'refusal to bless the state' is exactly right. A true political theology will take a negative stance towards the quasi-religious or messianic claims of politicians, because it will recognise the necessity of keeping open the transcendent dimension, rather than having it sealed up in any particular context.

On this view, Antigone stands alongside the extraordinary intransigence of political *refuseniks* of all shapes and sizes throughout the ages: from the Jewish and early Christian martyrs, challenging, at such terrible cost to themselves, the idolatrous pretensions of the Greek and Roman imperial powers; to Augustine's rejection of 'providential histories' (both pagan and Christian), and his desacralisation of the Roman Empire in *The City of God*; to the millennial insurgents of the radical Reformation. In the modern period, the same pattern appears in the protest of Karl Barth and others against the false messianism of National Socialism. Johann Baptist Metz's attack on 'bourgeois Christianity' is a similar protest, as is the *Kairos* Document (1978), the statement of the churches opposed to apartheid in South Africa.

In short, the splendid Antigone emerges as the patron saint of political theologians. We can recognise the attractiveness of the 'Antigone' mode of political theology, the proud resistance to injustice disguised as religion. The other style of political theology, represented by the ambiguities of the Eumenides, may be less palatable. W.H. Auden draws these out in a poem, 'Vespers', which tells of a strange twilight encounter: between the speaker, a romantic innocent, and his opposite, a cynical realist. 'Both simultaneously recognise his Anti-type: that I am an Arcadian, that he is a Utopian':

> He notes, with contempt, my Aquarian belly: I note, with alarm, his Scorpion's mouth.
>
> He would like to see me cleaning latrines: I would like to see him removed to some other planet.
>
> Neither speaks. What experience could we possibly share?
>
> Glancing at a lampshade in a store window, I observe it is too hideous for anyone in their senses to buy: He observes it is too expensive for a peasant to buy.
>
> Passing a slum child with rickets, I look the other way: He looks the other way if he passes a chubby one.[6]

At first the speaker emphasises the gap between these two world-views: 'between my Eden and his New Jerusalem, no treaty is negotiable'. And yet the poem does not rest with this antagonism, rather it speaks of the possibility that these perspectives, the 'Arcadian' and the 'Utopian', are perhaps complementary, and that the mysterious meeting forces each one:

> for a fraction of a second, to remember our victim
>   (but for him I could forget the blood, but for me he could forget the innocence),
>   on whose immolation (call him Abel, Remus, whom you will, it is one Sin Offering) arcadias, utopias, our dear old bag of a democracy are alike founded:
>   For without a cement of blood (it must be human, it must be innocent) no secular wall can safely stand.

Romulus, killer of his brother Remus, was the founder of Rome. According to Genesis chapter 3, Cain, the murderer of his brother Abel, is the founder of the first town: we are dealing here with foundational acts of sacral violence. The attitudes of the two men, 'Arcadian' and 'Utopian', may stand for the two possibilities opened up, between the 'Antigone' and the 'Eumenides' versions of politics. If Antigone stands for the *innocence*, the Eumenides represent the *blood*. We will recall that on this last account, political fellowship and belonging are the flip-side of the ferocious antagonism that needs to be projected outwards onto an enemy group. There is a strong tradition in political thought which sees this process – of containment and re-channelling of violence – as the fundamental meaning and purpose of politics: or at the very least, as an important aspect or criterion of 'the political'.

The doctrine of the katēchon

Another way of understanding this theme is to take up the New Testament notion of the *katēchon*. This is a Greek word, which is found in a rather mysterious passage in one of Paul's letters. Paul is trying to dampen expectation among his readers concerning the Second Coming of Christ (2 Thessalonians 2:1–12). The Greek word *katēcho* means 'to hold back, hold fast, to bind, restrain', and is used by Paul to refer to the restraining hand of God before the chaos of the end times is unleashed. Mark 13 and

Luke 21:5–36 make similar reference to a *delay or deferral of the apocalypse,* though the theme is most graphically depicted in the Book of Revelation, chapter 20:7–8.

The noun *katēchon* refers to the political force whose function is the restraint of chaos and disorder. This conception of politics as *katēchon* is important for understanding the work of Carl Schmitt, as we shall see. For now, we are able to identify two descriptions, in tension with one another, concerning how we account for violence and coercion in politics. We have specified an 'Antigone' and a 'Eumenides' motif. Antigone stands out as a brave protester against the idolatrous violence of the state. She sees this violence as a distortion of the political, not a dimension of it. With the Eumenides, the opposite holds: here, the problem of violence is at the very heart of the political, defined precisely in terms of how the aggressive forces of human society are to be managed: a terrifying curse if they are unleashed internally, but a blessing if they are channelled outwards onto a common enemy.

Political theology must arbitrate between these contrasting accounts of what is going on. For Jürgen Moltmann, we have two distinct anthropologies, differing views of what can be expected of human beings as political animals, which he explicates in terms of a 'Covenant' model versus 'Leviathan' (Moltmann, 1994). The former tradition allows for the possibility of human beings entering into covenant with God and with each other; the second, more pessimistically, sees the task in hand as that of restraining the 'war of all against all' which is our natural condition, and ensuring strong central government – a *katēchon* – to prevent chaos. And political theology has been resourced from both of these traditions, as a brief survey will indicate.

For Augustine, or at least on one 'tragic' reading of him, the primary purpose of institutions in society is dealing with the conflict and disorganisation resulting from the Fall – in other words, the restraining function of the *katēchon*: 'while they are feared, the wicked are held in check, and the good are enabled to live less disturbed among the wicked'. Augustine's argument for the necessity of *disciplina* for an inescapably recalcitrant human race has fateful consequences, as it forms the basis of his justification for religious coercion by the state – making him, it has been said, 'the first theologian of the Inquisition'. Martin Luther follows Augustine in understanding a conflict between the City of God and the earthly city: these are in tension until the end of time. Luther distinguishes between the 'saving' kingdom of Christ and the 'preserving' kingdom of the world: those under the first are motivated by the Sermon on the Mount, and are in no need of external constraints, because the authority which they recognise is persuasive rather than coercive. They are, however, only a tiny minority of the population (perhaps one in a thousand), and effective government of the majority requires coercive rather than persuasive measures: rulers, magistrates, laws backed up by the sword. Luther accepts that there is a two-tier morality in place: the high gospel standards to which Christians seek to attain, and a less demanding ethic, based on fear and coercion. Trying to run an entire society according to the first, minority gospel ethic would have predictable and disastrous consequences:

> If anyone attempted to rule the world by the gospel and to abolish all temporal law and sword on the plea that all are baptised and Christians, and that, according to the gospel, there shall be among them no law or sword – or need for either – pray tell, friend, what would he be doing? What do you imagine the effect will be? He would be loosing the ropes and chains of the savage wild beasts and letting them bite and mangle everyone, meanwhile insisting that they were harmless, tame, and gentle creatures; but I would have the proof in my wounds. Just so would the wicked under the name of Christian abuse evangelical freedom, carry on their rascality, and insist that they were Christians subject neither to law nor sword, as some are already raving and ranting.[7]

Hobbes, Schmitt and the Leviathan

So the *katēchon*, first encountered in the New Testament, is taken up by theologians reflecting upon the challenge of establishing a correct foundation and scope for the political and religious spheres. With Thomas Hobbes in the seventeenth century the same problem which confronted Augustine and Luther is addressed, but in a secularised form. In many respects his book *Leviathan* (1651) represents the 'birth' of modern political thought.

Hobbes announces his conviction of the equality of all human beings. This takes up Luther's *theological* insight that we all stand equal before God, and follows through on its sociological and political implications in a way that Luther did not. These are not at all good: the natural equality of humans has deadly consequences, as Hobbes argues in *Leviathan*, ch. 13: it engenders equality of hope, which in turn breeds envy. The direct result of equality, therefore, is universal competition and strife, the famous 'war of all against all', a condition 'of continuall feare, and danger of violent death; And the life of man, solitary, poore, nasty, brutish and short'. Christianity is a dangerous religion, inspiring the kind of human equality which leads to conflict; it nevertheless yields the solution to the problem, namely the secularised *katēchon*. Hobbes championed the notion of an absolute power that could prevent the outbreak of civil war, a mortal 'God' who would be sovereign of both politics and religion, even the sole interpreter of scripture. Absolute power is granted to this sovereign by the people, as a result of a social contract. So the State functions as a *katēchon*, with no positive goal other than the restraining of the apocalyptic state of war.

In *The Stillborn God* (2007), Mark Lilla praises Thomas Hobbes for bringing about the Great Separation between politics and religion: as we shall see in chapter 5, this judgement is open to contestation by political theologians. In the meantime, we consider a thinker who has been greatly influenced by Hobbes in modern times. Carl Schmitt has been described as the 'twentieth-century godfather of political theology' (Hollerich, 2004:107). Though scholarship on Schmitt is immense and growing, he has always remained a controversial figure, because of his complicity with the National Socialist regime from 1933 to 1936. Schmitt wrote legal studies defending the regime, including the Nuremburg racial laws and the 1934 'Night of the Long Knives', and there is also clear evidence of his anti-Semitism. Despite this dismal background, he was admired and sought out until his death in 1985; thinkers of both right and left have shown interest, including political realists such as Hans J. Morgenthau and Henry Kissinger. Many critics confirm his status as a brilliant but highly problematic theorist. We need to take note of Schmitt's diagnoses, but also to look for solutions that go beyond them. His key text, *Political Theology*, sets out the roots of sovereignty as a secularised theological concept. In a companion work, *Roman Catholicism and Political Form*, he presents the Church as a *Machtform*, a bulwark of authority against a chaotic world, while a third work, perhaps his most influential, *The Concept of the Political*, defines politics in terms of the *Freund–Feind* distinction, which we turn to now.

The Political as Friend–Enemy

As the 'German Hobbes of the twentieth century', Carl Schmitt's thought is firmly aligned on that of his seventeenth-century predecessor. His *'Freund–Feind'* distinction: 'friend or foe', is an extension of the concept of the state set out in *Leviathan*.[8] According to Schmitt, the world is divided into states which are aligned with or against one another, according to a 'friend/enemy' distinction. Political stability arises from the balance between them: a state needs alliances, but it also needs the unifying power which comes from having enemies. This division between peoples and states is in fact part of God's plan! Two passages from Genesis are cited here: the enmity which God sets between the woman and the serpent (Genesis 3:15), and the incident of the Tower of Babel (Genesis 11:9), where the name Babel or Babylon is related to the Hebrew word for 'mixed up'. It follows that any attempt to unite where God has instituted separation and strife, such as the League of Nations (precursor of the United Nations), is a grave mistake. This 'denial of difference' upsets the balance between states, and therefore has the opposite effect of what was intended.

The religious background of the *Freund–Feind* distinction is crucial to Schmitt's politico-theological critique of liberalism.[9] Behind the apparent neutrality of the modern liberal state is the brutal reality of the modern revolt against God; there is a *theological* enmity between Christianity and liberalism. The liberal search for 'perpetual peace' and a secure existence

deprives us even of our enemies (liberals, he says, would probably appoint a commission to investigate the question, 'Christ or
Barabbas?'!). From a gospel perspective, however, this search
for peace is a delusion. The decision 'for or against enmity':
what we have been calling Antigone or Eumenides, or Arcardian
or Utopian, is above all a political-theological criterion. Schmitt
did not believe in a world free of aggression, because the effort
to create such a world would itself have to be aggressive. He is
also sceptical about the weakened modern state's ability to
provide peace, while the substitution of economic competition
for war merely disguises the coercion between states. Like the
Eumenides, Schmitt proclaims the intensity of two sentiments,
love for fellow citizens, and hatred of one's enemies: 'The
distinction of friend and enemy denotes the utmost degree of
intensity of a union or separation, of an association or dis-
sociation'. Together with the dogma of original sin and the
Freund–Feind doctrine it becomes clear that 'the undifferentiated
optimism of a universal conception of man' is impossible.

Here, it is argued by Jürgen Moltmann and others, is the core
of *katēchon* theology – or rather mythology, as we defined it
earlier. As with the Grand Inquisitor (whom we meet below)
there is a failure of nerve, a panic at the delay in Jesus' return;
meanwhile political chaos threatens to engulf us. The paradox
remains, however, of the *katēchon* as a means of restraining
chaotic and unlimited violence through limited violence:
'Leviathan', the force of anarchy, is now itself a source of order.
This is Augustine's understanding of the *pax Romana*, the
strictly limited peace which comes from imperial domination,
and while he clearly understands the City of God to be offering
something else, Augustine is unable, ultimately, to break free of
the necessary violence of the political.

Covenant or Leviathan?

In his article entitled 'Covenant or Leviathan?', Moltmann
points out two strains of political theology, arising from the sixteenth and seventeenth centuries. The first of these positions,
'Covenant', derives from the Calvinist articulation of the right
of resistance against political and religious absolutism in France

(after the St Bartholomew's Day massacre of Huguenots in 1572). It represents a federal theology, whereby the covenant of human beings with one another is based on and preserved by God's covenant with them. 'Federal theology presupposed that God considers human beings to be worthy and capable of forming a covenant. Out of this trust of God comes the trust of human beings in their mutual ability to form a covenant' (Moltmann, 1994:25). This covenant theology is taken by Puritans into the New World (an 'exodus' from theocratic dictatorship), and the notion of America as a covenanted nation undergirds the American Revolution. 'Leviathan', as we have seen, is Hobbes' name for the Utopian security state that unites spiritual and secular power, and allows neither the division of powers nor the right of resistance.

Beneath each of these conceptions is a political anthropology. The covenant idea of the State has a positive anthropology, legitimating a critical theology of power as well as democratic institutions for its control: 'All men are created free and equal and endowed by their Creator with inalienable rights'. A foundation of power in the covenant of free citizens recognises in the polity both a created disposition of humankind, and an anticipation of the 'heavenly citizenship' in the Kingdom of God. However perverted by human sinfulness, the present State belongs to the essence and not just to the alienation of humankind. Human beings are social beings. The Leviathan, on the other hand, presupposes a negative anthropology in order to legitimate a positive theology of power, authority and sovereignty. 'Human beings are evil by nature, chaotic, and therefore need a strong State to protect them from other human beings and from themselves' (Moltmann, 1994:33–4).

Nomos *and Space in Schmitt*

To understand more precisely why Carl Schmitt positions himself in this pessimistic 'Leviathan' tradition, we need to look at his second major concept (after the *Freund–Feind* distinction), which is a reflection upon the relationship between *nomos* (law) and space or territory (Palaver, 1996). Schmitt uses the Greek word *nomos* in a broad sense, rather than the more abstract

German term *Gesetz*. Law always comes to us through a specific
set of social institutions and structures, so that *nomos* means a
'total concept of law that contains a concrete order and a community'. This total concept includes the religious dimension of
nomos; the term connotes originally a 'sacred location', empha-
sising a strong connection between religion and territoriality. We
may refer back to Detienne's description, above, of Apollo as
one of the deities associated with the building of a city. As
'founder' he was invoked as the one who measures out and
marks off its dimensions, including those of the *agora*, the place
of assembly.

Even this straightforward activity seems to have overtones of
foundational violence. Schmitt's linking of *nomos* and territory,
with *nomos* as a unity of order,[10] is impelled in part by his
support of Nazi policies, including the annexation of foreign
countries. 'The great primal acts of law … remain earthbound
locations (orientations). These are land appropriations, the
founding of cities and colonies.' Schmitt argues for resonances
between *nomos* and spatial categories: for example, *nomos* and
wall (Heraclitus), or *nomos* as spatial enclosure, 'the enclosing
ring, the fence formed by men, the men–ring' which is an image
of political community.[11] By 1953 he has worked out a number
of meanings of *nomos*, one of which is 'to take or appropriate'.
Land appropriations always come first: we have the biblical
stories of the appropriation of Canaan by the Israelites (see the
books of Numbers and Joshua). Another example is the
Conquista, the acquisition of land in the Americas – which
Schmitt charmingly regards as 'the last great European
adventure'.

It should be clear now why Schmitt set himself so firmly
against any kind of 'universalism' in international affairs:
'Throughout his life, Schmitt feared nothing more than a unified
world' (Palaver, 1996:111). Organisations like the League of
Nations (forerunner of the United Nations), which sought to
bring nations together in co-operation, not only ignored the
importance of the *Freund–Feind* distinction, but they were also
oblivious of this dimension of territoriality: namely, the arrangement of space as the foundation of international order. Whatever
the new post-war *nomos* was going to be – Schmitt did not

foresee the Cold War lasting very long – it had to be one of equilibrium between states, rather than undifferentiated universalism. Schmitt's own preference was for a *nomos* of the earth based on several independent large blocs, a pluralism of *Grossräume* (large living spaces).[12]

Matthew Lamb is trenchant in his judgement that Schmitt's is 'a completely immanent project with no trace of the transcendence of Christian faith', while Hollerich contends that his 'religious faith was more polemical and "dramaturgical" than substantive'. Critics have also objected, not surprisingly, to the dualism of the *Freund–Feind* distinction, and its Hobbesian reduction of the state to a mere question of power: not to mention Schmitt's negation of the gospel command to love one's enemy (though for Schmitt the biblical command applied to individual, not 'political' enemies!). Palaver recognises that Schmitt's two key concepts, the *Freund–Feind* distinction and the connection of *nomos* and space, need to be subjected to a twofold theological critique. Firstly, he recognises the presence in Schmitt's work of *katēchon* political mythology. Many of Schmitt's key themes and concerns – the dualism of friend and enemy, the reduction of politics to power, the instrumentalisation of religion – can be discussed under the heading of *katēchon*.

From a Christian perspective, as Palaver acknowledges, the idea of the *katēchon* is highly problematic. Its true status is conveyed in the figure of the 'Grand Inquisitor', from chapter 5 of Fyodor Dostoyevsky's novel *The Brothers Karamazov*. In this bitterly anti-Roman Catholic satire, the Inquisitor presides over an *auto-da-fé* when he recognises Jesus, who has silently returned. He arrests him, and explains to Jesus how he has worked to repair the damage done by the Lord when he called his followers into a dangerous freedom. Such a freedom, if taken seriously, can only lead to chaos, even cannibalism. The Grand Inquisitor fears this chaos and destruction, and tries to 'hold back' the apocalypse. Unsettled by the silence of Jesus throughout this interrogation, the Inquisitor decides to let him go. His final words – 'Go away and don't come again … come never, never again … never, never!' – contradict the concluding words in the Bible: 'Come, Lord Jesus!' And it is worth noting that the person of Jesus hardly features at all in the Leviathan tradition. Schmitt describes Hobbes as seeking to displace Christianity into marginal domains, and therefore to 'render harmless the effect of Christ in the social and political sphere; of de-anarchizing Christianity, while leaving it in the background a certain legitimating function'.

Above all, it does seem hard to understand how these themes in Schmitt can be prised apart from his dismal associations with National Socialism, though clearly many contemporary thinkers believe this is possible. Political theologians (especially the post-war generation of Metz, Moltmann and Sölle), have sought to distance themselves from Schmitt's version of political theology. Like the theologians of liberation, they voice an Antigone-like protest against the abuses of power. But this is not the same as addressing the problematic violence at the root of politics, the Eumenides part of the equation, as Schmitt attempted to do, however unsavoury some of his judgements. A further theological critique is needed, which is corrective of the problematic aspects of the *Freund– Feind* distinction and the *nomos*–space conjunction, while preserving what may be genuinely insightful in these concepts.

Wolfgang Palaver's own analysis does soften the edges of the contrasts we have explored here. He suggests that the 'Covenant or Leviathan?' options set out by Moltmann, with corresponding positive and negative anthropologies, is too schematic. In this respect René Girard's mimetic theory is a deeper and stronger overview of the conditions which lead to human violence (Palaver, 1999:353–70). Palaver also draws attention to Bonhoeffer's use of *katēchon* in his *Ethics* in a more positive sense than Schmitt (Palaver, 2007:86).

We began with two Greek tragedies that illustrate contrasting aspects of the 'theologico-political'. In *Tragedy and Revolution* Terry Eagleton sees these two aspects – the innocence of Antigone, the blood of *The Eumenides* – present in *Oedipus at Colonus*, in an analysis which resonates with those themes (unstable identity, scapegoating, exclusionary violence) which René Girard has made his own:

> Oedipus, broken and blind, stands before Colonus. As he once gave an answer to the Sphinx, his presence now poses a question to the nearby city of Athens. Is it to gather this unclean thing to its heart, or cast it out as so much garbage? (Eagleton, 2005:8)

The answer to the Sphinx was of course 'Man': 'four, two and three in one'. In the same way Athens needs to discern his humanity, as the *pharmakos*, the 'impossible homeopathy of poison and cure ... nothing is more fearful or opaque than ourselves and those akin to us, and nothing more pitiable than a humanity deformed alarmingly out of recognition'. This is the achievement of tragedy, that in Oedipus, Lear and in the tortured Christ, we 'come to pity what we fear' (8). Nothing could be further from our contemporary political world, says Eagleton, than this language of scapegoats and blood sacrifice. We are embarrassed by it, just as we are uneasy with the language of revolution. But what our reluctance amounts to 'politically speaking, is a choice between one kind of death-in-life and another.' Western hubris celebrates as energy what is in fact a nihilism secretly in love with annihilation; its death drive is the opposite of the existence of the dispossessed, who seek to flourish in the face of death, finitide and failure. The West

> cannot recognise its own visage in the raging fury at its gates. It is unable to decipher the symptoms of weakness and despair in that fury and therefore is capable only of fear rather than pity. (21)

Chapter 3

'LOVE OF THE WORLD'

Is Political Theology Possible?

Political theologians agree with Charles Davis, that '[t]he Christian religion has always been thoroughly political … Christians find God in their neighbour rather than in their consciousness or in the cosmos.' We are beginning to see that the picture is more complex. Political theology, even when it proclaims itself Christian, has often been resourced by something closer to pagan mythology, rather than by a genuinely biblical or ecclesial faith – as we have seen from the last chapter, where we discussed the mythology of the *katēchon*. We are beginning to see a distinction between 'political theology' and 'political mythology' has begun to emerge, but it is not always an easy one to draw.

There is a further complication. A powerful argument can be made for Christianity being inherently *apolitical* or even anti-political – directly contrary to what Davis proclaims. What I propose in this chapter is to assess the critique of Christianity put forward by Hannah Arendt (1906–75), with a view to answering the question: *is political theology possible*? Arendt is relevant here, because her answer is 'no'; she makes a case which requires attention, that politics and Christianity are in fact incompatible.

Hannah Arendt on Christianity

Hannah Arendt was a controversial political philosopher, who has been described as 'one of the most important and original thinkers of the twentieth-century catastrophes'. In her main works: *The Origins of Totalitarianism* (1951), *The Human Condition* (1958), and *On Revolution* (1963), she explores politics and society in the modern world, especially the terrible events of 'dark times'. These analyses are brought to bear in her famous and provocative coverage of the trial of Adolf Eichmann, who was accused of Nazi war crimes, tried and condemned in Israel in 1961. Arendt's 'report on the banality of evil', *Eichmann in Jerusalem* (1963), is a classic but highly controversial meditation on the roots of the National Socialist horror.

Arendt reads through the prism of two earlier periods: Classical Greece and Rome, and the early modern period, 1600–1900. By comparison with the first of these, in particular the classical ideal of politics which she associates with the city-states of Greece, she finds Christianity wanting. There is an 'other-worldliness' in the Christian faith, which Arendt interprets as an intrinsic hostility to the public domain, tending instead to a glorification of the self and individual destiny. The gospel calls for a shift from 'care of the world' and the duties connected with it, to care for the soul and individual salvation: 'For what will it profit them to gain the whole world but forfeit their life?' This 'unworldliness' makes a positive Christian engagement with the *polis* impossible. Arendt argues for the incompatibility of love and the public realm. In a letter to the Black liberationist, James Baldwin, in 1962, Arendt wrote: 'In politics, love is a stranger, and when it intrudes upon it nothing is being achieved except hypocrisy ... Hatred and love belong together, and they are both destructive, you can only afford them in private ...'

Arendt's logic is clear. Love is a 'stranger' in politics; Christianity is love; therefore ... As James Bernauer sees it,[1] there are three interrelated aspects to Arendt's critique. Firstly, Christianity's rejection of the classical viewpoints which fostered worldly engagement means a reversal of the Greek and Roman world-view, according to which our only hope of 'immortality' (as mortals in an immortal universe) is to make a lasting mark in the political world, through heroic action or leadership. For the Christian, however, it is the world that will pass away, while the individual soul endures. There is another reversal: the Roman emphasis on the past encouraged an emulation of the great deeds of founders and ancestors. The Christian steadfastly ignores these, his or her gaze directed to the future instead, a pilgrim on the way to Paradise.

Arendt's second objection, according to Bernauer, is Christianity's demeaning of the world of political action. The *negative* inner freedom of the gospel is also a 'freedom from politics' and secular involvement: hence, for example, the Church's indifference to social evils such as slavery. The Christian conception of the common good, namely 'the salvation of one's soul', is alien to the public realm, and remains *hidden from view*: Jesus declares that only God is good (Luke 8:19), and insists that acts of charity and other good works should be carried out in secret. As a result, the agent and the act are separated: this has serious consequences for Arendt's theory of action, which is fundamental to her political theory. Arendt draws a curious parallel with the status of the criminal:

> Although nobody knows whom he reveals when he discloses himself in deed or word, he must be willing to risk the disclosure, and this neither the doer of good works, who must be without self and preserve complete anonymity, nor the criminal, who must hide himself from others, can take upon themselves. Both are lonely figures, the one being for, the other against, all men; they, therefore, remain outside the pale of human intercourse and are, politically, marginal figures who usually enter the historical scene in times of corruption, disintegration, and political bankruptcy. (Arendt, 1958:180)

Thirdly, for Arendt, Christianity is not only indifferent to the public realm: it is actually the source and support of values that destroy political life. We have already mentioned 'love' in this regard. As a direct consequence of the Incarnation, which is the belief that the Absolute has been incarnated in human history, we have to live with the haunting spectre of absolute truth over human affairs and institutions. 'Truth as revelation' contradicts the political model of life, which rejoices in the necessary diversity of opinions, and in the values of consent, mutual agreement and freedom. This would correspond very much to the alleged incompatibility of 'utopian politics' (John Gray) or 'political theology' (Mark Lilla) with political life as such. A further legacy of Christianity is the tendency of certain moral experiences, such as compassion and pity, to be allowed to dictate human conduct in the political realm. Much of the violence of modern revolutionary theorists arises from the victory of moral feelings over political virtues: we are tempted to allow moral outrage or sentiment to lead the way, and to 'shun the drawn-out wearisome processes of persuasion, negotiation and compromise'. In other words, incarnational Christianity has brought into politics a dangerous fanaticism that is, inevitably, the opposite of freedom.[2]

Three key concepts: action …

Arendt's concerns about Christianity become clearer if we look at her own understanding of 'politics', especially at two closely related concepts. One is 'action', which she carefully distinguishes from labour and work, and the other is 'natality', a description of human beings which is the alternative to stressing our 'mortality'. These need to be discussed along with a third distinctive category in her thought, that of *amor mundi*: love of the world.

In *The Human Condition* Arendt seeks to recover a theory of politics that was alive in classical Greece but lost to the modern age. She follows the Greeks in distinguishing between *private* and *public* (a third realm, that of the *social*, comes in with the Romans). It is in these three realms that human activity takes place, namely 'labour', 'work' and 'action'. The first two are motivated by necessity and utility respectively, the interaction of the individual with the world in general; they are to do with means. Action concerns human ends: only here do we have free, unforced and direct interchange between human beings. The private realm is pre-political, the realm of hiddenness, and is very important for human well-being. Nevertheless, only the public, which is the sphere of speech, space and appearance, is 'political' in the proper sense. So *speech*, *action*, and *freedom from necessity* appear together.

The political is a fragile space, which is all too easily over-whelmed by the social, or subsumed under the concerns of labour or work. To live principally or exclusively in the social realm is to see our freedom reduced. And yet it is impossible for the Christian to move out of this realm. Because 'action' is always accompanied by discourse, the Christian is excluded, on account of his or her good deeds being 'silent', like the bad deeds of the criminal. In passing, we can note that Arendt is attempting to envisage a 'pure' form of politics, outside or beyond any form of violence or compulsion. We shall return to this, but we can see already that her conception of politics is the opposite of that of Carl Schmitt and philosophers of the *katēchon*.

... *natality* ...

Closely allied to this understanding of 'action' is the notion of 'natality'. Arendt offers a riposte to the Western philosophical tradition, here including Martin Heidegger, which has taken death as its point of reference. For Heidegger, a 'bracing aware-ness of one's finitude' in the sense of our anxious 'being-toward-death' is the necessary condition for truth, and a liberating source of freedom (another, less favourable, description has it as the confluence of two pessimistic traditions: Augustinian–Kierkegaardian isolationism and a 'Teutonic–Romantic' death obsession[3]). Arendt takes this in the opposite direction. Like Heidegger, she is concerned with what makes human life authentic, but she roots human difference, not in mortality, but in the condition of our being 'natal'. This is intimately bound up with the human capacity to begin new things, to *initiate*. To quote in full from *The Human Condition*:

> With word and deed we insert ourselves into the human world, and this insertion is like a second birth, in which we confirm and take upon ourselves the naked fact of our original physical appearance. This insertion is not forced upon us by necessity, like labor, and it is not prompted by utility, like work. It may be stimulated by the presence of others whose company we may wish to join, but it is never conditioned by them; its impulse

springs from the beginning which came into the world
when we were born and to which we respond by beginning something new on our own initiative.

(Arendt, 1958:176–77)

Arendt offers an etymological justification of this understanding of action as politics: the Greek noun *archein*, means 'to
begin', 'to lead', and eventually 'to rule'. She cites Augustine in
support of her reflections on natality:

Because they are *initium*, newcomers and beginners by
virtue of birth, men take initiative, are prompted into
action. *[Initium] ergo ut esset, creatus est homo, ante quem
nullus fuit* ('that there be a beginning, man was created
before whom there was nobody'), said Augustine in his
political philosophy. This beginning is not the same as the
beginning of the world; it is not the beginning of something
but of somebody, who is a beginner himself. With the
creation of man, the principle of beginning came into the
world itself, which, of course, is only another way of
saying that the principle of freedom was created when man
was created but not before. (177)

The distinguishing feature is 'startling unexpectedness', like the
emergence of life from inorganic matter by an infinite improb-
ability of inorganic processes, or the evolution of human out of
animal life. '[T]he new therefore always appears in the guise of
a miracle', and if someone is capable of action we can expect the
unexpected from them:

And this again is possible only because each man is unique,
so that with each birth something uniquely new comes into
the world. With respect to this somebody who is unique it
can be truly said that nobody was there before. If action as
beginning corresponds to the fact of birth, if it is the actu-
alization of the human condition of natality, then speech
corresponds to the fact of distinctness and is the actualiza-
tion of the human condition of plurality, that is, of living as
a distinct and unique being among equals. (1958: 7)

Arendt follows Augustine in describing birth as the entry into life of a singular and unrepeatable individual (the citation is from *The City of God*, xii. 20). 'Natality' makes action possible, that is, political action, which defines authentic self-disclosure. An individual has a capacity to stamp his or her actions as uniquely their own, and this has to be more than just the recoil we experience at the thought of our death. It is true, indeed, that we are born alone and we die alone – but it makes a difference which of these basic facts we choose to dwell on! For Arendt, the differentiation of self from self is primordial: every individual is marked, from the moment of birth, as the possessor of a unique *telos* or goal, which he or she may or may not fulfil during a lifetime.

... and love of the world

I have looked in some depth at Hannah Arendt's ideas because her intriguing, if lofty, ideal of the political life puts her critique of Christianity into perspective. That critique is idiosyncratic and overstated, and yet, I would contend, has enough uncomfortable home truths in it to merit our serious attention. Many Christians do seem to be allergic to politics, operating with what we described as a *cordon sanitaire* to divide (erroneously!) what is Caesar's from what is God's. An excessive or distorted concern for the 'spiritual', particularly in an individualised sense, has too often justified a downgrading of the social, and a consequent model of withdrawal, rather than engagement. As we shall see, much political theology is explicitly presented as a corrective of some of these aspects of the Christian tradition.

There is also something valid, if disquieting, in Arendt's observation that too often political reasoning is replaced by the certitude of moral sentiments: justified outrage or compassion. Having overwhelmingly strong feelings about an issue is no guarantee of wisdom about what to do about it – especially when the solution may require consensus or compromise. Arendt believes that Christianity's over-valuation of virtues such as pity has brought about this kind of distortion.[4]

To sum up Arendt's critique of Christianity, we turn to the third key concept in her work, by alleging that for her Christianity lacks an *amor mundi*:

> The all-absorbing passion of Hannah Arendt's life was a love for the world which exhibits itself in a relishing of human action's promise and in a respecting of the political structures which made action possible ... Human beings achieve worldliness to the extent that their lives are illumined by the recognition that care of the world is superior to care of the self. (Bernauer, 1987:1–2)

A love of or 'partisanship for' the world involves a decision to be responsible for it: such a decision was to be a 'founding act' of western culture's rebirth, the creation of a new political solidarity. Conversely, in *The Origins of Totalitarianism*, Arendt identifies anti-Semitism, imperialism and totalitarianism as crimes against the world as such. They arise out of a condition of alienation from the world and constitute a refusal to *share* the world, opting instead for 'non-worldly' processes organised around race, destiny and class. Like Carl Schmitt, Arendt is attentive to the spatial dimension of politics; the ideal of the public sphere is represented for her by the *agora* in the Greek *polis*, or in the town square of the earliest European settlers in America. It is a space to be entered into with relish, the space where we disclose ourselves.

Her objections to Christianity, when set against her own political conceptuality, can now be formulated in terms of a specific threefold deficit. First, Christianity lacks that concept of *action* (understood as a composite of deed and discourse) required for the activity of free and unforced interchange that she calls politics. Secondly, Christianity lacks, or has at least failed to nourish, our sense of *natality*: instead, through the centuries, it has been caught up in philosophies of mortality that paralyse with fear rather than energise with wonderment. Thirdly, Christianity lacks a genuine *amor mundi*, a love of the world that encourages us to respect it and take responsibility for it.

Testing Arendt's Critique: the Politics of the Early Christians

An effective retort to Arendt will consist of two strands. Firstly, it will be necessary to demonstrate that her view of Christianity as incompatible *in principle* with politics is one-sided and unfair; that those categories allegedly essential for political activity are not missing from Christian tradition in the way Arendt suggests. It is possible to argue that what Arendt sees as an antipathy between faith and the world is actually something very different, namely the birth of a new and transformed politics, and not to be judged according to the standard or model of the Greek *polis,* to which she constantly appeals. According to Duncan Forrester, Christianity is one of a number of religious and cultural forces in the ancient world which challenged and pulled apart the antique unity of society and religion; what he calls 'city religion';[5] perhaps Christianity needs to be seen in terms of this wider process.

The second tack is to look at Arendt's own political philosophy, and identify within her own work the religious (Jewish and Christian) themes which underlie what is intended as a secular political theory: themes which Arendt herself either ignores or downplays. What is of interest is the curious but striking argument of Walter Benjamin's parable of the 'puppet and the dwarf', which we examine below. Benjamin uses it to maintain that while 'theology' continues to play an important part in political discourse, nowadays it has to remain 'out of sight'. If this is true (both of Arendt and of political thought in general), then, to answer the question at the head of this chapter, *political theology is not only possible but necessary.*

To take the first of these strands, namely Arendt's case against Christianity, how true, in fact, is Forrester's description of early Christianity as a destructive, subversive force in the ancient world? The history of the early Church has been classically described as 'the story of the successful Christian revolution against the Roman Empire' (Frend, 1964:viii). But Frend goes on to acknowledge 'a very real contrast between violent and revolutionary theories and conservatism in practice' (97), so we need to be careful. Nevertheless, there is plenty of evidence of the intransigence of the early Christians – which seems to confirm Arendt's point about the gospel and the *polis* being irreconcilable.

We need only ask the crucial question: why, precisely, were the Christians persecuted?

The answer is clear: it is given to us over and over again in the sources. It was not so much the positive beliefs and practices of the Christians which aroused pagan hostility, but above all the negative element in their religion: their total refusal to worship any god but their own. The monotheistic exclusiveness of the Christians was believed to alienate the goodwill of the gods, to endanger what the Romans called the *pax deorum* (the right harmonious relationship between gods and men), and to be responsible for disasters which overtook the community ... [the Christians] openly maintained that the pagan gods either did not exist at all or that they were malevolent demons. Not only did they themselves refuse to take part in pagan religious rites; they would not even recognise that others ought to do so. (Ste Croix, 1963:25)

This is 'deity-orientated politics': the persecutions testify to Christianity's collision course with 'the living heart of pagan religiousness' (Fox, 1986:125), a religious passion which, while centuries old, was still capable of enflaming whole populations.

As early as 64 CE, when the Christians were scapegoated for the fire in Rome, the antagonism which was to flare intermittently over the following two centuries was already in place, resulting in 'a kind of schizophrenia in Christian attitudes towards government' (Chadwick, 1988:12). This ambivalence is, of course, already in evidence in the New Testament writings: from Pauline injunctions to respect the secular authorities (Romans 13), to the hostility expressed in Revelation 17 towards Babylon (Rome, the persecuting power). Once again, Frend's description of a 'revolutionary theory, conservative practice' would seem to apply. Chadwick asserts that there is no substantial change in Christian thinking regarding government and power, even with the conversion of Constantine to Christianity in 312 CE. The dominant tone seems to be one of *relativism* regarding the use of power in a fallen world, though there were alternative positions, articulated by Eusebius of Caesaria (who saw the Christianisation of the Empire as providential, and the earthly monarchy as a mirror of God's heavenly rule), and by the schismatic African Donatists, who rejected the legitimacy of the secular authorities. 'But between the two extremes there lay a passionately religious indifference to political power':

> The early Christians did not launch any particular political theory upon the Roman world. They simply ensured that subsequent political thought would be controlled by a greater debate, namely about the nature and destiny of man; that no-one should long suppose man capable of living by bread alone; that religion itself is abused if its function becomes that of providing an ultimate legitimation for whatever be the current order; and that, since individuals matter to God, they are objects of his care in this world and the next, and therefore have rights now meriting deep respect. (Chadwick, 1988:20)

Field (1998) recognises that '[a]ncient Christians regarded liberty as humanity's greatest and highest goal', a vision that survived differently in 'East' and 'West', to use terms which come to denote two distinct self-understandings:

> On the one hand, the Greek East became the Byzantine Empire, which saw itself as coterminous with, and indistinguishable from, the Church on earth. At once sacred and temporal, it possessed two hierarchies but ultimately only one absolute jurisdiction, which by right belonged to the emperor. On the other hand, the Latin West became medieval Europe, where most believed that two powers – the royal power and the 'bishops' consecrated authority' – ruled the world. (Field, 1998:xiii)

He draws attention to different trajectories within the New Testament: Paul's alleged 'monistic' view of a single principle of governance, namely divine authority; the 'dualism' of John's vision, and the martyrs' struggle against the Antichrist in an irreconcilable conflict. With these monistic and dualistic tendencies co-existing and qualifying one another, 'Christians thus expressed a deep ambivalence toward the Roman empire' (xvii).

However, this is not the full story. If the response of Christians is 'schizophrenic', we should note that we find a similar ambivalence when we examine the shaping influence of Greek and Roman political theory. Plato (the *Republic* and the *Politics*) and Aristotle (the *Politics*) are of course foremost authorities – but these philosophers do not influence the European political tradition until after the thirteenth century. What does take place is a shift of emphasis: from concern for governance of the *polis*, the small-scale city-state, to that of larger empires, which, experience showed, could only be adequately ruled by a powerful monarch. So classical political theory comes to centre more on questions of kingship and empire, and less on democracy.

Under the emperor Augustus and his successors, a *de facto* monarchy was carefully framed with respect to republican structures of government; but this balance always depended upon the goodness of the emperor. There was simply no defence against bad emperors, such as Nero or Domitian, other than assassination. The diversity of political ideals inherited from the Greeks was in fact irrelevant to the needs of the Roman Empire, whose lasting political legacy was to be an ideology of absolute kingship. Increasingly, the tendency was to revert to earlier practice, whereby the ruler derived legitimation from above, as a delegate or even incarnation of the godhead: 'From being a *princeps* greeted with *salutio* by his fellow-citizens, he became increasingly the *dominus*, hedged with divinity and approached by his subjects with *adoratio*, a ceremony of Persian origin.'[6] With the apotheosis of Constantine, as we find it in Eusebius (who describes the Emperor as the regent of God, and 'friend' of God's only begotten Word), this tendency takes an 'aggressively Christian guise'. There is no longer an attempt even to pretend that the ruler is answerable to a commonwealth.

R. A. Markus confirms this account when he speaks of the salvation of the Empire from anarchy and collapse by reforming emperors at the end of the third century.[7] This reform consisted primarily in the establishment of a centralised bureaucratic state, by emperors whose military background left little sympathy for the venerable traditions of Roman public life. The idea that governance was a shared enterprise between Emperor and Senate became increasingly fictional: it was finally dissolved in the third century, as the traditional republican political ideal of *concordia* came to be eclipsed by that of *disciplina* (Markus, 1988:83).

This same atrophy of Roman religious and political traditions is reflected in the growing appeal of Christianity, even before Constantine embraced the faith. With his conversion, Christian antipathy to pagan culture (manifested by the likes of Tertullian) was now out of place, so that by the middle of the fifth century there was a complete 'cessation of hostilities' between Christian and society. The 'Constantinian revolution' saw a religion that shortly before had been subject to persecution now being acclaimed as the legally enforced religion of the Empire. Such a radical change of status changed the self-perception of Christians. Under persecution,

> Judeo-Christian thinking about politically organised society had always stressed God's initiative and action in bringing about the only truly just society. In relation to His kingdom men were subjects rather than agents; in respect to all other, earthly kingdoms they were in some degree aliens, temporary residents, exiles from their true home. (86)

From the fourth century onwards this had to be rethought. The powerfully resonant theme of (Babylonian) *exile* had fortified Christian self-definition under persecution. Now that society was governed by Christian emperors and officials, 'exile' could hardly refer uniquely to Christians, though it might still be applied to the human condition in general. There were new issues to face: the relation of secular to sacred power, religious freedom and coercion. As the classical inheritance of Plato, Aristotle, Cicero had disappeared from view, a framework for addressing these issues was provided by the Bible and by Christian theology. The 'hints and mere seeds of ideas' relating to political thought have to be gleaned from the fundamentally religious writings of Ambrose, Augustine, and Gregory the Great.

More and more we have to recognise that Hannah Arendt's critique contains only an important half-truth about Christianity's relation to the political, at least regarding the earliest centuries of the Church's existence. Her tactic is, one might say, to use the Greek democratic ideal of the *polis* as a stick with which to beat Christianity. But the reality is more complex. It is not simply the case that Christianity 'refused' the noble Greek and Roman ideals of non-coercive political participation; in fact, these ideals were themselves already being consigned to the past, because the needs of empire dictated a very different political vision. The ancient world had already turned its back on the kind of classical politics envisaged by Arendt, in favour of a style of government that was more absolutist and coercive, and more explicit in its appeal to the trappings of religious transcendence. Post-Constantinian Christianity is taken up into this process and reinforces it, but cannot be said to have initiated it.

The persistence of the theological: Slavoj Zizek and the 'fragile absolute'

The second retort to Arendt concerns her own attempt to establish political thought on a purely secular ground. While this is never a question of 'claiming' Arendt as a tacit political theologian, the presence of religious motifs in Arendt's work is undeniable, and the possibility that her 'faith' has a greater significance than Arendt would admit has been explored (Bernauer, 1987).[8] It is interesting to note that this discussion has a similar pattern to the dialogue between critical theory and political theology (see chapters 8 and 9), in which theologians such as Metz and Moltmann try to follow through on the religious implications of 'secular' theorists like Ernst Bloch and Jürgen Habermas. More generally, the contemporary 'return to religion' which has been detected in recent philosophy, and described as the 'persistence of the theologico-philosophical' (Lefort, 2006:150), has to be accounted for.

Having begun with the question '*is political theology possible?*' we are now faced with its opposite. Is the attempt to think politically, without religious categories, itself a mistake? To take the third of Scott and Cavanaugh's definitions: both politics and theology are to do with the production of metaphysical images around which communities are organised: no *cordon sanitaire* is possible. Walter Benjamin, in his *Theses on the Concept of History* tells the parable of 'The Puppet and the Dwarf':

The story is told of an automaton constructed in such a way that it could play a winning game of chess, answering each move of an opponent with a countermove. A puppet in Turkish attire and with a hookah in its mouth sat before a chessboard placed on a large table. A system of mirrors created the illusion that this table was transparent from all sides. Actually, a little hunchback who was an expert chess player sat inside and guided the puppet's hand by means of strings. One can imagine a philosophical counterpart to this device. The puppet called 'historical materialism' is to win all the time. It can easily be a match for anyone if it enlists the services of theology, which today, as we know, is wizened and has to keep out of sight.[9]

In other words, political is theology not only possible, it is *unavoidable*. 'Theology' is still a motive force of history, even though it is ugly and unfashionable, to be 'kept out of sight' like the dwarf. For an orthodox Marxist, of course, this is heresy: surely the whole point of the doctrine of Dialectical Materialism is that it excludes any reference to the transcendent, still less the divine, in explaining human affairs. According to this view, 'political theology' is a nonsensical contradiction in terms.

Walter Benjamin is breaking ranks, which is why his work is significant for post-war political theology. In this he is not alone, since there is no shortage of socialist thinkers who have used religious language or motifs: Theodor Adorno and Ernst Bloch, as well as Benjamin come to mind. But much more recent critical theory has seen a proliferation of Marxist-inspired writers, who have taken what has been described as a 'religious turn'.[10] The list includes the work of Alain Badiou, Antonio Negri, Slavoj Zizek and Terry Eagleton.

Zizek's treatment of Christianity is as idiosyncratic as Arendt's, though he is moving in exactly the opposite direction. He seeks, from a Marxist/Lacanian perspective, to retrieve what he regards as valuable from the Christian tradition in the face of crass fundamentalisms (both Christian and non-Christian) on the one hand, and post-modern and New Age obscurantism on the other. 'Against today's onslaught of New Age pagan-ism, it thus seems both theoretically productive and politically salient to stick to Judaeo-Christian logic' (Zizek, 2000:107).

This logic is made clear in a chapter from *The Fragile Absolute*, entitled 'Christ's Uncoupling', where Zizek sees a contrast between *global* and *universal* religions. Global (or pagan) religions function by assuring the individual of his or her appropriate place in the cosmos. The ultimate good in this case is the cosmic balance of hierarchically ordered principles. By contrast, universal religions such as Christianity and Buddhism upset this global balanced cosmic Order, because they offer to the individual an *immediate* access to universality, not an indirect one. In universal religions, the hierarchical social order is fundamentally irrelevant, as we see with both Buddha and Jesus regarding their choice of disciples, and even more strikingly in the explicit injunction of Jesus to 'hate father and mother', and in his relativisation of kindred and ethnic relationships. To cite Schelling, Christ's appearance is the event of *Ent-Scheidung*: a 'slicing', a differentiating decision, which disturbs the balance of the pagan universe:

> We can see here how thoroughly heterogeneous is the Christian stance to that of pagan wisdom: in clear contrast to the ultimate horizon of pagan wisdom, the coincidence of opposites … Christianity asserts as the highest act precisely what pagan wisdom condemns as the source of Evil: the gesture of *separation*, of drawing the line, of clinging to an element that disturbs the balance of All. The pagan criticism that the Christian insight is not 'deep enough', that it fails to grasp the primordial One-All, therefore misses the point: Christianity is the miraculous Event that disturbs the balance of the One-All; it is the violent intrusion of Difference that precisely *throws the balanced circuit of the universe off the rails*. (2000:121)

The same principle of disturbance is at work in Christ's teachings about not returning insults and injuries, thereby breaking the unremitting circular logic of revenge and punishment. Passionate sexual love has something of this social 'uncoupling': witness the renunciation by Romeo and Juliet of their identities, of their 'belonging' to their respective families (remember, Arendt thinks love is a 'stranger' to politics). Zizek is careful to insist that this 'unplugging' or 'uncoupling' does not take the form of a perverted love of the victim as such: this, he claims, would merely invert the hierarchy, not subvert it. Nor does this uncoupling denote a passive withdrawal from the world, as Arendt maintains. Rather, Christian 'unplugging' is the active work of love – resisting what he has elsewhere called the temptation to 'decaffeinate' the Other!

> As every Christian knows, love is the *work* of love – the hard and arduous work of repeated 'uncoupling' in which, again and again, we have to disengage ourselves from the inertia that constrains us to identify with the particular order we were born into. Through the Christian work of compassionate love, we discern in what was hitherto a disturbing foreign body, tolerated and even modestly supported by us so that we were not too bothered by it, a subject, with its crushed dreams and desires – it is *this* Christian heritage of 'uncoupling' that is threatened by today's 'fundamentalisms', especially when they proclaim themselves Christian. Does not Fascism ultimately involve the return to the pagan *mores* which, rejecting the love of one's enemy, cultivate full identification with one's ethnic community? (Zizek, 2000:129)

Here is a paradox that leaves it unclear whether, finally, Zizek's reflections are to be read in support of Arendt's thesis about Christianity's hostility to the political, or against it. For Zizek, Christianity's essence lies in its 'uncoupling' from given ethnic and political identities. This makes it an important resource for countering fascism and nationalism ('pagan' ideologies), as well as the escapist vacuities of New Age thinking – hence the sub-title of Zizek's book: *The Fragile Absolute, or why the Christian legacy is worth fighting for.*[11]

But if the essence of Christianity is precisely this 'un-coupling', a refusal to be bound by ethnic or national ties, how can it contribute positively to the project of human conviviality?

Zizek and Arendt seem to differ considerably on precisely what is the nature of the 'pagan political legacy', and therefore on the desirability of retrieving or preserving it. In any case, for Zizek, the theologico-political contribution of Christianity is still relevant – even urgently so: 'It thus seems both theoretically productive and politically salient to stick to Judaeo-Christian logic.' But the ambiguity of that contribution suggests that, with regard to Arendt's judgement about the inadequacy of Christianity in the realm of the *polis*, the jury may still be out.

Part 2

THE HISTORY

Chapter 4

'THE DOCTRINE OF THE TWO'

Political Theology's High Traditions

This is the first of three chapters in which I attempt to establish the historical contours of political theology. The figure of Augustine of Hippo looms large, given his immense contribution in *The City of God* and elsewhere. An issue to confront is Augustine's alleged political pessimism, which can be rendered as a 'Leviathan' rather than a 'Covenant' option (chapter 3). This pessimistic strain is usually set against an optimistic brand of political theology, associated with Thomas Aquinas, and while one has to be extremely careful with such categories, I tentatively map out the territory in this chapter.

We take up the story from chapter 3, where we considered the early Church's attitude of 'revolutionary theory, conservative practice' towards the Roman Empire, in the light of Hannah Arendt's thesis about the incompatibility of Christianity and politics. What we found, instead of a straightforward confirmation of Arendt's charge, was a more complex interaction between Christian and pagan traditions, as well as within Christianity itself.

We have also begun to explore the notion of a 'doctrine of the Two', which draws on the formulation of Pope Gelasius: 'two there are by which this world is governed'. Field describes the dilemma caused by the intertwining of 'monistic' and dualistic' emphases: 'Politically, the Church had to endorse the status quo, because God had ordained all powers. Yet Christians also had to

resist it, since it was sinful' (Field, 1998:xviii). Field associates
these emphases with 'Pauline' and 'Johannine' tendencies in the
New Testament, which were eventually to blossom into the
distinctive political world-views of Eastern and Western
Christendom respectively.

Oliver O'Donovan posits a 'High Tradition' of political theology, which he dates from 1100 to 1650 (O'Donovan, 1996:4).
He maintains that the supposed 'novelty' of twentieth-century
political and liberation theologies is due to current theologians'
ignorance of this earlier tradition, bounded by the reforms of
Pope Gregory VII at the beginning, and at the other end by a
relocation of political theory in the early Enlightenment – from
theology to Moral Science. *The Desire of the Nations* is an
attempt to recover this lost tradition, and to ask why it should
have been eclipsed so effectively. This High Tradition is included within a much longer historical period known as
'Christendom', understood as 'the idea of a professedly
Christian secular political order' (195). This term also denotes a
temporal era: 'The doctrine of the Two' is, before all else, 'a
doctrine of two ages. The passing age of the principalities and
powers has overlapped with the coming age of God's Kingdom.'
This is an *eschatological* fusion, insofar as it stresses the hidden,
cosmic dimension of reality. Firstly, there is a confrontation with
the powers to be defeated, and in the longer term an attenuated
balance of the 'two rules'. The role of secular institutions in this
'overlapping' of epochs is real, but clearly subordinate:

> They are Christ's conquered enemies; yet they have an
> indirect testimony to give, bearing the marks of his sov-
> ereignty imposed upon them, negating their pretensions
> and evoking their acknowledgement. Like the surface of a
> planet pocked with craters by the bombardment it receives
> from space, the governments of the passing age show the
> impact of Christ's dawning glory. This witness of the
> secular is the central core of Christendom. (211–12)

Christendom, far from being a monolithic category, is read by
O'Donovan as a series of successive attempts 'to recover and
reassert the missionary impulse of Christianity' (196–7). He

suggests six signposts or phases, the first four of which will be summarised in this chapter:

a. the rout of the demons;
b. redefining the boundary;
c. 'two rules';
d. the supremacy of spiritual authority;
f. authority of word alone; and
g. restoring the balance.

a. 'The rout of the demons'

What O'Donovan identifies as a triumphalist phase of Christianity deserves closer attention. Christ's Resurrection – his overcoming of the power of death – understood as a cosmic 'victory' over the powers of evil, is one of the earliest Christian theological affirmations. This corresponds to the Pauline tendency mentioned above: we meet it in Paul's epistles and in the ancient and dramatic picture of the harrowing of Hell, Christ barging noisily into Satan's kingdom to release the captive souls and lead them victoriously into heaven. The notion of a victory procession is taken up by a number of patristic writers: Ignatius of Antioch, in his Epistle to the Romans, describes his journey to martyrdom as a victory procession, while Irenaeus recasts this image under the doctrinal notion of *recapitulation*. Winners as well as losers are led by Christ, in triumph, back to the Father.

This is, in short, the earliest political metaphor we have for Christianity: a glorious military victory over enemy powers.

Constantine's triumph at the Battle of Milvian Bridge outside Rome in 312, after his having allegedly been told by Christ that 'in this sign (of the cross) you shall conquer', makes this an affirmation about history, and not just a powerful metaphor. The fourth-century historian Eusebius captures the mood, in notoriously slanted fashion, with his *Ecclesiastical History* (323/4). Eusebius saw the hand of God at work in the conversion of the Empire to Christianity: Constantine, was 'an imitation of God himself', one who 'frames his earthly government according to the pattern of that divine original, feeling strength in its conformity to the Monarchy of God'. The emperor participates, at the level of politics, in the action of the *Logos* who governs nature and the cosmos; he is therefore the reflection and counterpart in the visible world of God's invisible Logos, an intermediary between the earthly and heavenly kingdoms. In his *Life of Constantine*, and in shorter panageyrics to the emperor, he writes with wonder about revolutionary events, and about a definitive revelation of God's glory which has overthrown the tutelary deities of the Empire. The conversion of Constantine and the subsequent growth of public Christianity are nothing short of miraculous. Markus summarises:

> Church and Empire were both reflections of a heavenly kingdom; the monarchy of Constantine brought that kingdom to men, and with his conversion the earthly city became the city of God ... Christianity and the Empire became indissolubly united: Christianity was the Empire's religion and the Empire its proper, divinely intended, setting. (Markus, 1988:93)

What is missing is an eschatological perspective. The triumph Eusebius is recording is totally in the present, and totally identified with the person of the Christian emperor. There is no future dimension to God's victory: idolatry has set in. Eusebius sets the tone for other historians, such as Rufinus (composer of another *Ecclesiastical History*) and Orosius (who writes expansively of another Christian emperor, Theodosius I). With the court historian Eusebius and his successors, two previously distinct ideas had been effectively fused together: 'Roman' and 'Christian'.

b. *'Redefining the boundary'*
O'Donovan sees Ambrose (338–97 CE) and Augustine (354–430) struggling with the new problem of authority arising from these developments: with whom did ultimate authority rest in a 'Christian society'? Eusebian assumptions are occasionally but not systematically challenged by Ambrose of Milan, though his rebuke and disciplining of various emperors (Valentinian II in 386, Theodosius in 390) are a powerful demonstration that in his judgement the Emperor was in the church, not above it. There are new lines beginning to be drawn, but in general the identification of 'Christian' and 'Roman' is presupposed by

Ambrose, and by most of the historians of this period – even, initially, by Augustine himself.

For pagan and Christian commentators alike, a 'providential-ist' view of the Empire denoted a belief in the special mission of Rome, which carried with it a tendency to interpret world events e.g. military success or failure, in moral terms. Divine protec-tion was expected, which makes the incursions of the Goths and the sacking of Rome in 410 as traumatic an event as the September 11th atrocities for the United States in our own time. The faithful found themselves open to two charges from their pagan adversaries: firstly, that the ascendancy of the Christian religion had angered the gods, secondly that Christian other-worldliness left Christians indifferent to the fate of the Empire in any case (Hannah Arendt's charge). But Christians too were traumatised: how could such a disaster have happened, if God was the protector of the Christian empire and its Christian emperor?

Augustine responds with *The City of God* (written between 413 and 427) as an argument against two forms of 'city theo-logy', one pagan, one Christian. He means to show that there was nothing special or unique about the Roman Empire as such, and nothing special or unique about the Empire in its baptised version. In each case, Augustine asserts a neutral or agnostic view of the significance of history: 'The Roman Empire (and by implication, any earthly society) is of itself neither holy nor diabolical. Like all human work, its ultimate value is determined by the ultimate allegiances of its creators: their piety or impiety' (Markus, 1988:105).

As we shall see, the key word here is 'ultimate'. Augustine's 'refusal to bless' Eusebian political theology is also a refusal to think apocalyptically, to regard the Roman Empire as a special instrument either of God or of Satan. The fundamental distinction runs between two 'cities', the *civitas* of God and the *civitas* of the Devil. These extend beyond the human community, originating in the choice of angels to serve or not to serve God. On a human level, we have Cain (earthly city) and Seth (the heavenly), two lines which progress through biblical history. The earthly city is represented in the empires of Assyria and Rome; the Church re-presents the heavenly city ... 'The two cities were created by two kinds of love: the earthly city was created by self-love reaching the point of contempt for God, the heavenly city by the love of God carried as far as contempt of self.' (Bk XIV, 28)

Our temporal history is called the *saeculum*, in which the two cities are mixed into one another, until they shall be separated at the end of time (Bk I, 35). These two cities are eschatological realities, co-existing in the present *saeculum*. They do not differ externally, but only internally, in how they respond to the same experiences: both feel the same vicissitudes of fortune, good or bad; but they do so not with the same faith nor the same hope, not the same love – until they shall be separated in the last judgement. Christians are therefore exiles, registered aliens, existing in this disordered world.

> For Augustine, the *saeculum* is a sinister thing. It is a penal existence, marked by the extremes of misery and suffering, by suicide, madness, by 'more diseases than any book of medicine can include', and by the inexplicable torment of small children … Like a top set off balance, it wobbles up and down without rhyme or reason. (Brown, 1965:11)

Brown goes on to note that 'there are no verbs of historical movement in the City of God, no sense of progress to aims that may be achieved in history'. Christians are in the *saeculum* as a vast experimental laboratory (the image of the olive press, squeezing the olives for oil, is used). The earthly city was founded by a murderer, and has inherited the sin of Adam. Augustine famously asks: 'Set justice aside, and what are kingdoms but great robberies?' (Book IV, 4). Human nature, being fundamentally dislocated, cannot sustain moral goals such as justice, and the earthly city is driven by the desire to dominate:

> [T]he outward expression of this 'lust' in the form of organised states is merely a symptom. The extent and even the admitted injustice of the state-building that Augustine observed, and commented on in his blistering terms, was of purely secondary importance … so to say, as Lord Acton would, that 'all power tends to corrupt, and absolute power corrupts absolutely', would have struck Augustine as being

rather like saying that a man caught measles from having spots. (Brown, 1965:10)

In his seminal study on Augustine's political theology, Markus agrees with Brown's pessimism:

> Augustine saw the whole course of history, past, present and future, as a dramatic conflict of the two cities, that is to say, in terms of a tension of forces which will appear in their naked reality beyond temporal history. From this point of view the sphere in which human kingdoms, empires and all states have their being is radically ambiguous, and all social institutions and human groupings are radically affected with this ambiguity ... in Augustine's mature thought there is no trace of a theory of the state as concerned with man's self-fulfilment, perfection, the god life, felicity, or with 'educating' man towards such purposes. Its function is more restricted: it is to cancel out at least some of the effects of sin.
>
> (Markus, 1988 [1970], 62–3, 94–5)

There is, therefore, a place for an ordered hierarchy of established power that holds in check the human desire for domination and vengeance – a pragmatic acceptance of the need for order in society. Even so, political life is 'downgraded', having no straightforward connection to the ultimates of human destiny. Social institutions meet only limited needs, and have no immediate relation to perfection or salvation.

Augustine is significant as the only major orthodox figure of the fourth century who was disturbed by the Eusebian sacralisation of the Empire, rejecting 'the fundamental assumption that any slice of secular history, any nation, institution or society, could have an indispensable place in the historical realisation of God's purpose' (Markus, 1988:57). The fulfilment promised to man is revealed as a unique possibility given in Christ and only achieved in his kingdom. No historical conditions can provide so much as a shadow of this fulfilment, no historical process can lead either towards or away from it, so optimism and pessimism are equally irrelevant.

c. 'Two there are ... by which this world is ruled'

Despite Augustine's eschatological vision, his views were used in the Middle Ages to justify the creation of 'Christendom', in which human history was seen as the growing together of the earthly and heavenly cities. With figures like Otto of Freising in the twelfth century, and the emperor Frederick Barbarossa, Christianity and the empire became fused once more; with the coining of the Holy Roman Empire, protest against Christendom was left in the hands of fringe groups and protest groups throughout the Middle Ages.

Pope Gelasius I, writing to the Emperor Anastasius in the generation after Augustine, reworks the formula of the 'Two Cities' in a way that is significant, namely as a more general and ambiguous formula about government.[1] The unclarity of this 'doctrine of the Two' shifts the delicate eschatology of Augustine, and in the high and late Middle Ages the problem of the 'theologico-political' is recast as a search for the correct balance between two legitimate jurisdictions: the consecrated authority of priests, and royal power. The sense of a qualitative differentiation between them has been lost. Cavanaugh refers to a 'flattening out'; the two spheres now struggle with each other for ascendancy over the one city which is to be ruled, namely Christendom. Quoting O'Donovan, Cavanaugh sees 'differentiation being sacrificed to equilibrium, the two offices turning into each other's shadows' (2006:309).

With Pope Gregory the Great (590–604) we see how far the Augustinian vision has been eclipsed. Gregory worked with a conception of all rule and authority in terms of service, influenced as he was by traditions of monastic life, especially Benedictine: in this spirit, the tension between the 'Two Cities' is spiritualised. While Augustine had been arguing against the fascination of a sacralised Roman conception of the political, by the time of Gregory, these seductive pagan traditions were simply no longer a viable alternative to the Christian world-view. The earthly powers have been absorbed into the spiritual community, and all authority is conceived in religious terms, so that the term 'rector' could refer both to 'ruler' in the general sense and to the presider (bishop) over the Christian community.

For Gregory I, the principal challenge of political life is to keep the active and contemplative elements in balance. It is this simpler, less nuanced vision that proves to be more acceptable and more enduring than the complexity of Augustine's careful synthesis.

d. The supremacy of spiritual authority

Several centuries later, the eschatological tension is revived once more, with Pope Gregory VII (1020/1025–85) and his definitive assertion of spiritual authority as supreme over the secular powers. The high ideals of monasticism give a reform-ing spiritual energy to these claims, so that by the time of the Investiture Crisis in the eleventh century we have, as it were, an arm-wrestling contest between 'imperial power with its toady-ing bishops, or a papacy influenced by the monastic model of strict religious separation from the world' (Ozment: 1980:141). O'Donovan senses in Gregory's reforming energy a renewed eschatological edge: a recovery of the patristic sense of conflict with the supernatural powers, which depreciates the secular political order and reinforces its subordination (1996:205).

The Investiture Controversy is most dramatically represented by the stand-off between Gregory and the German emperor Henry IV over the existence of mutual privileges of appointment and legitimation. The attempt by Gregory and the Reformers to rescind secular involvement in church appointments led to mutual 'dethronings' of Pope and Emperor in 1075/6, and a conflict which saw the Emperor excommunicated twice and Gregory eventually deposed and exiled from Rome in 1085. Resolution of the controversy does not come into view until the Concordat of Worms in 1122, by which date the political theo-logical landscape, not least in Germany, had been altered out of all recognition.

Predominant in the Gregorian reform is a break with the early medieval search for equilibrium and a new assertion of the priority of the spiritual. The Church was founded by God alone, therefore the papacy was the sole universal power, entrusted with the task of embracing all humanity in a single society, with divine will the only law. The pope, as head of the Church, was vice-regent of God on earth, and disobedience towards him implied disobedience to God and a defection from Christianity. In the two centuries following the investiture crisis we see the persistent assertion of the uncompromising claim for papal authority which so scandalised Martin Luther. Gregory represents the high water mark, along with Innocent III (1198–1216), who effectively proclaims a theocracy by which popes and kings are related 'as sun and moon'; and by Boniface VIII (1294–1303), whose bull *Unam sanctam* asserted the subjection of the secular to the spiritual power. Innocent puts it thus:

> You see then who is this servant set over the household, truly the vicar of Jesus Christ, successor of Peter, anointed of the Lord, a God of Pharoah, set between God and man, lower than God but higher than man, who judges all and is to be judged by no one.

It may be assumed that many of the problems that afflicted the popes in subsequent centuries stemmed from their trying to assert this high ideal in increasingly hostile and unrealistic circumstances. O'Donovan offers a relatively benign reading: indeed, Gregory's papal apologetic marks the beginning of what he terms the 'High Tradition' of political theology. At its best, the reforming papal arguments appeal to a vision of 'a universal jurisdiction bringing order to the jungle of competing claims and interests', something like the United Nations (O'Donovan, 1996:206). Without the explicit guidance, involvement and legitimation of sacred leaders (that is, the pope), the struggling 'new order' of fractious kings and barons is only sheer conflict and brute force, incapable of providing justice. That is, it lacks true political authority.

From Investiture to the Conciliar Movement

In fact the power struggle between the papacy and secular rulers, which is graphically symbolised in the stand-off at the Investiture Controversy, should be seen as one of two versions or expressions of the same late medieval controversy in the late Middle Ages. The fifteenth-century Conciliarist crisis, arising from the competing claims of multiple popes, addresses from *within* the Church those issues of authority which had up to then been pressed from 'outside', that is, from secular rulers. In each case we can speak tentatively of two ways of justifying authority from 'top down' to 'bottom up'.[2]

Regarding popes versus princes: papal pre-eminence was justified from three sources: scripture (Matthew 16:19, Christ's commission to Peter); a patristic and Augustinian theological tradition which saw the political community as secondary and artificial; thirdly, from historical precedents of princely submission (including a fraudulent document from the ninth century, entitled the *Donation of Constantine*). From the other side, arguments in favour of secular autonomy are likewise marshalled from the New Testament (Romans 13 and Luke 20.25, 'Give unto Caesar'), as well as from traditions of Roman law, freshly retrieved in the twelfth century, and, from around 1260, the works of Aristotle, especially the *Politics*. Here was a tradition that saw political communities as part of the natural order of things, and not of a sinful world after the Fall.

Each side had its extreme positions. Giles of Rome is the extreme apologist for papal power. Marsilius of Padua, whose account of power devolving directly from God to 'the people', who then empowered both king and pope, anticipates some aspects of the Reformation, and would be as good a patron of the position usually referred to as 'Erastian'. Between these extremes, John of Paris and Thomas Aquinas represent moderate positions, which attempted to see the tension in terms of equilibrium between parallel jurisdictions: this middle ground was more theoretical than actual, however, and under pressure, John tilted towards royal power, Aquinas in favour of the papal/ecclesiastical:

> The ecclesiopolitical history of the Middle Ages was never marked by true equilibrium; temporal and spiritual power struggled for dominance within Christian Europe in a contest secular rulers won decisively both in theory and in fact by the eve of the Reformation. (Ozment, 1980:178)

The Conciliarist crisis replays these issues in a debate that is internal to the church but with considerable ramifications beyond it. The Council of Constance (1414–17) brought to an end a thirty-six year long schism, which at its darkest point saw three rival claimants to the throne of Peter. The need to adjudicate between them makes this a period of rich juridical and theological reflection upon the nature of both ecclesial and, inevitably, political power. This has meant that this short-lived 'conciliar experiment' and the Council's decree *Sacrosancta* (1415) have been given an enormous, if perhaps exaggerated, significance:

> Probably the most revolutionary official document in the history of the world is the decree of the Council of Constance asserting its superiority to the pope, and striving to turn into a tepid constitutionalism the divine authority of a thousand years. (Figgis, 1931:32)

Sacrosancta is seen to be the religious equivalent of the *Magna Carta*, 'a classic defence of the rights of the privileged many against the claims of the one' (Ozment, 1980:157). The enormity of the stakes is conveyed by Ozment's comparison: deposing a pope is like executing a king. The procedure was psychologically and legally difficult, and conciliarist supporters delayed over it as long as possible. In this interval, as stated, considerable intellectual work was done, with the resources of Aristotle to the fore, above all the principle of *epikeia*, or equity, requiring that universal laws had to be adjusted to particular circumstances. On these grounds, the deposition of a pope by a council becomes both conceivable and justifiable. Though the council itself was more cautious than Figgis' judgement implies, its implications were taken up by the Reformers, not least Calvinists articulating a 'right of resistance' against unjust rulers: if a council had the power to depose a pope for the sake of the well-being of the larger community, then the same arguments applied to the removal of political tyrants.

Finally, mention should be made of a classic and groundbreaking attempt to formulate a 'doctrine of the two', namely Ernst Kantorowicz's, *The King's Two Bodies* (1957), 'a book that would be the guide for generations of scholars through the arcane mysteries of medieval political theology … a wonder-

fully exciting and constantly rewarding book': thus writes
W. C. Jordan in his introduction to the 1997 anniversary edition
(p. xv). In his own words, Kantorowicz's study

> deals with certain cyphers of the sovereign state and its
> perpetuity (Crown, Dignity, Patria and others) exclusively
> from the point of view of presenting political creeds such
> as they were understood in their initial stage and at a time
> when they served as a vehicle for putting the early modern
> commonwealths on their own feet.
>
> (Kantorowicz, 1997:xix)

The particular cypher that interests him is a 'mystic fiction', the
'fiction of the King's Two Bodies, its transformations, implications and radiations' (ibid). Kantorowicz works back from this
metaphor in Tudor political doctrine in order to reconstruct its
unknown medieval precedents: kingship is seen to be centred
variously on Christ, law, polity, or man (as in Dante's treatise on
Monarchy). Apart from the inherent value of this historical
study, Kantorowicz's investigation of 'political mysticism' provides an interesting counterpart to his German contemporary,
Carl Schmitt, whose 'political theology', as we have seen, is not
free of mythological content.

Augustine and Aquinas

O'Donovan's six-point scheme covers a range of different
expressions of the Christian faith, veering from a triumphalism
which eclipses the secular order altogether, to an accommodation between the secular and religious powers which sees them
in fragile equilibrium, to different versions of reform which
insist on the primacy of the spiritual once again, followed by an
attempt to restore the balance once more.

Among these vicissitudes, we need to examine what is sometimes presented as a kind of 'showdown' between two great
political-theological traditions. The theology of Thomas
Aquinas is alleged to fit into the optimistic 'theonomous' tradition, of participatory reflection upon God as Intelligence and
Love; as humanity's 'common good' (for a summary of this

argument, see Tracy, 1994). The Augustinian tradition, by contrast, refuses this hopefulness for a decidedly more pessimistic take on how sinful humanity stands before God. In each case the consequences are felt in terms of what kind of political order can be built on their respective foundations – Covenant and Leviathan, once again. We need to proceed very carefully, as it is nearly impossible to say anything that is not a distorting caricature, particularly where Augustine is concerned. But provided we recognise that these are very broad brushstrokes, I will attempt to set out the parameters.

In broad terms, the story runs as follows. The great classical heritage of political reflection (comprising Plato, Aristotle and the Stoics) was eclipsed during the early centuries of the Christian era, for the reasons we saw in chapter 3, so that religious-political questions came to be resourced directly from scripture and the Christian tradition. Augustine's synthesis in *The City of God* is a clear high point, whose remarkable fruitfulness, even today, makes him the 'godfather' of Christian political theology. Nevertheless, his synthesis was not maintained: less nuanced versions of the 'theology of the Two' came into play, so that political theology became largely a question of negotiating the correct balance between the 'spiritual' and 'secular' realms.

Thomas Aquinas (c.1224–74) frames the 'theologico-political' with the help of Aristotle, though it may be important to note with contemporary scholars (Bauerschmidt, 2004) that discussion of, for example, natural law and virtue in Aquinas should never be divorced from their theological context. Thomas' appropriation of 'the Philosopher' runs contrary to the neoplatonist Augustinian tradition, which for the most part saw earthly politics as 'a regrettable and squalid business', at best a necessary evil, but a product of the Fall and inevitably tied up with the sinful condition of humankind (Dyson, 2002:xxiv). This theocratic tradition held that a complete submission of earthly princes to the spiritual powers was the only way forward for humanity, a view reinforced by the Investiture Crisis, and summed up for Dyson by the Augustinian assertion that '[t]rue justice, however, does not exist other than in that commonwealth whose founder and ruler is Christ'. (*City of God*: 2.21).

Thomas' appropriation of the *Politics* and *Nicomachean Ethics,* always controlled by scriptural and theological tradition, lays the foundations for a 'milder and more optimistic' political theory (Dyson, xxv). Where Augustine saw the individual faced with a choice between two loves and two cities, St Thomas sees no irreconcilable tension between the pursuit of earthly and eternal goods: he agrees with Aristotle, that 'man is by nature a political animal' (*Summa Theologiae,* Ia 96:4). There is here a new confidence in political society and justice as natural qualities and possibilities, which do not, after all, need to be underwritten by the pope (as the papal apologists had been arguing). And political society begins to look like something a bit more respectable than the thinly-legitimised banditry scoffed at by Augustine in *The City of God*.[3] Government is 'not ordained to do little more than hold the lid on human destructiveness by force and fear. It is a benevolent administration suited to the kind of sociable and co-operating creature that man is by nature' (xxvi). The end of political activity is virtue and happiness, not the suppression of rebellion. Dyson points out that Thomas' position is less explicitly set out, as he is never called upon to explicate his view in the way that Augustine was, in response to the crisis of 410. Thomas seems to be firmly within the mainstream of tradition, which acknowledges that spiritual and secular powers are both derived from Divine power, but 'in those things which pertain to the civil good, the secular power should be obeyed before the spiritual, according to Matthew 22.21'.[4] This leads to differences of emphasis from Augustine (though never explicit disagreement) on matters such as resistance of tyrants, private property and analysis of law (xxix–xxxv).

R. W. Dyson depicts a strong contrast between the two theologians: it is at least arguable that he overstates the case, but if so he is far from being alone. The view that Augustine's pessimism infected his thinking about the political is fairly widespread; put bluntly, he does not believe in the capacity of human beings to establish a decent society for themselves. The earthly city is marked by sin, that is, the denial of God and others, in favour of self-love and self-assertion, of *dominium* as an end in itself. Augustine denies the viability of a *res publica* or commonwealth, since human beings are unable to achieve true unity by agreeing on the things they love ultimately. The fulfilment offered by the earthly city can only be intermediate or provisional, a view that makes for a political vacuum. To use Moltmann's terms, it seems Augustine belongs firmly in the 'Leviathan' rather than the 'Covenant' camp. Once again, we have politics understood as *katēchon*, as restraint of social chaos. And the disturbing outcome of this view, it is alleged, is the ease with which Augustine was able to justify coercive measures against the Donatist schismatics, leading to the accusation that he is 'first theologian of the Inquisition'.

As suggested above, Thomas Aquinas seems to speak in a different tone of voice, though his questions are much the same. His treatise on law and political theory (*Summa Theologicae* vol. 28:1a, 2ae, 90–9) investigates political authority, and the recognition that we are obliged to obey just rulers: what are the *roots* of this obligation? By what warrant does a legislator bind the consciences of men? Suffice to say that Thomas' answer is different from a 'Hobbesian' or Leviathan view; rather, human government is based on a premise of harmony rather than con-flict – a belief that all can achieve complete freedom. With Aristotle, Aquinas holds human beings to be social by nature, drawn into the common good, which is God, by the 'beauty of order' (1.96.3 ad.3). 'Thus we might say that, on the level of human community, the common good is the good of ordered common life itself, a goodness that is a participation in the goodness of God' (Bauerschmidt, 2004:56).

We need to be very careful about buying too readily into the caricature of Augustine as a deeply pessimistic thinker – and by the same token, building up the optimistic rationality of the Thomist position. As we have seen in chapter 4, the Greek ideal of the *polis* was already losing its hold on the classical imagina-tion at the time of Augustine's writing *The City of God*. The problem now was how to govern an empire, rather than a *polis*, and scepticism towards the Platonic, Aristotelian and Stoic ideals had come to be a widespread, not just a Christian trait.

Jean Bethke Elshtain argues for a clear distinction between scepticism (which Augustine shared with many of his contem-poraries, though his own version was theologically grounded), and the pessimism of which he is often accused, as we have seen. She warns us that the view of Augustine as a 'political realist', scathingly dismissive of the political order, is too easily gleaned by narrowly selective excerpts from *The City of God* – what she describes as 'Augustine Lite' (Elshtain, 2004:35). Far from his views representing a pessimistic *realpolitik*, they advocate a high ideal of human social life. Augustine's criticism of the Roman commonwealth's falling short of this ideal should not be read as a dismissal of all human attempts to live socially: Elshtain cites Rowan Williams to the effect that 'Augustine's condemnation of "public" life in the classical world is, consistently, that it is not public enough' (Williams, 1987:68).

We may note once again the central importance of Augustine's refusal to absolutise any specific political regime. Elshtain and Markus each recognise that this is what makes Augustine so contemporary with us, after the collapse in our own time of various forms of political utopianism. These fiascos are invariably established on mistaken assumptions about human malleability and potential. Given such nightmarish distortions, perhaps it is the 'optimistic' doctrine of Aquinas which comes under the closest scrutiny: how does a Thomist work out a system of government which will realise, in fact, the theoretical harmony between law and freedom? For Augustine's part, it is important that he be rescued from those who wish to enlist him on the side of political 'realism' or limitation. This would be to ignore his positive contribution concerning hope and *caritas*: 'he can never be enlisted on behalf of the depredators of mankind' (Elshtain, 2004:47).

Chapter 5

'A STORMY PILGRIMAGE'

Political Theologies of the Reformation

Endings – things falling apart – are usually a lot easier to trace than origins. Early modernity, coinciding with the end of the High Tradition of political theology, can be identified by some of the key markers of the collapse of 'Christendom', such as the end of the Thirty Years' War (specifically the Treaty of Westphalia, 1648), and the publication of Hobbes' *Leviathan* (1651). Westphalia marks the end of the 'Wars of Religion', and the enshrinement of the doctrine of *cuius regio eius religio* ('religion according to the ruler of the territory'), the formula that announces the pre-eminence of the secular authorities in matters of religion. Thomas Hobbes is generally regarded as the father of modern secular political theory, and the justification of secular authority we find in *Leviathan* parallels and reinforces the important shifts symbolised by the Westphalian doctrine.

Making sense of the two centuries that precede this event and this publication is harder work; this chapter can do little more than note the principal figures and influences. Even so, there is inevitably a high degree of selection, with scant room for important figures such as John Wyclif, Jan Huss, Niccolò Machiavelli, Desiderius Erasmus or Thomas More. I will dwell instead on three thinkers whose achievement is especially important or representative. Scholars speak of a mainstream reformed tradition of *magisterial reformers*, so-called because they depended upon the support (i.e. the coercive power) of the magistrate or civil authority to carry out their reforms. This group includes Martin Luther, Zwingli, John Calvin, and Thomas Cranmer. The more *radical reformers* rejected this alliance, however, and in doing so left behind the notion of Christendom as a unitary society, comprising a balance of secular and spiritual authorities. The key strands here are Thomas Müntzer and the Anabaptist traditions. So an overview of key themes as they are played out in the thought of Luther, Calvin and Müntzer will open this chapter.

I will then examine W. T. Cavanaugh's revision of this history, which he undertakes as part of his critique of political liberalism. Cavanaugh seeks to construct a political theology that takes seriously those ecclesiological and liturgical dimensions neglected or downplayed since the post-Westphalian collapse of 'Christendom'. In order to do this, a dramatic reconsideration of the origins and function of the modern state is needed – which turns out to have significant implications for contemporary political theology.

The Magisterial Reformers: Luther and Calvin

We begin with the mainstream or magisterial reformers, who accepted the necessity of the civil powers, though this does not mean they were of one mind as to how civil and spiritual powers should collaborate. The two distinct theological understandings of the political which open up within the mainstream Protestant Reformation in fact diverge on this issue: the 'Two Kingdoms' doctrine of Martin Luther, and the Reformed (Calvinist) doctrine of the 'Lordship of Christ'.

Martin Luther's political theology is only comprehensible in terms of his devastating experience of the 'justice of God', as prefigured by Paul and Augustine. Luther's proclamation of the individual's fundamental and unmediated relation before God both challenges the Church's claim to be a mediator of salvation, and leans in the direction of modern ideas of individualism and modern democracy. He takes up the baton of articulating what we have been referring to as 'the Doctrine of the Two' ('Two there are, by which this world is ruled'). Luther's championing of the doctrine of the 'priesthood of all believers' is a refutation of the medieval Catholic notion of separate compartments, the spiritual and secular 'estates': '[a]ll Christians are truly of the spiritual estate, and there is no difference between them except that of function.'[1] Equally unacceptable is the subordination of the secular to the temporal, specifically in the assertion of papal supremacy over the temporal powers.

Luther's theory of the 'Two Kingdoms' or 'Two Governments' in *Temporal Authority* gives an alternative to the 'two estates' theory. Like Augustine, Luther finds himself arguing in two directions at once: he also needs to refute the religious separatism of the Anabaptists, whose refusal to recognise or take part in the coercive power of the state was, of course, a flat denial of the state's divine origin. Given these tensions, Luther addresses fundamental questions. What is the purpose and task of secular authority? What are its proper limits, and how should it relate to the spiritual? How should Christians exercise secular authority if and when they are called to do so?

His answer, directed against the Anabaptist rejection of the secular powers, is framed by Romans 13:1–7, and by 1 Peter 2:13–14: 'Be subject to every human institution for the Lord's sake, whether it be to the king as supreme to governors as sent by him for the punishment of evildoers and the approval of those who do good'. The 'Two Kingdoms' position runs as follows:

> For God has established two kinds of government among men. The one is spiritual; it has no sword, but it has the word, by means of which men are to become good and righteous, so that with this righteousness they may attain eternal life. He administers this righteousness through the word, which he has committed to the preachers. The other kind is worldly government, which works through the sword so that those who do not want to be good and righteous to eternal life may be forced to become good and righteous in the eyes of the world. He administers this righteousness through the sword.

There is no uniform doctrine of the Two Kingdoms; even today the notion is used to justify quite varied political options. Stephenson (1981) suggests there is often a conflation of two distinct theories or assertions: firstly, the Augustinian doctrine of the Two Cities, intermingled in the present age like 'mouse droppings among the peppercorns, tares among the grain'; secondly, an assertion about God's sovereignty in the world, operating in two distinct ways or orders of government: through the spiritual and secular authorities. 'Luther's "so-called" doctrine of the two kingdoms is in fact a pragmatic combination of these two conceptual pairs, the first of contrasts and the second of correlates ... it could be used as a kind of conceptual clotheshorse on which to spread out the whole of his theology' (Stephenson, 1981:322–3). So if we emphasise the *eschatological* antagonistic dualism of the first assertion, then the term 'two kingdoms' is usually preferred. If we are discussing the inter-related nature or method of God's activity, then reference to two 'governments' (*Zwei-Regiment-Lehre*) is more common.

As is largely recognised, the inherent dualism of the anthropology of the 'Two Kingdoms' and the two regiments eventually takes its toll. Martin Luther sees the spiritual regiment as concerned with the soul and the inner person, and the worldly regiment concerned with the body, external goods, and relationships in the world. Jürgen Moltmann points out how an inversion of this doctrine becomes an affirmation of the Protestant world, with an understanding of Church and State as distinct and separate dimensions of the world, as well as a separation of private and public, or inner and outer. 'With that, faith was made world-less and the world was made faith–less. God became unreal and reality God-less. The world was left to unfaith, and faith retired into the shell of the introspection of the pious soul' (Moltmann, 1989:75).

The inherent danger and instability of the Two Kingdoms position is that a separation of the two realms, the religious and the political, results too easily in an other-worldly form of piety on the one hand, and an unbridled and unaccountable nationalism on the other. McGrath notes: 'The way was opened to the eventual domination of the church by the state which was to become a virtually universal feature of Lutheranism'. Above all, Luther's scheme (unlike Augustine's) does not allow for a Christian critique of structural injustice, specifically for any kind of effective resistance to tyranny or unjust governance – a weakness the twentieth-century consequences of which are all too evident. Stephenson commends the doctrine of the Two

Kingdoms as 'a salutary antidote to the idolatry of enthusiasm which would identify law and gospel, summoning heaven to earth and producing hell' (1981:337). More generally, however, commentators see Luther's opinions on allegiance and resistance as pragmatically or even opportunistically motivated.

The other pole of mainline Protestant thought is the Reformed teaching that the 'Lordship of Christ' permeates every aspect of life, and therefore demands of the Christian an unconditional discipleship. John Calvin writes as a second-generation reformer, when the Protestants themselves are breaking up into sectarian factions, and when the Catholic reformation is also under way. He has therefore to differentiate his position from the extreme millenarianism of groups like the Anabaptists, whose anarchy provoked fear in Lutheran and Catholic alike.

Calvin's position is set out in the *Institutes of the Christian Religion*, Bk IV ch 20: 'On Civil Government'; only in this final section does he speak of the scope and nature of the civil political. He reinforces the understanding of the two kingdoms as distinct, but acknowledges the dangers of anarchy and absolutism if the affairs of the state are divorced completely from those of religion.

> The end of secular government, however, while we remain in this world, is to foster and protect the external worship of God, defend pure doctrine and the good condition of the Church, accommodate the ways we live to [the requirements of] human society, mould our conduct to civil justice, reconcile us to one another, and uphold and defend the common peace and tranquillity. (para 2)

The Reformed Church developed in city-states, such as Zurich and Geneva, which already had democratic forms of citizenship (in contrast to Lutheran origins in the principalities). The Christian city was already much more a fusion of faith and politics, and there is not such a strong divide between human and divine justice; Calvin wants to explore the relation between them, rather than stress their distinction. Even in politics, there is a personal call to the discipleship of Christ: 'According to the

Reformed view, the Christian does not live in two different worlds; he or she lives in the one encompassing lordship of Christ in the various relationships of this world' (Moltmann, 1989:81). In addition, where Martin Luther had expounded the doctrine of the 'general priesthood of all believers' in opposition to the clerical tyranny of Rome, the Reformed recovery of the language of covenant and the 'general kingship of all believers' were articulated in the face of the danger posed by political, not ecclesial, tyrants.

Calvin was the least orginal of the main Reformers, yet provided the Reformation's most eloquent theological statement: the *Institutes*; and its most disciplined institutional form: the Genevan church (Ozment: 1980:372). His lasting achievements are well-recorded, especially the coherence of Calvinist doctrine with modern capitalist economic developments: Max Weber's familiar account of capitalism's indebtedness to the doctrine of predestination as an incentive to strive for signs of God's favour in the economic sphere. It is probably fair to say that this was a grudging adjustment to sixteenth-century realities, rather than inherent to Calvinism. A similar point applies to the 'right of resistance' which is associated with Calvinist thought, but may owe more to historical circumstances. Regarding Moltmann's distinction of 'Covenant versus Leviathan' (chapter 2): the development of a 'Covenant' theology arises from the vulnerability of French Calvinists during the Wars of Religion; other scholars argue for a Lutheran rather than Calvinist provenance of the doctrine, however. More evident is Calvin's preference for 'collegiality' over 'singularity', which lends itself to the Covenant model; his positive attempt to construct a new society on Christian principles is most clearly inspirational for those who constructed 'one nation under God' in the New World.

In some respects, Calvin's position is intermediate between that of Luther and a radical reformer like Müntzer: Calvin clearly believed (with Luther) in the importance of order and good governance, but (unlike Luther) saw 'Church' and 'state' as equal partners in a complementary work, namely good government according to scriptural norms. 'For Calvin, then, politics was important and not secondary in God's pecking order to so-called purely spiritual matters' (Bradstock, 2004:73). At

the same time, as with Luther, his is a theology of 'restraint';
Harro Höpfl sums up the differences thus:

> Fallen humanity is constitutionally prone to wickedness,
> for which Calvin had a wide range of terms which modern
> English cannot match; the passions in each man are con-
> ceived by Calvin to resemble a boiling cauldron or a
> smouldering fire. Where there is no external restraint (as is
> notably the case with kings), the fire 'breaks out' and
> 'rages' (to use Calvin's and Luther's favourite terms for the
> conduct of the wicked and tyrants). The imposition of a
> 'bridle' or 'brake' is therefore indispensible. But restrain-
> ing is not enough: for there is God's work to be done, and
> people must be *directed* to it. So that, whereas Luther's
> metaphor for the polity is the 'sword', Calvin's is the
> school or the 'bridle': the twofold government imposes
> 'discipline', direction and restraint together.
>
> (Höpfl 1991:xxiii)

'A Stormy Pilgrimage': Thomas Müntzer and the Radical Reform

It is this concern for 'restraint' that distinguishes Luther and
Calvin from the radical reformers, who are often loosely and
probably not very acurately grouped together as 'Anabaptists'.
For many critics, Luther's hardening against any support for the
peasants meant a narrowing of the social promise of the
Reformation: his writings on freedom and religious equality
were taken up by desperate people and applied to broad-based
social and religious demands, going well beyond what he envisaged, forcing him to distance himself. And yet the logic of the
radical reform position is that taking seriously the grievances of
the peasants (which even Luther himself tried to do), could only
entail a radical community of goods, and an acceptance of the
provisionality of private property ('the greatest enemy of love').
Not 'reform', but a radical reconstruction of the Church along
New Testament lines was called for, as well as a pacifist and
separatist break with the Church's 'Constantinian' past. The
political implications are summed up in the insistence on ex-

clusively adult baptism, a practice which w
concept of a national 'Church', and was
ferociously by the authorities.

The 'radical left' reformers are of perennia
much to do, perhaps, with the thesis of the n
historian Ernst Troeltsch, in *Protestantism ar*
the Anabaptists, spiritualists and others were the modern and
progressive wing of the Reformation, and therefore politically
more significant than mainstream reformers. The thesis can take
several forms: 'modern and progressive' here can mean that they
are precursors of liberal democracy, human rights advocacy,
religious tolerance, and so on; or, more radically, that they are
harbingers of modern socialist or communist awareness and
commitment. Mennonite scholars (heirs to the Anabaptist
tradtion) and Marxist historians have been most favourable to
the nonconformists of the sixteenth century, and there is much
here that is of interest, though two dangers need to be recognised: a romantic exaggeration of their influence, and an
appropriation of their beliefs and actions for nationalist or ideological purposes.

A good case study here is Thomas Müntzer, 1489/90–1525,
though his fomenting of violent revolt clearly places him outside
of the Anabaptist tradition. Under Luther's influence during his
three years at Wittenberg, he moved to a more radical position
which recognised scriptural warrant for rebellion in certain circumstances. His thinking was rooted in a mystical spirituality,
which in a way reads Matthew's parable of the wheatfield in
precise opposition to Augustine. A 'Two Cities' model calls for
the wheat and tares to grow together until the harvest time;
Müntzer, on the other hand, saw the urgency of uprooting the
'weeds', of all that is inauthentic and sinful in the individual
human soul. His political theology emerges from the conviction
that this must be an *outer* as well as *inner* cleansing: godless
leaders and false teachers, all who hinder the people of God
from reaching perfection, must be ruthlessly purged (Bradstock,
2004:67). Another clear difference from Luther is that Müntzer
expected the civil authorities to assist positively in the process
of transformation, and not merely provide the peaceful
conditions for it by protecting the godly from wrongdoers.

is a difference of emphasis in reading Romans 13
ther stresses verse 1: 'Be submissive to the authorities';
Müntzer is looking at verse 3, which speaks of the positive
responsibilities of those authorities). He reads Romans 13
alongside the Book of Daniel: in the Sermon which Müntzer
allegedly delivered to Duke John of Saxony and his advisors in
Allstedt in July 1524, he presents himself as the 'new Daniel',
interpreting the dreams of the princes to them (see Daniel 2), in
order 'to bring about a reconciliation between the wrath of the
princes and the rage of the people'. Müntzer understood the
fifth and final 'worldly kingdom' of the vision to be the Holy
Roman Empire, and explicitly ascribes to the Princes an active
involvement in this purification, not the passive role advocated
by 'Brother Soft-Life' (Martin Luther) and his followers:

> For they have made such a fool of you that everyone swears
> by the saints that in their official capacity princes are just
> pagans, that all they have to do is to maintain civic order …
> as Christ says in Matthew 10: 'I am not come to send
> peace, but the sword.' But what is one to do with the
> sword? Exactly this: sweep aside those evil men who
> obstruct the gospel! Take them out of circulation! …
> The tares have to be torn out of the vineyard of God at
> harvest-time.

Convinced of the 'apocalyptic inevitability' of conflict, and that
God's 'harvest-time' had arrived, Müntzer led a group of about
eight thousand peasants at the battle of Frankenhausen, on 15
May 1525; a definitive struggle which would clear the way for
the Kingdom of God. The rebel forces were comprehensively
defeated, and Müntzer was captured and tortured, before recant-
ing his views and being reconciled to the Roman Catholic
Church. He was beheaded in Mühlhausen on 27 May, 1525.

For most scholars, Thomas Müntzer was a short-lived radical;
there is little in his ideas about the form society will take in the
new age, beyond a call to hold all things in common, and
distribution of goods according to need. It is interesting to note
how his example was adopted by socialists, such as Friedrich
Engels, as a symbol of early class struggle. The most interesting

study for us, however, comes from Ernst Bloch (1885–1977), an important figure for twentieth-century political theology, since his monumental work *The Principle of Hope* profoundly influenced Johann Baptist Metz, Jürgen Moltmann and the liberation theologian Gustavo Gutiérrez. In one of his earlier works, written in 1921, some of Bloch's main hypotheses concerning messianic hope are tested out on a historical 'case study' entitled *Thomas Müntzer, Theologian of the Reformation.*[2]

So how does Bloch read Müntzer? Firstly, he gives a summary of the Reformer's life and then an analysis of his theology and preaching, in comparison with the alternative theologies of his day. Bloch chastises Luther for his 'secret Manicheesm', and for his justification of the atrocious treatment of the peasants, which amounts to a *Tyrannophilie* ('love of tyranny'). By contrast, Bloch sees in Müntzer's experience a 'phenomenology of God-preparation' (*Gottbereitung*), an explosive combination of the German mystical tradition with the Reformation rediscovery of the Word of God, that went beyond even the radicality of Luther's comparatively 'secure' experience of grace. The individual's state of abandonment anticipates Kierkegaard: 'the soul's abyss is finally made perfectly empty, and man, in the quietest and most profound abandonment and detachment, becomes at last aware of God's word'(Bloch, 1969 [1921]:189).

Müntzer is describing a universal human experience, a stretching towards the future. Bloch seeks to connect, perhaps better, re-connect, a religious striving for the divine with that structure of human self-understanding which we find in Romanticism and elsewhere. The final section of the Müntzer study is entitled 'The Absolute Man: or the way of the Breakthrough', and sets out envisaging a miracle (*Wunder*) of entry into a new world, in which the relations of lordship and slave are reversed:

> To this world of faith rises the smoke of the pure dawn of the Apocalypse, and precisely in the Apocalypse it gains its final criterion, the metapolitical, indeed metareligious Principle of all revolution: the beginning of the freedom of the children of God'. (Bloch, 1969 [1921]:210)

This is of course very strange language for a Marxist to use! For Roberts, this is why it is not a good idea to regard Bloch as primarily a Marxist thinker: he argues that in important passages of *The Principle of Hope* Marxism is 'rhetorically present but in substantial terms predominantly supportive, even marginal' (Roberts, 1990:16). What Ernst Bloch is working toward is a positive recovery of the divine in the human, rather than the negative and exclusionary view of God as illusory projection asserted by orthodox Marxism. The study of Thomas Müntzer prefigures *The Principle of Hope* and its attempted fusion of Marxism and universal (including spiritual) culture. It is precisely this idea of a 'joint campaign' between Marxism and the religious dreamers of history which is suppressed in the icy chill of 'orthodox' Marxism. Nevertheless, this utopian, anticipatory spirit – an inheritance both Western and universal – animates the whole of Bloch's project; and Thomas Müntzer, the 'prototypical religious man', is one of its heralds:

> High above the ruins and fractured spheres of the culture of this world the spirit of unobstructed Utopia shines in, certain of its centre only … in the house of the absolute appearance of ourselves. In this way at last Marxism and the dream of the undetermined join forces in an identical campaign; that is as the driving force of the end which brings to an end the voyage of the whole world around us, in which man is an oppressed, a despised and lost being; as reconstruction of the planet earth and all creation, the forced entry of the kingdom: Müntzer with all the Chiliasts remains the one who summons us to this stormy pilgrimage.[3]

William Cavanaugh: A Fire to Consume the House

The 'Two Kingdoms' doctrine (Luther), the confession of the 'Lordship of Christ' (Calvin), and the proclamation of apocalyptic hope (Müntzer), are three distinctive responses to the convulsions that accompanied the death throes of 'Christendom' in the fifteenth and sixteenth centuries. Which, if any, of these three extraordinary figures holds the key which will help us solve the conundrum of the 'doctrine of the Two'?

Each of these traditions has been called upon, four hundred years later, to resource Christian reflection in a very different situation of collapse and crisis. In his commentaries on Luther and Calvin, Moltmann spells out the inadequacy of the vision of these 'magisterial' reformers in the face of the Nazi Leviathan. Similarly, Bloch's vision of an anti-fascist alliance between Marxism and the religious dreamers of history, such as Müntzer, failed to materialise. And yet, as we shall see in chapters 8 and 9, it is Bloch's project which has intrigued comtemporary political theologians such as Moltmann and Metz – at the same time, such a project is the nightmare of secularist thinkers who believe in the Great Separation.

By way of polemical conclusion to this chapter, I will refer to an important if provocative essay by W.T. Cavanaugh that offers a 'rereading' of the history which we have just been considering.[4] As even the distinction between 'magisterial' and 'radical' Reformers makes clear, there was no single response to the challenge of how to relate Church and State under the new conditions of early modernity. During this period of immense political and social instability, the overriding concern is the Christian use of the coercive power of the State. The acceptability of calling upon the secular authorities is what distinguishes the magisterial and radical Reformers: but we should be clear that in both cases there has been a break with the 'traditional concept of Christendom as an all-encompassing, unitary society' (O'Donovan), even if the break is more defined with the extreme position of Thomas Müntzer *et al*. The exact nature of the interplay of temporal and spiritual authorities is now up for debate.

Cavanaugh takes up this history in order to set up a critique of political liberalism, and to demonstrate why certain patterns of thinking about political theology are misguided insofar as they follow liberal assumptions about the State and about religion. His concern arises from the way we apply a certain *double standard* to the question of violence; our revulsion towards killing in the name of religion is used to legitimise transfer of our ultimate loyalty to the state, the violence of which is never scrutinised in quite the same way. This is because, according to its own 'official' history, modern liberalism originated in the need to overcome the religious enmity of the early modern period; specifically the so-called 'Wars of Religion' which afflicted Europe from roughly 1550 to 1648. The liberal 'story' is that liberal principles and a secularised public discourse developed as the only alternative to societies being torn apart by religious factionalism. The modern secular state arose precisely as a peacekeeper between warring factions; or, a more patronising description, 'the State stepped in like a scolding schoolmaster on the playground of doctrinal dispute to put fanatical religionists in their proper place' (Cavanaugh, 1995:408).

Let me remark, in passing, on a remarkable similarity: between Cavanaugh's accusation of our double standards regarding violence, and the same accusation made against Luther regarding the Peasant Wars. As we have seen, Luther judged the princes' violent suppression of the revolt to be legitimate, while under no circumstances could he approve of the peasants' rebellion, however just their grievances might have been.

Cavanaugh challenges the 'official' history by suggesting that it has the sequence back to front. 'The "Wars of Religion" were not the events which necessitated the birth of the modern State; they were in fact themselves the birth pangs of the State' (398). At the heart of these conflicts was not a denominational struggle between 'Catholic' and 'Protestant', but differences around the rise of the emerging State as a replacement of the declining medieval ecclesial order. For the princes of this period, including those who instigated the worst of the killings, doctrinal loyalty took second place to this political decision, namely whether they were in favour of or opposed to the centralisation of power. The Thirty Years' War (1616–48) is cited as the bloodiest of the conflicts: yet Protestants and Catholics fought on both 'sides', and in its last, most violent phase, this was essentially a conflict between two rival Catholic dynasties, the Bourbons and the Hapsburgs.

The growth of the state predates the modern notion of 'religion' as a privately held set of beliefs without direct political relevance, and in fact goes towards the shaping of this notion. It follows, then, that to speak of these wars as primarily 'religious' is an anachronism. What Cavanaugh intends by this historical survey is to challenge the soteriology of the modern state as peacemaker. *Soteriology* means the theory or doctrine of salvation: what is in question is the myth of the state as the community's 'saviour' from our own implacable religious fury and fanaticism.

There is a crucial development here, broadly illustrated by a shift from the medieval 'Two Swords' metaphor to the Lutheran idea of the 'Two Kingdoms'. The 'Two Swords' doctrine acknowledged joint political responsibility between Church and Prince for the ordering of society, a situation of equilibrium in which the Church was, nevertheless, the supreme power. By the middle of the seventeenth century this equilibrium had been upset and the hierarchy reversed: the secular ruler was now the dominant partner. Though the 'Two Kingdoms' doctrine was a laudable attempt to disentangle the Church from its inappropriate worldly involvements, its effect was to reinforce this dominance of the secular. The Church no longer had its own judicial powers, because these had been handed over to the secular authorities: 'What is left to the Church is increasingly the purely interior government of the souls of its members; their bodies are handed over to the secular authorities' (399). Granted the attractiveness of this doctrine for Lutheran princes, this was a 'Catholic' as well as a 'Protestant' development.

A final word about Christendom. It is worth noting that any contemporary political theology, in needing to establish its post-Christendom (and now, increasingly, post-Westphalian) credentials, should resist the temptation to simply dismiss the phenomenon of Christendom as an unfortunate mistake, or worse, a 'fall from grace' from the Church's original political innocence. William Cavanaugh reminds us that 'Christendom' is a very complex series of attempts to take seriously the Church's political role. Its inheritance of civic responsibilities with the collapse of the Roman Empire was in a sense accidental – but the conflicts of the subsequent centuries were due to the inseparability of politics and religion, not to the fact that these had been illegitimately yoked together.

Oliver O'Donovan makes a similar plea for the baby not to be ditched with the bathwater, when he reminds us that

Christendom, 'the idea of a professedly Christian secular political order ...' is the womb of late modernity: it gives us a reading of political concepts and a reading of ourselves and our situation. Christendom's legacy is the fruitful constellation of social and political ideas that forms the 'early modern liberal' tradition, and is reflected in the institutions of Europe and America. Whatever misgivings or critiques are made against it, the liberal tradition has right of possession: 'there is no model available to us of a political order derived from a millennium of close engagement between state and church. It ought, therefore, to have the first word in any discussion of what Christians can approve, even if it ought not to have the last word' (228). We should surely be attentive to a historical challenge which the Church has already heard and responded to, rather than trying to construct an abstract statement which bypasses what is, after all, a church tradition worthy of respect. With this in mind, O'Donovan goes on to 'to venture to characterise a normative political culture broadly in continuity with the Western liberal tradition' (230 ff), by pointing to a family of political structures which have carried forward, with varying degrees of success, the traditions of Christendom.[5]

Cavanaugh is less sanguine than O'Donovan about the merits of political liberalism. In any case, his argument has enormous implications for how we shape the problem of political theology, and we shall examine these in more detail later. For the present, we need to note the paradoxical claim that in a sense the State has 'created' the problem (religious diversity) that it is supposed to have come into being to solve. And the self-understanding and self-justification of the modern State continues to rest on this: if it were not for its protective power, all hell would break loose (literally). Once again we encounter the myth of the Leviathan, or *katēchon*: here, we can see that it is fundamental to the *raison d'être* of the State. Thomas Hobbes, as was shown earlier, is the principal theorist of the Leviathan: according to him, the religious impulse and the urge to political co-operation have a common source:

> The war of all against all is the natural condition of humankind. It is cold fear and the need for security, the

foundation of both religion and the social contract, that
drives humans from their nasty and brutish circumstances
and into the arms of Leviathan. This soteriology of the
State as peacemaker demands that its sovereign authority
be absolutely alone and without rival. In Hobbes it is not so
much that the Church has been subordinated to the civil
power; Leviathan has rather swallowed the Church into its
yawning maw. (Cavanaugh, 1995:406)

It is with the soteriological presumptions of the State, and the
interaction of fear and hope that such a description implies, that
the stage is set for an examination of 'political religions' and
State utopias, to which we proceed in the next chapter.

Chapter 6

'STILLBORN GODS'

The Enlightenment Roots of Political Theology

After Westphalia: Political Religions

With this and the preceding chapter, we are entering a white-hot intellectual war-zone. Theological readings of the sack of Rome in 410, or the Investiture Controversy in the late eleventh century, are unlikely to arouse very much controversy today. However, the four and a half centuries since the 'end of Christendom' – the epoch of 'Westphalia' – form the historical matrix out of which emerge our present anxieties regarding 'the persistence of the theologico-political'.

And we have been shocked into awareness of this 'persistence' by men with beards who are willing to kill us, in the name of God, as we travel to work on the Underground. It is little wonder that passions are running high.

And yet the diagnoses vary wildly. Richard Dawkins sees suicide bombers as an atavistic return to the violence which has always accompanied this dreadful 'virus' called religion; Jürgen Habermas (see chapter 10) judges extremist fundamentalism to be 'entirely a modern phenomenon', a product of imperfect processes of secularisation. As indicated above, there is evidence of a new *Kulturkampf* between believers and non-believers. The nervous aggression in which these groups mirror each other betokens nothing less than the 'fall of Westphalia': the fragile *cordon sanitaire* between religion and the public, between Church and State, seems ready to give way. For some this is an event of euphoric liberation, for others it is a prospect of enormous anxiety and frustration.

Our reading of the early modern period gave air-time to one theologian, William T. Cavanaugh, who argues for a re-thinking of the traditional 'narrative' of Church and State relations, by which the modern secular liberal State came into being and persists as the only protection against our religious aggressivity: the State is the schoolmaster in the playground, ensuring that we play nicely. Arguing the case against 'political theology', we have Mark Lilla, to whom I am indebted for the title of this chapter, adapted from *The Stillborn God* (Lilla, 2007). Lilla holds the Enlightenment's Grand Separation of religion and politics to be a precious and fragile achievement, one that requires especial vigilance on our part if we are not to lose it. Lilla argues in favour of the narrative Cavanaugh rejects. Like many commentators, he is frankly concerned by the re-appearance or the persistence of the 'theologico-political', and while his take on religion is a lot more subtle and respectful than the clunking diatribes of Dawkins, Christopher Hitchens and others, many of the basic presuppositions are the same. The student of political theology probably needs to be exposed to these arguments before proceeding much further.

But before the polemics, some scene-setting. In an important but extremely challenging essay entitled 'The permanence of the theologico-political?' Claude Lefort identifies two essential moments in modernity.[1] In the sixteenth century we begin to see the first signs of a modern reflection on politics and religion. With the collapse of the *Ancién Regime*, the king no longer held the regime together, nor was he any longer the point of contact between God and man, between the political and the religious. So a sustained attempt to re-order politics ensues, 'to conceive the state as an independent entity, to make politics a reality *sui generis*, and to relate religion to the domain of private belief'. Religion is made private and politics is made public.

But a much wider debate opens up in the nineteenth century, inaugurated by the French Revolution in 1789: the feeling that a break has occurred, but not within time: 'it establishes a relationship between human beings and time itself, that it makes history … and society … a mystery' which cannot be encompassed in political or economic institutions. It is the *religious* meaning of this break which haunts thinkers of very different persuasions, restorationists and revolutionaries alike: '[T]hey all speak the same language, and it is simultaneously political, philosophical and religious' (149). G. F. W. Hegel protests against the attempt at separation described above: 'It has been the monstrous blunder of our times to try to look upon these inseparables as separable from one another, and even as mutually indifferent'.[2] Hegel insists that the state rests on the ethical sentiment, which in turn rests on the religious.

Lefort comments: 'The "monstrous blunder" which Hegel denounces in 1817 would therefore appear to designate the truth of modern times, the truth of our own times'. Nevertheless, Lefort wishes to stay with these earlier thinkers, caught in the throes of revolutionary events, who:

> may, even if they were mistaken, have had a singular ability to grasp a symbolic dimension of the political, of something that was later to disappear, of something that bourgeois discourse was already burying beneath its supposed knowledge of the real order of society. (150)

He wonders if in fact Hegel did get it wrong, after all. Did the religious *actually* recede from and become compartmentalised against the political?

> Can we not admit that, despite all the changes that have occurred, the religious survives in the guise of new beliefs and new representations, and it can therefore return to the surface, in either traditional or novel forms, when conflicts become so acute as to produce cracks in the edifice of the state?

There is little space here to do other than establish the broader picture, which I attempt with the help of two theologically attentive historians, Michael Burleigh and Adam Zamoyski. Burleigh (2005, 2006) discusses notorious 'political religions', taking in the civic cults of the Jacobins during the French Revolution, as well as Bolsheviks, Fascists and National Socialists, all of whom evoke the transcendence of religion for their respective political projects:

> These were meant to forge a sentimental community – in which emotional plangency was the norm – by refashioning space and time to envelop 'the masses' within a dominant ideology. This would involve wider discussion of related utopian projects, based on the creation of a 'new man' or 'new woman' from the old Adam, an exercise that presumed that human personality is as malleable as wet clay. (Burleigh, 2005:1)

Burleigh points how the rise of Enlightenment thought worked to unravel this alliance of throne and altar in France. For all its appeal to the tranquil detachment of Reason, however, Enlightened thought was haunted by the bloodshed of the Wars of Religion. 'The desire, fanatically pursued, to eradicate the infamy of fanaticism was a reflection of these collective memories'(41). The striving for 'Enlightenment', in its English, French and German versions, was haunted by the nightmare of widespread fanatical violence, and saw in an enlightened appeal to Reason and reasonableness the antidote to such fanaticism. Zamoyski concurs in his history of the Age of Revolutions (Zamoyski, 1999):

> Fired by the urge to redeem mankind and themselves, many young men struggled and died in a kind of crusade whose Jerusalem was an idealized projection of 'Our Lord Mankind'; the nation, death in the service of which brought martyrdom and life everlasting.
>
> (Zamoyski, 1999:5)

This is in effect to echo the argument of Alexis de Tocqueville, who remains a magisterial commentator:

> Because the Revolution seemed to be striving for the regeneration of the human race even more than for the reform of France, it lit a passion which the most violent political revolutions have never before been able to produce. It inspired conversions and generated propaganda. Thus, in the end, it took on that appearance of a religious revolution which so astonished contemporaries. Or rather,

it itself became a new kind of religion, an incomplete religion it is true, without God, without ritual, and without life after death, but one which nevertheless, like Islam, flooded the earth with its soldiers, apostles, and martyrs.

(Cited in Burleigh, 2005:3)

The Stillborn God

Mark Lilla argues differently: that the European Enlightenment, through moral philosophers such as Thomas Hobbes, Baruch Spinoza and John Locke, successfully removed ideas of divine revelation and redemption from politics (Lilla, 2007). This is the happy resolution of 'the theologico-political problem', and the story of the 'West's auto-emancipation' from what Lilla calls 'political theology' (defined as 'discourse about political authority based on a revealed divine nexus'). Political theology differs from political philosophy or political science, because it seeks for the best form of government by asking about God, rather than about man. Lilla speaks of the prising apart of political theories from theology, begun with Hobbes in the sixteenth century, as the Great Separation.

Hobbes prescribes the vital 'cure', namely, a translation of religious questions into psychological and anthropological form. By asking what humanity needs from its God, rather than the other way round, Hobbes sets aside the political theological approach that had obtained previously. Enter the 'Leviathan', the sovereign who becomes an 'earthly God', and whose totalitarian overtones are softened by the more liberal vision of other sensible Britons such as John Locke, followed by David Hume and John Stuart Mill.

However, if we think that this emancipation was an inevitable and definitive achievement, like the Copernican revolution that overturned the geocentric view of cosmology, we are sadly mistaken. The 'theologico-political' persists – much to the frustration and incredulity of secularist critics. Lilla concedes that religion is a default position: our natural impulse is to transcend and connect beyond ourselves, and very exceptional circumstances are required for us to decide to *dis*connect. He notes another strain of Enlightenment thinking which has a more positive take on religion. These are the 'children of Rousseau', a continental tradition of philosophers which includes Jean-Jacques Rousseau himself, G. F. W. Hegel and Immanuel Kant. In different ways these three philosophers are unsympathetic to the Enlightenment's disparagement of religion, and offer instead an account of religion as an expansive response toward the universe, and towards morality and freedom.

Jean-Jacques Rousseau is of course best known for his articulation of a 'Social Contract' as the basis for political harmony, and as such is to be linked with the political philosophy of Thomas Hobbes. Where he differs from Hobbes, to repeat, is over the validity of religion, or perhaps more accurately religious experience and emotion. Rousseau championed the individual conscience, what he called 'the inner light', in each human being. We find this set out most clearly in the fourth book of Rousseau's novel *Emile*, which contains the 'profession of faith of a priest from Savoy' (*Profession de foi du vicaire savoyard*). This liberal, basically deist, priest explains his approach to religious belief, referring not to the doctrines of Christianity, or to the authority of the Bible, but above all to his own conscience: 'I believe all particular religions are good when one serves God usefully in them ... the essential cult is that of the heart'. Rousseau seeks to preserve the spiritual advantages of religion, without resurrecting its fanatical dogmatism. The implication of this chapter is that humanity cannot do without the affective, personal dimension of religious belief: the sense of connectedness that goes with 'signing' a Social Contract is simply not enough for us.

Kant was deeply influenced by Rousseau, and saw the role of religion in similar terms, basically as supportive of our moral striving (which was why everyone should belong to a church: so that they can be helped in their quest for the good). He does not ultimately think that morality can stand alone without religious 'postulates'. Both thinkers, in other words, stress the importance of religious sentiment – whatever 'enlightened rationality' may say.

With German Idealism and Romanticism, this importance becomes inevitability. We have already noted that Hegel thinks the attempted separation of religion and the political is the 'monstrous blunder' of his time. In Hegel's *Lectures on Philosophy of Religion* we read:

> The object of religion as well as of philosophy is eternal truth in its objectivity, God and nothing but God, and the explication of God ... Philosophy explicates itself when it explicates religion, and in explicating itself it explicates religion ... Thus religion and philosophy come to be one. Philosophy is itself in fact worship [*Gottesdienst*]; it is religion inasmuch as it renounces subjective notions and opinions in order to occupy itself with God.

The project implicit in these philosophers, of articulating a Romantic liberal theology with no contradiction between religious belief and the full development of human intellectual and affective capacities, is the 'stillborn God' of the book's title. Not only did this deity fail to materialise: worse, in its stead came an apocalyptic version of political theology, which Lilla sees as a preparation for the totalitarian state religions of Nazism and Communism, with the messianic hopes of these Enlightened philosophers somehow paving the way. Of the two strains of Enlightenment thought, it is the fine surgeons of the English tradition who save the day: Hobbes, Locke and Mill manage to excise all the religious malignancies in the body politic. With the French and Germans it is a different story; by leaving these apparently 'benign' growths alone, they allow them to spread insidiously, eventually breaking out as the disastrous tumours of twentieth-century totalitarianism. In the case of the 'children of Rousseau', even allowing for the considerable differences between the French and German Enlightenments, their 'surgery' was nowhere near thoroughgoing or whole-hearted enough.

There is much food for thought in Lilla's thesis. Though not totally hostile to religion, he clearly subscribes to the reigning orthodoxy that Cavanaugh seeks to dethrone. As Lilla understands it, 'political theology' is bad news, and because it can never be definitively consigned to history, we should be on constant guard against it. Nevertheless, we need to note a glaring imbalance in Mark Lilla's book: while he is a careful and thought-provoking commentator on the modern period, he is much more slipshod on what comes before Hobbes and company. The Introduction and Chapter 1 of *The Stillborn God* do not merit a single footnote – and yet it is in these opening fifty-four pages that Lilla makes extremely sweeping claims about the origins, nature and 'crisis' of religion. Only with Chapter 2, entitled 'The Great Separation', does Lilla deign to offer some back-up for his analysis, with appropriate citations of Hume, Hobbes, Pascal, and Locke. It seems the case against pre-modern 'political theology' is so self-evidently watertight as not to require proper argument.

Given this uneven analysis, we may want to press Lilla on why the Great Separation of 1651 (do we really need those capitals?) should be taken as such a definitive marker. We have already seen how it is possible to discern elements of rupture within the ancient world, where the 'theologico-political' fabric of the city-state is torn apart (not just by Christianity, of course). Is it not possible to see in Augustine's 'refusal to bless the state' in *The City of God*, and in the 'doctrine of the Two' which issues from it, an equally decisive turning point? The answer is, presumably not, because this would interfere with the neat storyline built around the bloody Wars of Religion. Which leads to a further question: how does Lilla's narrative fare against Cavanaugh's revisionary account, above all Cavanaugh's dismissal of the 'soteriology' of the modern state as 'saviour' from our religious violence?

Immanuel Kant: Daring to Know, Daring to Hope

My argument from Immanuel Kant, which will help explain his significance for later political theology, proceeds from three important writings: *The Critique of Pure Reason*, the *Critique of Practical Reason*, and an essay, written in 1795, entitled *Towards Perpetual Peace*. If space permitted I would have liked to dwell on a fourth work, his intriguing essay on theodicy, 'On the miscarriage of all philosophical trials in theodicy' 1791, where Kant dismisses traditional theodicy (justification of evil and suffering), before focusing, surprisingly, upon the Book of Job.[3] Perhaps the reader can bear this striking 'theological turn' in mind. As it is, with Kant's first two *Critiques* and *Towards Perpetual Peace* we have two distinct but related issues to address:

• How can the individual's belief in God be justified?
• On what grounds can we hope for lasting peace between nations?

We may recall that Kant asks three questions at the close of the *Critique of Pure Reason*: What can I know? What must I do? What may I hope for? An answer to this third question, about the grounds for our hope, is consequent on the first two. The rather dispiriting outcome of the *Critique of Pure Reason* is that, strictly speaking, we cannot claim knowledge of *anything* other than 'phenomena' – the way in which the world presents itself to us. For Kant, this meant the demolition of all alleged metaphysical 'proofs' of the existence of God, such as the cosmological or ontological arguments. 'Pure reason' cannot help us to God: it is only under the heading of 'practical reason' that indications of God's existence can be found.

By considering the scope and nature of our ethical obligations ('what must I do?') in his second *Critique*, the *Critique of Practical Reason*, Kant frames the following argument. We can only make sense of our ethical existence if we assume or *postulate* three facts that cannot be formally proved: that we are free, that God exists, that there is an afterlife. The first of these is clear enough; but why does morality require us to postulate God and the afterlife? Because, says Kant, fundamental to our moral convictions is the belief that good ethical behaviour should be rewarded and bad behaviour punished. When this does not happen (as plainly it does not, in so many cases) we are scandalised and tempted to despair – like Job. For ethics to operate at all we need to imagine some way in which the balance is redressed. That can only mean a just God, who gives people what they deserve in the afterlife.

As an argument this looks about as trustworthy as a syllogism which runs: 'We are surrounded by hostile Cherokee Indians; only the cavalry appearing over the hill can save us; therefore the cavalry are coming over the hill'! Supposing the world just *is* an unjust place, where people's behaviour is rewarded inappropriately? (to quote Oscar Wilde: 'the good end happily, the bad end unhappily: that is what fiction means.') Kant's argument is that to believe this would be to open ourselves up to moral despair – and this would destroy us. There *must* be a God and an afterlife, if ethics is to make sense.[4]

Thomas McCarthy summarises Kant's argument as follows:

> [W]e are commanded by the moral law to pursue certain ends that would be impossible to achieve if God did not exist and the soul were not immortal. The inherent tension between our moral-rational duties and aspirations, on the one hand, and our finite limitations, on the other, would lead to moral despair without God and immortality. Thus, it is a practical necessity that we postulate them; not to do so would be to commit moral suicide.
>
> (McCarthy, 1991:201)

In *Towards Perpetual Peace*, we find a marked contrast from the two Critiques in the way Kant argues. Put very briefly, while the Critiques and the essay on theodicy could be said to 'deny knowledge so as to leave room for faith', there isn't even an implicit faith dimension in Kant's account of what is needed for perpetual peace between nations. As we have seen, the 'postulates of practical reason' are necessary, because for the individual, ethical existence is unthinkable without religious hope. One might expect a similar proviso in this important essay, where Kant looks at what is needed for lasting and peaceful political coexistence. Doesn't this activity, too, require to be 'underwritten' by religious hope? Kant does, after all, begin the essay with a sardonic remark concerning the phrase 'Towards Perpetual Peace', found on an innkeeper's sign depicting a graveyard! Is this the best and the only 'peace' we can hope for? Surely, our collective striving for the good is just as prone to moral despair as the individual's – and is in equal need of religious postulates?

Towards Perpetual Peace is a remarkable, even inspiring and moving work – and also troubling. It comprises six preliminary articles for perpetual peace among states, and three definitive articles, with two supplementary points. The three 'definitive

articles' express a preference for 'Covenant' over 'Leviathan':
republicanism, with its separation of powers, he sees as the only
alternative to despotism. The virtues of federalism become evident: as a powerful and enlightened people becomes a republic,
other nations are inspired to imitate it and enter into alliance
with it, gradually spreading its benign influence. The right of
hospitality, grounded in the common possession of the earth's
surface, has an Arendtian ring to it, particularly when Kant lists
examples of *inhospitality*: colonial domination and enslavement
in the Americas, East Indies, Africa. There is an angry denunciation of the European powers 'that make much ado of their piety
and, while they drink wrongfulness like water, want to be known
as the elect in orthodoxy' (330).

The first supplementary point is especially important for our
purposes: 'On the guarantee of perpetual peace'. Who, or what,
underwrites the optimistic vision Kant sets out in this 'philosophical project', in order for us to avoid the evident temptation
to moral despair? What are the 'postulates of perpetual peace?'
The answer is intriguing, and troubling:

> What affords this guarantee (surety) is nothing less than
> the great artist *nature* (*natura daedala rerum*)[5] from whose
> mechanical course purposiveness shines forth visibly,
> letting concord arise by means of the discord between
> human beings even against their will ... if we consider its
> purposiveness in the course of the world as the profound
> wisdom of a higher cause directed to the objective final
> end of the human race and predetermining this course of
> the world, it is called *providence*.

The deployment of 'providence' at this juncture is very eccen-
tric. Kant discourses about nature's foresight in scattering
people throughout even inhospitable regions of the world, providing the wherewithal for human life, even in the Arctic, in
Mongolia and so on. There are also 'natural' reasons why
republicanism is both possible and compatible with human
instincts and capacities. So: nature uses two means 'to prevent
people from intermingling and to separate them' and thus avoiding despotism, namely differences of *language* and of *religion*

(336). Nature 'wisely' ensures that states which might otherwise be inappropriately joined together are kept separate; and sooner or later, the spirit of commerce takes over every nation, and the *power of money* compels states to promote honourable peace and avoid warfare.

To put it mildly: a little 'suspicion' towards this providentialist outlook would not go amiss!

The postulates of practical reason (freedom, God, immortality) filled in a gap, allowing us to connect up 'goodness' and 'happiness'. But with perpetual peace, there is no question of things not working out. Provided 'wise nature' is allowed to take its course, and statesmen make sure to consult the philosophers before going to war, then perpetual peace between states will certainly come to pass! We do not need to postulate God, nor an afterlife – and we certainly don't need to invoke the inspiring figure of Job.

Kant's reticence here merits our attention. There seems to be a need for a directly religious guarantee in one case (individual practical reason), but not in the other (the project for perpetual peace). But why is it necessary to invoke God to safeguard the individual moral order, while the political order – republican, federal, pluralist, even capitalist – can simply be entrusted into the 'wise' hands of 'providence'? Why does Kant dare us to hope in one case, but not in the second?

Living in Truth: G. W. F. Hegel

Hegel's more robust and confident assertion of the 'theologico-political' seems to have no room at all for hope, since there is no need: revelation is understood by Hegel as 'the process of the human spirit coming to understand itself', so that 'humanity itself' is seen to be the manifestation of what was once called God. The wars of religion, whose bloodiness haunts the Enlightenment imagination, are to be seen as merely the birth pangs of the revelation of our own divinity. In religion's 'completion' in philosophy, we encounter the ambiguity of Hegel's notion of *Aufhebung*, which connotes abrogation or cancellation, but also 'preservation'. In one sense, it looks as if religion is annulled, left behind; in another sense its validity is maintained, but on a higher level. In the end, this lack of clarity is the weakness of Hegel's religious philosophy.

One of the most accessible and useful commentaries is Andrew Shanks, who takes us through Hegel by way of Prague. *Hegel's Political Theology* opens with the Czechoslovakian novelist Milan Kundera, who introduces in his best-known novel the phenomenon of 'kitsch'.[6] *Kitsch* is defined as '[a] largely self-censored perception of reality – governed by indulgence in a common narcissim, the desire to feel good about what one is a part of'; it is a 'pervasive, basic evil', exemplified, in the words of Sabina (the novel's heroine), by the image of 'a parade of people marching by with raised fists and shouting identical syllables in unison' – whether those people have been marshalled by party leaders into a May Day parade, or whether they are protesting Western students who 'can't wait to spit their innocence in the cops' faces' (Shanks, 1991:2, 3).

Kitsch is therefore a kind of false consciousness, which Shanks equates with Hegel's 'Unhappy Consciousness'. In the Conclusion this contrasts with the idea of 'Living in Truth', set out in Vaclav Havel's well-known 'parable of the greengrocer'.[7] Havel is examining 'post-totalitarian' ideology, the phase of a dictatorship when no one seriously believes any more in the innocence and idealism of the revolution. The Emperor is naked, but everyone goes through the motions – because it is the easiest and safest thing to do. Until, one day, a greengrocer decides otherwise.

For Shanks, Hegel's political theology is about the transition from a false to an authentic consciousness: how do we resist and overcome the deeply authoritarian seduction of ideological *kitsch* – as political parade, as circle dance, as religious liturgy – and learn to 'live in truth'? Shanks insists that the central logic of Christianity – the cross – provides this resistance, but like any spiritual tradition Christianity is open to corruption. This is where Hegel comes in. His affirmation of 'the infinite value of the individual as such' is at the core of his struggle with the problem of Christian religious *kitsch*.

Between the two 'Czech' moments, Shanks makes more explicit links between Hegel's concerns and some prominent figures in twentieth-century political theology (149–83).

Dorothee Sölle and Jürgen Moltmann are explicit dialogue partners, since they engage with Hegel in their key works. Sölle's *Christ the Representative* takes Hegel's Christology to be a restoration of the balance between two opposed doctrines of the atonement (Luther's 'imputation' of forgiveness and Anselm's doctrine of 'satisfaction'). Her book *Suffering* and Moltmann's *The Crucified God* are seen by Shanks as exemplars of a wider movement in twentieth-century German theology, towards a 'fundamental de-Platonizing of the Christian tradition' (64) – a development which Hegel has pioneered.[8]

We have noted in chapter 3 how Hannah Arendt argued that Christianity lacks an *amor mundi*; it promotes an inner withdrawal from the world, and is therefore incompatible with politics. For Shanks this coheres with Hegel's critique of Stoicism as a 'flight from action', and of the anti-political Romantic ideal of the 'Beautiful Soul' (156). Shanks goes on to draw a parallel between Arendt's portrayal of the 'thoughtlessness' and the 'banal evil' of Adolf Eichmann, and Hegel's Unhappy Consciousness; other common concerns would include the decline of the State, and of political freedom (159–65).

As we shall see, Johann Baptist Metz likewise offers a critique of the privatised bourgeois Christianity that so spectacularly failed when put to the test in Germany in the 1930s. This critique matches very closely Hegel's own comments about the state of the Church in his day. Hegel may therefore be seen as a 'lonely pioneer' of political theology (150) even if there are other important themes where he and Metz diverge – not least in Metz's resistance to an 'evolutionary' and elitist ideology which permits an unfeeling amnesia towards the victims of history (152).

In brief, Andrew Shanks argues cogently for continuing to take Hegel seriously as a pioneer of, and dialogue partner for, contemporary political theology. For Shanks, Hegel's potential contribution is benign and necessary. Not all agree, as we have seen: Chapter 4 of *The Stillborn God*, entitled 'The Bourgeois God' (Lilla, 2007:163–213) is Lilla's account of how Christian suspicion of Hegel is fully justified, not least concerning whether his apparent indifference to the immense suffering of history – which Hegel shockingly described as a 'slaughter-bench' – can be 'justified' by its ultimate reconciliation. Hegel's system is a nightmarish distortion of Christian faith, precisely because it operates without the 'eschatological' checks and balances we find in the traditional understanding of salvation and reconciliation (Lilla, 2007:211–13). The Hegelian legacy, so the argument runs, is to be found in the mass death of the twentieth century. Stranger still, however, and perhaps more disturbing, is his rendition of the world as a 'sensible, well-designed bourgeois home', and his sanctification of modern bourgeois life (212–13), making Hegel a more problematic dialogue partner for Arendt and Metz than Shanks would imply.

Conclusion

From the 'children of Rousseau', Kant and Hegel, we have two very distinctive expressions of a 'theologico-political' vision. Over the next three chapters we will see whether contemporary political theology is best understood, above all, as an act of the 'eschatological imagination': a daring to visualise the outcome of our wager on God, and of God's wager on us. Though both these thinkers loom large, this imagining will lean more towards the implications of the Kantian 'postulates of practical reason', albeit in ways that Kant would not necessarily recognise.

The 'postulates of practical reason' are precisely geared towards God rewarding the good and punishing the wicked at the end of time, while Kant's essay on theodicy turns at the crucial moment to the Book of Job, whose 'truthfulness' validates a certain kind of theodicy (Kant: 1795). Hope acts as a postulate, it is a *heuristic* device: a 'what if?' Only by assuming the existence of God and of an afterlife do our lives make sense.

This is important, but the understanding of hope that is offered here is anaemic, deliberately passionless. It hardly resonates with the scriptural witness: the desperate clinging to God of the psalmist, of the Suffering Servant in Isaiah, of Job, or of Christ in his abandonment; nor with the burning hearts on the road to Emmaus. There seems to be little correspondence between Kantian hope, and what we will encounter over the next few chapters: the messianic hunger of Ernst Bloch and Walter

Benjamin, the 'suffering towards God' which animates the work of Johann Baptist Metz, Jürgen Moltmann, and liberation theologians of every hue. And yet the structure of the argument for all of these theologians: that the only alternative to a rationally-expressed political hope is despair – is the same as that of Kant's postulates, without which ethical existence would not be possible.

The map we have sketched over the last three chapters is inadequate for any purpose other than the most general orientation, in what can be bewildering territory. While Section 1 may have helped to establish the parameters of political theology, some sense of the history is also necessary. In particular, the seemingly endless debates about 'modernity' and 'postmodernity' very often hinge on some sense of a fall from a 'golden age', or more likely our taking a wrong turning somewhere: which leaves us with the intellectual task of getting back to Eden, or to the crossroads where we went astray. Is it the case that Augustine got it absolutely right with *The City of God* and everything that has happened since has been a struggle to regain the fine synthesis he achieved? Or does sanity begin in 1651, with Thomas Hobbes' *Leviathan* and the Great Separation of theology and politics; a benchmark for our survival which must be preserved at all costs?

These are options set before us by William Cavanaugh and Mark Lilla, from the perspectives of faith and secularity respectively. One regards political theology as essential for the wellbeing of human communities, the second sees political theology as a menace, against which constant vigilance is needed.

The next three chapters take us into the twentieth century, and the catastrophic unfolding of the 'dialectic of Enlightenment'. Whichever narrative we go with must attempt to explain why 'the fully enlightened earth radiates disaster triumphant'. Meanwhile it is always good to let Franz Kafka have the last word. In his parable entitled *The City Coat of Arms*, he gives us his version of the biblical myth of the Tower of Babel (Genesis 11:9). The plan to build a tower to the heavens is normally a symbol of human arrogance in the face of God, therefore stands nicely as a parable of the Enlightenment's attempt to 'do without

God', or to 'take the place of God'. In the biblical version, God frustrates the builders' plans by instilling divisions of language among them, thereby making common action impossible. Franz Kafka tells it differently, brilliantly illustrating how the dream of progress turns back on the dreamer and becomes the heaviest of nightmares:

> At first all the arrangements for building the Tower of Babel were characterised by fairly good order; indeed the order was perhaps too perfect, too much thought was given to guides, interpreters, accommodation for the workmen, and roads of communication, as if there were centuries before one to do the work in. In fact, the general opinion at that time was that one simply could not build too slowly; a very little insistence on this would have sufficed to make one hesitate to lay the foundations at all.

The townspeople put off proper work on the tower until they are adequately prepared – but because technical progress and innovation is constant, there is always a reason for further delay. This does not matter, as they believe the vision itself is safe: 'The idea, once seized in its magnitude, can never vanish again; so long as there are men on earth there will also be the irresistible desire to complete the building.' But generations pass, the vision of the tower takes second place to constructing a town for the workmen, rivalries and fights break out, and the sense of unity behind the project disappears:

> To this must be added that the second or third generation had already recognised the senselessness of building a heaven-reaching tower; but by that time everybody was too deeply involved to leave the city. All the legends and songs that came to birth in that city are filled with longing for a prophesied day when the city would be destroyed by five successive blows from a gigantic fist. It is for that reason too that the city has a closed fist on its coat of arms.

Part 3

THE CRISIS

Chapter 7

THEOLOGY IN A LAND OF SCREAMS

The Crisis of National Socialism

As I write this chapter, I have before me a haunting photograph, one of the most disturbing images of the *Shoah* (Holocaust) I have come across. It is an RAF aerial reconnaissance photograph of Auschwitz, taken at 11 a.m. on August 23 1944, when Hungarian Jews were being exterminated at a frenzied rate.[1] Details are all too apparent, despite the altitude: the grid layout of the camp is clearly visible, and the neat rows of huts; it is possible to discern large groups of inmates assembled for roll call; on the outskirts of the camp, a thick cloud of smoke issues from a mass burial pit.

This image is peculiarly distressing, for several reasons. There is the helplessness of the prisoners, so distant and so small; perhaps also, the thought that such an aerial perspective is too much of a 'God's eye-view' for comfort. What also disturbs, however, is the 'oversight', as in thoughtlessness, which the photograph betrays. This piece of hard evidence of Nazi atrocity, which, if analysed properly and acted upon, might have saved hundreds of thousands of lives over the remaining five months of the death-camp's operation, was only discovered in 2003, during the digitalisation of aerial reconnaissance photographs at the National Archives. It seems that its significance was overlooked in the sheer volume of film – running to millions of images – brought home by RAF photographers: analysts were busily scanning these images for military data, not for evidence of genocide. The paradox that this recording technology should be so efficient as to overwhelm remembrance of the victims is one that we should bear in mind.

The catastrophe befell a nation that regarded itself as the high repository of European artistic and philosophical culture. Many of the key figures discussed in this book were German and, to differing degrees, directly affected by the events of 1933 to 1945. This is dramatically the case with Johann Baptist Metz and Jürgen Moltmann, each of whom narrowly escaped death while serving in the German armed forces: only to be confronted, at the close of the war, with the 'cold horror' of discovering the true nature of the cause they had been defending.

In Primo Levi's memoir of his arrest and transportation to a Nazi death camp, we find the following passage:

> The doors had been closed at once, but the train did not move until evening. We had learnt of our destination with relief. Auschwitz: a name without significance for us at that time, but it at least implied some place on this earth.[2]

Primo Levi's words are unbearable. But there is more, namely the way that 'Auschwitz' has, increasingly, come to seem anything *but* 'some place on this earth'. It has become a signpost, a marker, and in many ways the signpost itself takes more of our attention than the 'place', the 'city' Auschwitz.

To take two examples among many, Susan Neiman (2002) has written an 'alternative' history of western philosophy, which she understands as a reflection upon evil. She takes 'Lisbon' – the scene of a devastating earthquake of 1755 – and 'Auschwitz' as the compass points for modernity's reflection upon evil, with September 11th, 2001 now being a further marker. 'Between Lisbon and Auschwitz' denotes a shift of emphasis, from an event that is clearly acknowledged as a 'natural evil', to one that is the product of human choices. Neiman's principle argument is that '[e]ighteenth-and nineteenth-century philosophy was guided by the problem of evil' (Neiman, 2002:7), which therefore serves as an organising principle for understanding the history of philosophy. Whether expressed in theological or secular terms, this is a problem about the intelligibility of the world as a whole.

Neiman discerns two broad philosophical traditions: one (from Rousseau to Arendt) insists that we have a moral duty to make evil intelligible; the other (stemming from Voltaire) insists that evil cannot be encompassed rationally. She asserts that these two sets of philosophers are united by a moral imperative in thinking about evil, and one of the deficiencies of modern philosophy is its divorce of epistemology from ethics, and therefore an absence of the ethical urgency which guided Kant, Hegel and so on.

Richard Bernstein's *Radical Evil* takes an analogous approach, though his book is a more tentative series of 'interrogations' arising from his work on Hannah Arendt, quoting Arendt's response to the revelations of the Nazi death camps: '[T]he problem of evil will be the fundamental question of postwar intellectual life in Europe'. Contemporary philosophy finds itself ill equipped and reluctant to address this theme. However, as his eight chapters on different thinkers indicate, this has not always been the case. For Bernstein, 'Auschwitz' necessitates a re-reading of Kant, Hegel, Schelling (on evil, will and freedom), Nietzsche and Freud (the moral psychology of evil), and the post-Holocaust questionings of Emmanuel Levinas, Hans Jonas and Hannah Arendt.

We should note the largeness of this undertaking: to reshape the entire history of modern philosophy around events that took place in central Europe over twelve ghastly years. What should surprise us more is that there is nothing surprising about what Neiman and Bernstein propose. 'Thinking after Auschwitz' is pretty much a defining characteristic of 'post-modern' thought, and no field of human reflection – philosophy, history, politics, literature, even architecture – has been untouched by the reality of the *Shoah*.

Theology is no exception, and political theology has been shaken in two ways: firstly, because as a political and philosophical discipline it has been caught up in the intellectual and rational upheaval indicated above, and secondly because as Christians coming from Germany the key political theologians find themselves directly involved. As well as the general crisis of rationality, these theologians wrestle with specifically theologico-political challenges on at least two levels: the ineffectiveness of the Christian churches in resisting the 'political religion' of the Nazis; and the lines of complicity and culpability of Christians in the fate of the Jews, arising from theologically-justified Christian anti-Semitism.

There is also of course, a considerable body of Jewish theological responses to the Holocaust, as the victims themselves seek to make sense of what happened. These voices need to be heard before their Christian counterparts. I will consider the challenges to theological reflection under three programmatic questions:

1. What have been the Jewish theological responses to the *Shoah*?
2. Why were the Churches unable to resist the Nazi 'Leviathan'?
3. Does the *Shoah* represent a unique and radical 'rupture' within rational thought, conditioning 'theology after Auschwitz'?

Jewish Theologians and the *Shoah*

Dan Cohn-Sherbok is probably the foremost and most accessible Jewish theological commentator on the Holocaust (*Shoah*). His 1989 overview, *Holocaust Theology*, was reissued as *God and the Holocaust* (1996), and he has subsequently provided a study on the history of Christian anti-Semitism (1997) and a *Holocaust Theology Reader* (2002). In these works he has specified three groups of theological responses: those who seek to work within a traditional Jewish religious framework; those who, by contrast, offer radically revised versions of this tradition; and those who are inspired by the theology of liberation as a springboard for Jewish empowerment.

The first group are trying to salvage what they can from Jewish tradition. To mention three: Bernard Maza takes an Orthodox perspective, according to which God punished his people in the death camps for their failure to observe and protect the Torah; Ignaz Maybaum depicts the Jewish victims as God's suffering servant, atoning for the sins of humanity (he recognises the Christian overtones here by describing Auschwitz as

'the Golgotha of modern mankind'); Emil Fackenheim attempts
to recover traditional motifs, in particular the notion of *tikkun*,
or cosmic repair. He insists on the 'Commanding Voice of God
in Auschwitz', a voice that forbids granting a posthumous victory to Hitler: God demands, therefore, the primal importance of
Jewish survival. Fackenheim also asserts the uniqueness of the
Holocaust, citing five 'basic facts' which are found together
only in the event of the *Shoah*, as the criteria for its uniqueness.
Though Cohn-Sherbok does not mention the work of Emmanuel
Levinas in this category, Levinas' highly suggestive account of
Judaism as a 'religion of adults', in which Jews are called to an
unimaginable ethical responsibility, to 'love the Torah more than
God', surely belongs here.

A second group of responses comprises revisionist accounts
of the nature of God, to such an extent that, in Cohn-Sherbok's
view, these theologians have abandoned the Jewish tradition in
the name of humanist protest. He cites Rubenstein and Cohen:[3]
for Richard Rubenstein the only acceptable response to the
Holocaust is an acknowledgement of the irrevocable collapse of
traditional religious belief, and a new urgency in establishing
human solidarity in a desacralised world. Rubenstein quotes
from Elie Wiesel's *Night*: 'Never shall I forget those flames
which consumed my faith forever'. Elsewhere Wiesel asserts the
impossibility of understanding Auschwitz without God – even
though it is just as inexplicable with him. Rubenstein holds
belief in an omnipotent, beneficient God to be no longer acceptable, especially if this means making the Nazis instruments of
God's purposes. Judaism lives on for him, without God, but in
the form of a cosmic mysticism rather than Jewish secularity.

Another revisionist, a theistic one, is Arthur Cohen, who
conveys a sense of unfathomable mystery about the Holocaust
by his articulation of the *tremendum*. Here, the horror of the
Holocaust is brought into proximity with the magnificent
immensity of God: with this notion, the inadequacy of theological monarchism is exposed, as an archaic structure of interpretation. God acts in the future, not in history, and to have
expected His intervention during the *Shoah* merely betrays our
infantile understanding of the divine–human relation.

The third group of responses draws upon the model of the

theology of liberation as the way forward for a Judaism seeking to go beyond the Holocaust. Cohn-Sherbok has explored this (1987), while Marc Ellis asks: 'Can a Jewish theology of liberation become the catalyst to break through the paralysis confronting the Jewish community today?'[4] Ellis expresses his concern with the conservative tendency of most other Jewish post-Holocaust theologians, for whom the fact and necessity of Jewish empowerment, meaning an impregnable Israel, is the overriding priority. 'The dynamic balance between Holocaust and empowerment found within their analyses of the Holocaust is lost when they enter the realities of the post-Holocaust world' (Ellis, 1986:37). Seeking to move forward from this *impasse* Ellis cites movements of progression and renewal within Judaism; he sees a solidarity between these and the Christian liberation struggles (Black, Latin American, Asian) nourished by the emancipatory motifs of the Jewish scriptures.

Ellis criticises the ways liberation thought can too easily use the Jewish scriptures, while ignoring the Jewish people themselves: a common trait throughout Christian history. In particular, the post-Holocaust experience of the Jewish community does not accord readily with the triumphalism of Exodus language, as used by Christian liberationists. Nevertheless, these two traditions, liberationist and Jewish, can begin to 'probe the night together' when two questions are set alongside each other: 'Activist, what do you see in the night?' and that put to the Holocaust victim: 'What did you see in the night?'

In his overview of these three sets of responses, Dan Cohn-Sherbok shows how many are problematic, because their view of God is either humanly unacceptable, or revised beyond recognition by traditional Jewish belief. In other words, we are, agonisingly, caught within the classical problem of theodicy, of reconciling God's omnipotence and goodness. What is absent from all of the accounts he looks at, revisionist or traditional, is an affirmation of immortality. He comes up with his own version of the Kantian postulate we examined in the last chapter: if the Jewish faith is to survive, Holocaust theology will need to incorporate a belief in the Afterlife in which the righteous of Israel who died in the death camps will receive their just reward. He reminds us that the Jewish biblical belief in life after death comes to the fore in the narrative of political resistance and martyrdom in the Books of the Maccabees. Holocaust theologians have not affirmed this doctrine strongly, and yet for Cohn-Sherbok there can be no other way of reconciling a loving God with the horror of the death camps.

One final area needs to be mentioned. We have seen how Ellis is concerned that for some Holocaust theologians there has been an overriding priority given to Jewish empowerment in the aftermath of the *Shoah*. The *impasse* he refers to is the State of Israel, insofar as its aggressive stance towards Palestinian autonomy and its understandable defensiveness in the face of Arab neighbours detracts from Jewish integrity in the face of oppression. He cites the 'great leap': from Marc Bloch, accompanying a child as they went to their deaths together in the camp, to Baruch Goldstein, who massacred Moslems during their Ramadan prayer in the Hebron in February 1994. And yet, for many Israelis, God's 'saving word' after the catastrophe of the *Shoah* is exactly and concretely this vulnerable political entity – which makes its survival and protection an absolute, theological priority, overriding the claims to justice and autonomy of others. The establishment of Israel in 1947 could be said to be the most dramatic and fateful 'political theological' project of the twentieth century.[5]

Why Were the Churches Unable to Resist the Nazi 'Leviathan'?

The phrasing of this question comes from Moltmann, who, we will recall, explored the distinction between 'Covenant' and 'Leviathan' as alternative modes of political existence. Here, the Third Reich is clearly identified as an all-powerful Leviathan or *katēchon*. Burleigh tells how Nazi totalitarianism positioned itself as an alternative religion, consciously rivalling Church networks, educational and welfare institutions, social and pious associations and workers' syndicates so as to claim the kind of total allegiance that was normally reserved for Christian denominations, whether Catholic or Protestant.[6]

The success of this process of assimilation varied with demographic and geographical factors, but the general outlines are clear. Catholic opposition to Hitler was heavily weakened by the desire of the Vatican to conclude a Concordat with Hitler's regime: one fateful consequence of this was that it permitted the collapse of the Catholic Centre Party. The situation of the Protestant churches was different. The so-called German Christian movement, which sought to 're-invent' the faith along nationalist and anti-Semitic principles, was tempting in part because it held out a reconciliation of sorts between Lutheran and Reformed. It is probably the failure of this movement to win broad support that convinced Hitler that the Churches could not in the long run be co-opted, and hardened his attitude towards Christianity.

Explicit resistance is another matter, however. Apart from the example of the Confessing Church and a number of heroic individuals, it is the quietism and passivity of the majority of Protestant Christians that give cause for concern. Moltmann and others are forthright about the weakness of Luther's 'Two Kingdoms' doctrine in this regard (Moltmann, 1989:75; though Moltmann points out that this essentially pragmatic doctrine was also appealed to *against* Hitlerism). As seen in chapter 5, this doctrine insisted on allotting spheres of influence to Church and State, which resulted in a withdrawal into interiority for the faith, as the political realm was left in the hands of the princes. Coupled with this quietism, Luther's uncompromising refusal of the right of resistance, even against unjust rulers, was of course, a disastrous precedent.

The other mainline Reformation political theology, namely John Calvin's doctrine the 'Lordship of Christ', infuses the spirit of the *Barmen Declaration*. This was a document produced by the Confessing Church in 1934 (first version); one of its prime architects was Karl Barth, the great Reformed theologian. This remarkable text challenged very directly, and on theological grounds, the messianic pretensions of Hitlerism. It arose as a response to the temptations of the German Christian movement, which some of Karl Barth's own colleagues had joined. What will become clear, however, as we examine this text, is that the Lordship of Christ doctrine also has its problems and limitations.

In the *First Barmen Declaration*, Barth and the other signatories are clear about why Christian witness in the face of Nazism has been feeble. They speak of a *theological*, rather than a political or sociological collapse. They also stress that this is a problem that has been in place for some time, rather than a specifically new crisis. A 'disastrous theological error', which had infected the Roman Church and distorted the Reformation, is now made manifest in the events of 1933. This theological error is, simply, the forgetting of 'the Lordship of Christ':[7]

> For in these events an error has become ripe and visible, which has had a devastating effect upon the Evangelical Church for centuries. It consists in the opinion that beside God's revelation, God's grace, and God's glory, a justifiable human arbitrariness has authority to determine the message and form of the church, that is to say, the temporal path to eternal salvation. The view is thereby rejected that the development of the church since the Reformation has been a normal one and that the problems of our church today are only a temporary disturbance upon the removal of which that development might proceed normally … this error must today be recognised and opposed, even in its subtlest and purest forms; and the old confession must be opposed to the old error with a new joyfulness and explicitness.

The shorter *Barmen Theological Declaration* establishes Jesus Christ as the one word of God, such that 'we repudiate the false teaching that the church can and must recognize yet other happenings and powers, images and truths as divine revelation alongside this one Word of God, as a source of her preaching' (thesis 1) and 'we repudiate the false teaching that there are areas of our life in which we belong not to Jesus Christ but another word, areas in which we do not need justification and sanctification through him' (thesis 2).

The basic theological position as Moltmann (1984) evaluates it is a 'Christological eschatology': the sole Lordship of Christ had to be asserted in view of totalitarian claims of state or nation, in order to liberate the church from 'political religion'. God reveals himself in his Word, not in history, in nature or in political movements. 'Because Christ has already won the victory, the whole world is already objectively in Christ and under his lordship'. The world is no longer subject to demonic powers, but finds its peace and freedom in Christ. Moltmann's concern with this 'Christological eschatology' is that it repeats the temptation of the Corinthian community, whom Paul accused of forgetting that it is the *Crucified* One who is Lord. A triumphalist and theocratic position can hardly be a suitable retort to overweening Nazi claims. This theology, says Moltmann, cannot provide the foundation for engaging non-believers: 'The lordship of Christ reaches according to our experience as far as human beings, freed from sin by his death, are obedient to it ... Christocentric ethics can only be discipleship ethics.'

More than one commentator has pointed out the irony that the right of resistance articulated by the Covenant theology of the sixteenth century did not surface here, and that the Reformed theologians were as hamstrung as their Lutheran counterparts about the legitimacy of challenging an unjust tyrant. It is also significant that this position held together only until the outbreak of war, when national unity became a stronger priority. This last point looks eerily similar to the discussion by Cavanaugh (2006:319–20), when he argues against the assumption of many Americans that protests against the war in Iraq should cease once the decision to go to war has been taken by the Commander in Chief. Dissent, however principled, is expected to give way to the exigencies of national unity in a time of war, however questionable.

The most serious objection to the theology of Barmen, however, must be to do with the thinness of its critique, by comparison with the nature of the crisis it seeks to address. Its overwhelming concern is with the Nazi regime's quasi-religious pretensions and rivalry to the Lordship of Christ. The crisis is (for Barth) a long-standing one, but is brought to light by the controversy of the German Christian movement: it is discussed here, and in Barth's history of the conflict, almost entirely in ecclesiastical terms. The history contains a few scattered references to actual events in Germany, and only one reference to the fate of the Jews (Barth, 1965:45). Barth criticises the Confessing Church for its silence about these events – and yet his own allusion to them is almost in passing (an imbalance which he himself was to recognise later). Willmer (2004:128) warns against an anachronistic reading here, as if 'we who come after' should expect from the Barmen texts a full-blooded critique of the evils of National Socialism. Certainly, in 1934, the full horror of the death camps was not yet revealed: but surely enough *was* known for a stronger protest than we have here?

To return to the question at the head of this section: the verdict upon the theological resistance to Leviathan, whether from Catholic, Lutheran or Reformed sources, is a sad one. In each case a mistaken or inadequate 'doctrine of the Two' left the churches and theologians unable to withhold their blessing in a persuasive and articulate manner. There were indeed exceptions, but it is precisely as they were exceptions that they reinforce the general verdict. Dorothee Sölle's questions – 'How did this happen? … Didn't you smell the gas?' – for the most part remain unanswered. As we shall see, it is out of this crisis that the first generation of political theologians emerges after the war, with an urgently felt need to do better.

Finally, however, a consideration of Barth and his theological resistance of Nazism needs to take account of Mark Lilla's long section on Barth and the Jewish theologian Franz Rosenzweig (Lilla, 2007:258–95), perhaps the most controversial section of *The Stillborn God*.[8] Amazing as it may sound, Lilla points up uncomfortable similarities of style and method between Barth and his theological opponents who signed up to Nazism. They too believed that Germany in the years after World War One had arrived at a moment of crisis, that the collapse of liberal theology necessitated a decision. For the 'dialectical' theologian Barth and the Confessing Church the choice was 'Christ or Hitler'. For opponents such as Friedrich Gogarten and Emanuel Hirsch this moment of historic destiny enveloped both figures with messianic expectation; the propaganda of the so-called German Christians could declare that 'Christ has come to us through Adolf Hitler' (Lilla:280). Similar startling charges are brought against Rosenzweig, whose Jewish messianism is contrasted here with that of the unorthodox Marxist Ernst Bloch. What Lilla perceives to be the relationship between these thinkers really goes to the heart of the argument of *The Stillborn God*:

> But every orthodoxy spawns heterodoxy. That is what the explosive youthful works of Barth and Rosenzweig revealed: the possibility of a new heterodoxy that could exploit the gnostic potential embedded in the Bible's promise of redemption. The idea of redemption has been one of the most powerful forces shaping human existence in all those societies that have been touched by the biblical tradition. It has inspired individual human beings to endure suffering, overcome suffering, and inflict suffering on others. It has offered hope and inspiration in times of darkness; it has also added to the darkness by arousing unrealistic expectations and justifying those who spill blood to satisfy them. All the biblical religions cultivate the idea of redemption – and all fear its power to inflame minds and deafen them to the voice of reason. In the writings of Friedrich Gogarten and Ernst Bloch, we encounter what those orthodox traditions always dreaded: the translation of gnostic notions of apocalypse and redemption into a justification of political messianism, now under frightening modern conditions. (Lilla, 2007:294)

Does the *Shoah* represent a unique and radical 'rupture' within rational thought?

For many, the Auschwitz death camp is a kind of cultural and rational 'ground zero'. Everything that preceded the *Shoah* by way of civilisation, culture, science, and technology, needs to be thought anew or reconstructed 'after Auschwitz'. Philosophy, theology, poetry, even architecture are all subjected to what Susan Shapiro calls a 'radical negation' (Shapiro, 1984:4). Even the language with which we work is impossible to the task: and yet the urge to testify to what happened is a categorical imperative – that is, it is non-negotiable, since silence would be a concession of the final word to the executioner. Above all, Hitler must not be granted a posthumous victory. Shapiro therefore attempts to remain true to the radical negativity of the event, but also to leave open the possibility of a recovery of the sacred. She speaks of a 'double rupture': of the coherence and meaning of language in general, and of theological language (as the discourse of ultimate meaning) in particular: 'The negating character of the event cannot be understood, therefore, as either external or occasional to thought'. She notes the importance of narrative and symbol in the writings of Primo Levi and Elie Wiesel and the poetry of Paul Celan. Whatever the rupture in thought and word, however lamed our religious and intellectual traditions, the testimony of these survivors of the camps (Levi and Celan subsequently committed suicide) cannot not be heard.

One imperative of political theology 'after Auschwitz' is that never again can the Jewish voice be ignored; on the contrary, it must be allowed to shape and transform Christian reflection. Needless to say, this makes for a potentially agonising dialogue, as history must be reread, and formerly non-negotiable doctrines and patterns of thinking need to be looked at afresh. Of the Christian political theologians, Johann Baptist Metz has been foremost in 'facing the Jews after Auschwitz'.

If it is true, that Christian theology can only proceed with this new imperative at its heart, then one Jewish interlocutor who has probably done as much as anyone to shed light in this terrible darkness is George Steiner. His essays of literary criticism and cultural analysis in *Language and Silence*, and *No Passion Spent*, as well as his other writings, probe salient themes: the collapse and catastrophe of language (especially of the German language, abused by the Nazis themselves, and by post-war Germans in denial); and, agonisingly, the contortions of enmity and self-hatred which scar the historical and theological relations of Christian and Jew, and which prepared for the 'season of barbarism'.

What makes Steiner an important voice is the theological sensitivity of his writing. As with the other Jewish thinkers mentioned above, he finds himself scouring the tradition for some way of understanding what has happened, why God's fury should have been poured out. There are occasional Gnostic or kabbalistic speculations, but these are not pressed home. Once again, the futility of 'theodicy' is apparent, above all where it is

a question of getting God 'off the hook'. What is striking, however, is the frequency with which Steiner draws on Christian as
well as Jewish images and themes. In the end he proposes a kind
of negative theology, which falls short of assenting belief in the
traditional sense: yet he cannot let go of the sense that there is a
transcendent guarantee of the human adventure in language and
in art.

Steiner's 1989 essay, *Real Presences*, is a broadside against
certain convoluted and dispiriting academic trends. It is also a
postulate of the existence of God, offered not on ethical grounds
(as with Kant), but on aesthetic ones. All great art, says Steiner,
is a wager on transcendence, predicated on a God who underwrites our efforts at meaning. The essay proposes a 'necessary
possibility':

> that any coherent understanding of what language is and
> how language performs, that any coherent account of
> human speech to communicate meaning and feeling is, in
> the final analysis, underwritten by the assumption of God's
> presence.

This is a wager on the meaning of meaning: 'it is that of
Descartes, of Kant and of every poet, artist, composer of whom
we have explicit record'. Towards the end of the book he asserts
that having cited some of those who know best – the poets, the
artists – 'I have found no deconstructionist among them.' The
'density of God's absence, the edge of presence in that absence'
he finds both in the death camps, and in the master-texts of our
age (he lists Beckett, Kafka, Paul Celan).

The book closes with a rich extended image, of 'one particular day in Western history about which neither historical record
nor myth nor Scripture make report. It is a Saturday. And it has
become the longest of days.'[9] Steiner invites Christian and non-
Christian to see themselves between the Friday of waste and
brutality, and the Sunday which for the Christian speaks of a
justice and love which have conquered death, but which all of
us conceive of as the day of liberation from inhumanity and
servitude. We look to resolutions, be they therapeutic or
political, social or messianic. The lineaments of that Sunday

carry the name of hope (there is no word less destructible).

On the Friday the apprehensions and figurations of art are helpless and inappropriate; on Sunday they are unnecessary. It is only on 'the long day's journey of the Saturday' that such things make sense. 'They have risen out of an immensity of waiting which is that of man. Without them, how could we be patient?'

Here is a new twist to the wager, however. The catastrophe of Nazism underlined that humans are mysteriously and terribly capable of torturing prisoners during the day, and being moved by Mozart in the evening. Such an observation too quickly becomes a cliché, and Steiner's persistent probing is all the more remarkable for somehow avoiding this. Three specific points will be mentioned, before we look at Steiner as an inspiration for the political theologian. Firstly, though his life's work has unfolded in the shadow of the camps, he has refused to raise a standard over the exclusivity or uniqueness of the Holocaust, insisting with Marc Ellis on our answerability for the holocausts going on around us, even as we sleep. As for the paradox of Israeli self-empowerment: 'let us never forget that each time a Jew humiliates, tortures or makes homeless another human being, there is a posthumous victory for Hitler'.

Secondly, Steiner is adamant that Christian complicity in the Holocaust be fully acknowledged, insofar as two millennia of 'theological enmity', of Christian longing to be rid of the Jew, prepared the way for the Final Solution. As with Johann Baptist Metz, he sees the very credibility of the Church and of Christianity staked on the capacity to undertake this acknowledgement and repentance – something, he regrets, that has yet to happen on a convincing scale. Christianity itself, he conjectures, is 'sick at heart ... lamed, perhaps terminally, by the paradox of revelation and of doctrine' which produced the *Shoah* and its antecedents in European history.[10] 'Catholicism and Protestantism hardly know themselves', though Jewish identity has been similarly wounded, by the failed experiment of our effort to become fully human: 'After Auschwitz, Jew and Gentile go lamed, as if the wrestling bout of Jacob had been well and truly lost.' In neither case has the laming generated a theologico-philosophical renewal; perhaps it cannot do so.

Nicholas Lash judges that *Real Presences* 'stands firmly in the great tradition of Jewish and Christian prophecy' in its challenge to repentance, and to the remaking of a broken contract and a betrayed covenant. With Steiner's moving image of our Sabbatarian journey, we have a Jewish commentator (a theologian in all but name), engaging with a Christian patterning of time, in such a way that it becomes a universal description of our predicament. Political theology is a discipline of many such 'translations', as we shall see, when we examine, over the next two chapters, the messianic legacy of Walter Benjamin and Ernst Bloch, as well as the communication theory of Jürgen Habermas.

Should it be a cause of concern that, at face value, the scope for developing a political theology from Steiner's intuition appears limited? He has recently made no secret of his dismay at the extremists in all the main religious traditions, and seems pessimistic as to the capacity and willingness of religious communities to withstand and overcome fundamentalist pressures. In a way that echoes Zizek's praise of Christianity's metaphysic of 'uncoupling' (see chapter 3), Steiner speaks warmly of the Jewish destiny of homelessness, as a reproach to humanity's obsessional belonging to race, fatherland, church, or synagogue. A hotel room in Paris, he reminds us, afforded enough space for Marcel Proust to write his great novel.

Lash draws out some of the themes in Steiner which could resource political theology: for example, 'the modulation, where possible, of stranger into guest', a theme which, intriguingly once again, Steiner evokes by reference to the Christian Easter narrative, the stranger encountered on the road to Emmaus. 'Making the world habitable … making a home for others and making others at home' is also our Sabbatarian task. Lash also offers a corrective to Steiner's neglect of the mythological resonances of the Saturday, since the ancient symbolism of the Harrowing of Hell needs to be evoked here. We might add that this makes Saturday a day of intense political activity, having recognised earlier that Christ's victory over and rout of the demons, exemplified by the violent storming of Satan's kingdom, is perhaps the first Christian political theological metaphor.

Finally, we may note that the conversation to which Steiner

invites us is theological, because it is conducted on the premise 'that any coherent account of human speech to communicate meaning and feeling is, in the final analysis, underwritten by the assumption of God's presence.' With this claim, Steiner implicitly joins the company of those political theologians who listen in to the messianic whisperings underneath Critical Theory's account of language as emancipation of victims. It is to theology's engagement with Critical Theory, and its challenge 'to stay, awaken the dead, and make whole what has been smashed', that we now turn.

Chapter 8

'WE WHO COME AFTER'

Critical Theory and the Theologian[1]

In the early months of 1940, Walter Benjamin was waiting in Paris, wondering if he should escape to the USA before the Germans moved into France. He held back from fleeing because he did not want to give up writing his book on Baudelaire. He renewed his reader's card for the *Bibliothèque Nationale*, and contemplated the gas mask in his room, which reminded him of a skull adorning a monk's cell.

During this time he composed a series of eighteen meditations or *Theses on the Concept of History*, the last piece he wrote. He fled Paris, and on 26 September reached a Spanish border town with a group of refugees, only for them to be told that Spain had closed its border that same day, and that their visas would not be recognised. They were to be sent back to France the next morning. That night, Benjamin took his life.

Benjamin and the Angel

We have come across one of his 'theses' in chapter 3: Benjamin's parable of the 'Puppet and the Dwarf'. In this curious tableau, Benjamin indicates how 'theology' is still a motive force of history, but nowadays it had to be 'kept out of sight', like the ugly dwarf manipulating the chess-playing puppet. As we shall see, Benjamin holds us to be under a paradoxical obligation: to think in theological terms, while being forbidden to write in *directly* theological concepts: 'My thinking relates to theology like the blotting page to the ink. It has entirely soaked itself full with it. If the blotting paper had its way, nothing that is written would remain.' Yet another parable, likewise taken from the *Theses,* helps us to understand what is at stake in the 'dark times' Benjamin is trying to chronicle. It is called 'Angelus Novus' ('new angel') or the 'angel of history':

> A Klee painting named 'Angelus Novus' shows an angel looking as though he is about to move away from something he is fixedly contemplating. His eyes are staring, his mouth is open, his wings are spread. This is how one pictures the angel of history. His face is turned toward the past. Where we perceive a chain of events, he sees one single catastrophe which keeps piling wreckage and hurls it in front of his feet. The angel would like to stay, awaken the dead, and make whole what has been smashed. But a storm is blowing in from Paradise; it has got caught in his wings with such a violence that the angel can no longer close them. The storm irresistibly propels him into the future to which his back is turned, while the pile of debris before him grows skyward. This storm is what we call progress.[2]

Even though this stormy wind goes by the name of 'progress', it leaves in its wake an ever-rising tide of catastrophe and human wreckage. This paradox has a name, the 'Dialectic of Enlightenment'. Horkheimer and Adorno summarise thus: 'In the most general sense of progressive thought, the Enlightenment has always aimed at liberating men from fear and establishing their sovereignty. Yet the fully enlightened earth radiates disaster triumphant.' How is this possible, that an Enlightenment that sought to overcome fear and empower humanity should have ended in disaster? This is what 'dialectic' means here: something that is basically or apparently good turns out to have dreadfully negative consequences. And there can surely be no more poignant image of this than a cultured and humane scholar like Walter Benjamin being hounded across Europe to the point of suicide.

The problem of the 'theologico-political' in Benjamin's work is, precisely, the possibility of redemption for the victims of history. Is there some way in which the Angel can disentangle his wings from the storm, and come to the aid of the victims: 'to stay, awaken the dead, and make whole what has been smashed'? We have seen in chapter 7 how Kant addressed this issue, by arguing for three 'postulates of practical reason': that we are free, that God exists, that there is an afterlife. If these are not operative, if there is no chance of virtue and happiness coinciding, then we open ourselves up to moral despair. 'Thus, it is a practical necessity that we postulate them; not to do so would be to commit moral suicide'(McCarthy, 1991:201). When we look at the nature of our ethical obligations we are confronted with not just the possibility, but the 'necessity', of religious hope.

To return from the eighteenth to the twentieth century: one way of understanding contemporary political theology – by which I refer to the tradition of German Political Theology which arose after the Second World War, and therefore in full knowledge of the 'Dialectic of Enlightenment' – is to see it as a return to the approach taken by Immanuel Kant, namely addressing the philosophical foundations of religious belief from the point of view of *practical* rather than theoretical reason (*ethics* instead of epistemology). These theologians echo the theme explored in chapter 7; they maintain that human attempts at 'enlightenment', 'progress', and 'modernity', conducted independently of God, are doomed to fail, precisely because of the serpent's tail of destructiveness, the 'dialectic' which brings catastrophe in the wake of any project of human improvement. In this situation we are like Klee's angel as described by Benjamin, wanting 'to stay, awaken the dead, and make whole what has been smashed', but the storm of progress sweeps us on. And that terrible helplessness is a recipe for despair.

Benjamin and Horkheimer on Theology

We have seen that for Kant this temptation to despair is the only alternative to the 'postulates of practical reason'. The temptation recurs, one hundred and fifty years later, in a correspondence between Walter Benjamin and Max Horkheimer, set out in McCarthy's essay *Philosophical Foundations of the Political*

Theology (McCarthy, 1991). First of all, Horkheimer insists on the irrecoverability or 'closedness' of the past – in effect stressing the hopelessness of the parable of the Angel: 'Past injustice has happened and is over and done with. Those who were slain were really slain' (McCarthy:30). The materialist feels that humanity has been abandoned:

> What happened to those human beings who have perished cannot be made good in the future. They will never be called forth to be blessed in eternity. Nature and society have done their work on them and the idea of a Last Judgement, which the infinite yearning of the oppressed and the dying has produced, is only a remnant from primitive thought, which denies the negligible role of the human species in natural history and humanizes the universe. (30)

Walter Benjamin, by contrast, continues to explore the theme of redemption of the past, with a view of history as a form of remembrance, of empathetic memory that can open up and transform what was closed and done with. 'This is theology; but in recollection [or empathetic memory; *Eingedenken*] we have an experience that forbids us to conceive of history as fundamentally atheological, which is not at all to say that we can write history in directly theological concepts.' This extraordinary assertion reminds us once again of the parable of the Puppet and the Dwarf, where theology is as operative as ever, but is 'wizened, and kept out sight'. Horkheimer protests once again:

> The thought that the prayers of those persecuted in their hour of direct need, the prayers of the innocents who die without comprehending their situation, the last hopes for a supernatural court of appeals – are all to no avail, and that the night in which no human light shines is also devoid of divine light – this thought is monstrous. But is monstrousness ever a cogent argument against the assertion or denial of a state of affairs? (McCarthy, 1991:31)

The Critical Theorists of the Frankfurt School

The problem articulated here by Horkheimer and Benjamin is the twentieth-century attempt to answer Kant's third question, *what may we hope for*? It forms the kernel of post-war political theology's engagement with the social sciences. We shall see this especially with Habermas and the theologians in the next chapter; firstly, however, a more general outline of Critical Theory is required. Edmund Arens (1997) and Charles Davis (1998) sketch the history of Critical Theory as a series of contributions from a variety of disciplines, associated with the philosopher/sociologists Max Horkheimer and Theodor Adorno, and with others names such as Erich Fromm (social psychologist), Herbert Marcuse (philosopher) and Walter Benjamin (literary critic). Its initial aim, before the Second World War, was to develop 'a theory of the historical development of the present epoch', one which sought to examine the relationships 'between the economic life of society, the psychic development of the individual, and the changes in various sectors of culture in the narrower sense.' It was intended that a combination of Marxist social theory and Freud's psychoanalysis would uncover hidden psychic and social structures.

With the onset of Nazism (which forced most of this first generation of the Frankfurt School to flee Germany, as most were of Jewish origin), the agenda was radically transformed. We have referred already to Horkheimer and Adorno's classic text *The Dialectic of Enlightenment.* The guiding question here was 'why humanity, instead of attaining a truly human condition, is sinking into a new kind of barbarism?' Was the spirit of reason and Enlightenment merely nothing other than the expression of a will to self-assertion and domination? As Arens points out, the investigation of Horkheimer and Adorno produces a pessimism, even a despair, regarding the possibility of rationally-based emancipative action; Horkheimer eventually turns to religion (ironically, given his resistance to Benjamin's use of 'theology' in the correspondence cited above), Adorno to art and aesthetics.

Edmund Arens suggests two approaches in political theology

which emerge as a result of engagement with the Critical Theory
of the Frankfurt School: Johann Baptist Metz, who takes
Theodor Adorno and Walter Benjamin as his guides; and
Helmut Peukert, whose conversation partner is Jürgen
Habermas, and his Theory of Communicative Action ('an
integrated theory of the subject and of intersubjectivity, a theory
of society and of history'). These two approaches Arens calls
'apocalyptic political theology' and 'communicative political
theology' respectively. We shall look at the second of these in
the next chapter; here, our attention will focus on the recovery
of apocalyptic and eschatological themes in Johann Baptist
Metz and Jürgen Moltmann.[3]

Interruptions and Hope

Metz gives two examples of experiences he calls 'interruptions',
because their traumatic impact shattered forever the idyllic
complacency of his conservative Catholic childhood: firstly, the
mass death of his young soldier comrades during an Allied
assault towards the end of the Second World War (Metz himself
was sixteen); secondly, the realisation of the huge difference that
Auschwitz and the *Shoah* should have made to theology, and to
German society, but didn't. It is interesting to note that
Moltmann tells of strikingly similar experiences: during a
firestorm unleashed on Hamburg in July 1943, the friend standing next to him was torn to pieces by a bomb which left
Moltmann unscathed, while Moltmann also recalls the 'cold
horror' with which, as a nineteen-year-old prisoner of war in
Scotland, he was shown photographs of Bergen-Belsen and
Auschwitz for the first time. For Metz, however, and for
Germany as a whole, the full horror of this second memory only
surfaced gradually: 'There was no theology in the whole world
that talked so much about historicity. Yet they only talk about
historicity; they did not mention Auschwitz.' Metz detects in
theological idealism a huge and worrying apathy in this regard,
which perhaps connects with the theme of cultural 'weariness'
we will examine below.

Prior to these shattering experiences, Metz's childhood was
spent in Auerbach, Bavaria, which he presents as a symbol of

pre-Enlightenment Catholicism, indeed a place which seemed caught in the Middle Ages, and which required of him a 'journey from Auerbach' to the secular world of modernity.[4] His early work is heavily influenced by the Transcendental Thomism of Karl Rahner, but the divergence of their intellectual paths that takes place from 1963 marks a change of emphasis for Metz. In many ways the work of Rahner and the Transcendental Thomists should be seen as an attempt to respond to Kant's challenge to religion in the First *Critique*, while Metz moves to attend more to practical philosophy, or ethics, as we find in Kant's second work, the *Critique of Practical Reason*: the shift from 'what can I know?' to 'what must I do?' Metz's meeting with the revisionist Marxist Ernst Bloch confirmed this change of direction.

Moltmann had been similarly impressed by Bloch's massive work *Das Prinzip Hoffnung* (*The Principle of Hope*), which he read in 1960. Bloch's extremely intriguing philosophical project consisted in seeking to transform religious space into a privileged site of utopian expectation; Moltmann was struck by the paradox that a Jewish Marxist was writing more articulately about scriptural hope than Christian theologians! *A Theology of Hope* appeared in 1964, intended by Moltmann not as a 'baptism' of Bloch's book (as Karl Barth had suggested), but as a 'parallel action in Christianity on the basis of its own presuppositions'. Rather than coming under the Marxist's influence, it may be said that Moltmann was in fact drawing attention to those Jewish messianic elements in Bloch's thought which Bloch himself, trying to be a good Marxist, was playing down. To repeat the judgement which was made when we looked at Bloch's reading of Thomas Müntzer (chapter 6): in important passages of *The Principle of Hope*, Marxism is 'rhetorically present but in substantial terms predominantly supportive, even marginal.'[5]

Marxism, it seemed, had appropriated the fire of human hope and longing for itself; Moltmann and Metz were catalysed by reading Bloch to reclaim this vital human capacity for Christian theology.

A Theology of Hope is Moltmann's attempt to do this, building on a sense of anticipation of God's future for the world, insofar as we can tell what this will be like from the Resurrection of Christ. There is a 'dialectic', or tension, between present and future: God's raising his Son to life is a contradiction of the present world of suffering and death, so that '[p]eace with God means conflict with the world'. Anticipation is the action of the political visionary, who allows a perception of future possibilities to inform present practice. What for Bloch is a quality inherent in nature, of course, needs to be given a different ground by the Christian theologian (Adams, 2004:229–30).

Saving Modernity's Subject

Meanwhile, Metz sought to construct a 'practical fundamental theology'; in many ways the same move made by his teacher, Karl Rahner, only expanded. Rahner had come to the aid of the individual subject, battered into agnosticism by Kant's demolition of the traditional proofs of God's existence. Metz is also concerned for the 'endangered subject', but this subject must be seen in his or her social and political embeddedness, not in isolation. For Metz, 'theology should address believers at those points at which their identity as persons is most threatened by the social and political catastrophes of history' (Ashley, 2004:247). But rather than seeking to anaesthetise ourselves against this vulnerability, we need to accept that Christian faith 'is just the capacity to affirm and live an endangered identity'. His work is oriented towards 'subject concepts': that is, he attends to the ways in which we struggle to become subjects and to maintain our fragile subjectivity, in the face of those forces which would undermine it.

In this vein, Metz offers a scathing analysis of the distorted middle-class subject that has emerged in modernity, as well as the distorted 'bourgeois Christianity' to which this subject piously subscribes. As Marx had argued previously, this subject is not, as in the past, established through cultural conditions or political systems; he or she is determined by the pervasive principle of *exchange*. The marketplace – the primary location for the principle of exchange – adjudicates all norms and values of human life by supply and demand, by replacement and substitution. In modernity anything can be bought and sold; nothing – not even values, traditions, and relationships – can stand in the way of the market system. Having begun, in the 1960s, to construct a social anthropology on the basis of a positive appraisal of modernity and its quest for freedom, Metz now realises the ways in which modernity actually undermines the subject to which it gave birth, and in fact threatens its very survival.

He detects in post-modern currents of thought a paralysing weariness, indeed a 'second immaturity': do we want to become subjects in the Enlightenment sense after all? It is essential that the theodicy question is continually brought before society, in order to counteract this malaise. His growing awareness of this indolence brings about another significant shift in his work, a new emphasis upon *eschatology*. By 1969 Metz had allotted a specific eschatological function to the Church, called to be an 'instance of critical liberty'; That is, the Church was to stress that any present political arrangement, however benign, was non-identical, or *non-contemporaneous*, with God's future. The Church is the guardian of an 'eschatological proviso', a 'refusal to bless the state', once again. This concept is not without its difficulties, and came in for criticism from the liberation theologian Juan Luis Segundo (Kirwan, 2006).

The Weariness of Evolutionary Time

In fact Metz's later theology (from the 1970s onwards) hardly refers to the concept, partly because of Metz's sense of this 'growing weariness with being a subject'. The danger now is not of the Christian message being swallowed up and cancelled out by rival 'messianisms', but rather losing its edge in the paralysing numbness Metz calls 'evolutionary time'. This theme is treated by Metz in a form with which we are familiar, since he writes a chapter in *Faith in History and Society* entitled 'Hope as immanent expectation, or the struggle for forgotten time', which is very reminiscent of Walter Benjamin's *Theses on the Philosophy of History*, though the chapter is explicitly a tribute to the apocalyptic wisdom of Ernst Bloch: 'Christian theologians can learn from Bloch even if they have to contradict him' (Metz, 1980:169):

V

Catastrophes are reported on the radio in between pieces of music. The music continues to play, like the audible passage of time that moves forward inexorably and can be held back by nothing. As Brecht has said, 'When a crime is committed, just as the rain falls, no one cries: Stop!'

VI

The shortest definition of religion: interruption.

VII

The first categories of interruption: love, solidarity which as M. Theunissen has said, takes time, memory, which remembers not what has succeeded, but also what has been destroyed, not only what has been achieved, but also what has been lost and in this way is turned against the victory of what has become and already exists. This is a dangerous memory. It saves the Christian continuum.

VIII

There is a new form of metaphysics, called evolutionary logic. In it, time has been made indifferent and has come systematically to control man's universal consciousness. Everything is timelessly and continually reconstructed on the basis of this philosophy. This includes the religious consciousness and the dialectical criticism of religion.

(Metz, 1980:170–1)

I have found it very striking to look at some of these theses with students, and to realise how startlingly resonant they are, even thirty years after Metz wrote them. *'Timelessness as a system'*: Metz alerts us to the sinister ability of capitalist modernity to 'evacuate' sacred time, holy seasons when the spirit of resistance can and needs to be nurtured and renewed (Benjamin makes this point in his fragment, 'Capitalism as a Religion'). We know about the disappearance of the 'sabbath' in modern societies, and the co-option of feasts like Christmas by consumerist capitalism: but what are we to make of a market system that gives us Chelsea FC or Kylie Minogue *Advent calendars*?

Even this great Christian season of messianic hope and
anticipation has been trivialised.

As for our response to catastrophe and suffering: is there
anything more dispiriting about modern communications media
than watching a television news report on a human tragedy – an
earthquake, a campus massacre – while the latest football scores
or stock market prices scroll across the bottom of the screen?
'No one cries: Stop!'

The 'evolutionary' logic referred to in Thesis VIII denotes
how the paradoxical undermining of the modern subject by
modernity itself takes place. The *bourgeois* subject is defined in
terms of his or her 'freedom from suffering', which means
insulating himself from the suffering of others. In place of this
middle-class subject, Metz turns to *the subject of suffering*. As
with Walter Benjamin, attention is drawn not to the optimistic,
evolutionary history of the victors, but to the forgotten history
of victims. The freedom of the human subject is now defined as
the freedom *to* suffer, which includes 'the freedom to suffer the
suffering of others'. The categories in which this new historical
consciousness unfolds are *memory, narrative and solidarity*.
Christianity represents human freedom as the 'dangerous
memory' of the passion, death and resurrection of Jesus Christ:
'through this memory we experience history as a history of the
dead and of those who suffer'.

The Eschatology of Suffering

Metz takes up the idea of *apocalypse* as an antidote to evolutionary thinking. Apocalyptic thinking is a 'rhetorical device'
against sleepiness – though it is important to stress that, in
contrast to the blood and gore of the *Left Behind* visionaries
whom we will consider in chapter 10, Metz sees apocalypse as
a radical 'hope for the other, even for one's enemies'. It is
characterised, not by resentful violence, but by a prayerful disposition which he names *Leiden an Gott* (Ashley translates this
as 'suffering unto God'), making clear this is an active, not
passive stance, towards the suffering of myself and of others: the
stance once again of Job, or the Jesus of Mark's Passion. This
spirituality endures the remembrance of suffering, and coheres

with Metz's re-description of the Enlightenment subject in terms of the 'freedom to suffer the suffering of others'.

'Suffering' is at the heart of Moltmann's other notable achievement in theology: the reconsideration of the nature of God and the recovery for political theology of the Reformation 'theology of the Cross', which we find in *The Crucified God*, his second major work after *A Theology of Hope*. As with Metz, the cross has an interruptive role; it stands over against human certainties and cannot be incorporated into history, nor even be smoothed over by an optimistic 'eschatological' stance. Insofar as Moltmann is still working with German philosophical traditions, it looks as if Bloch is being 'corrected' or complemented with a darker, more pessimistic strain of thinkers like Rosenzweig, Benjamin, and the analysts of Enlightenment's 'dialectic', Adorno and Horkheimer.

Moltmann at times gets into knots trying to appropriate essentially atheistic philosophical insights for his theology (Adams:231–20). The same has been said about the problematic presence of Hegel's philosophy of negation and sublimation in *The Crucified God*: while the emotional power of an appeal to a God who is not apathetic towards the suffering of Auschwitz is undeniable, there are questions about Moltmann's 'revision' of our traditional concept of God, and his allegedly unacceptable restrictions on God's freedom. Moltmann's response is to change the terms of our notion of 'freedom', ascribing to God not our bourgeois 'freedom of choice' or 'self-determination', but an alignment of freedom with friendship. We shall note below some specific problems raised by Dorothee Sölle regarding his book, but these criticisms aside, the implications of a 'Crucified God' for theology are evident, and consonant with the judgement of Metz:

> Christian theology … must adopt a critical attitude towards political religions in society and in the churches. The political theology of the cross must liberate the state from the political service of idols and must liberate people from political alienation and loss of rights.
>
> (Moltmann, 1974:328)

A Fiery Cloud in the Night: Dorothee Sölle[6]

The achievements of Metz and Moltmann are considerable. Under the heading 'political theology' their work is usually linked with a third theologian, whose impact is in many ways very different, even if she has not shaped the landscape in quite the same way as her better-known male colleagues. Dorothee Sölle, also spelled Soelle (1929–2003), differed from them in that her career included a visible and sustained political and peace activism; one might say at the expense of an orthodox academic career in Germany, where such 'extra-mural activities' were frowned on. Sölle never held a professorship in her native land, and between 1975 and 1987 she divided her time between Union Theological Seminary in New York and activism in Germany. One of Sölle's most famous activities was the *Politisches Nachtgebet* (Political Night Prayers), which she helped organise in Cologne from 1968, originally as a protest against the Vietnam War, but taking in other issues of social concern, including the arms race and poverty in the developing world. A member of the Evangelical Church, her concern for the social relevance of the gospel made her a very visible figure, who was widely mourned when she died in 2003.

Her theological interests show a similar breadth, as she has written from feminist and liberationist perspectives, has shown an interest in mysticism (especially its 'anarchic' dimensions), and has also written poetry: her doctorate from Stuttgart was on the relation between poetry and theology. It is striking how many of the themes she addresses are close to those which govern the thinking of Metz and Moltmann, which is why it is appropriate that these thinkers are linked together. First of all, and once again, they share a wartime background, overshadowed by the catastrophe of the Holocaust, though Sölle was slightly younger than Metz and Moltmann. Her parents were opposed to Hitler and were shocked by the way the Churches had made their peace with him. In an essay on sin, Sölle shows herself to be very much a German of her generation: 'I was born in 1929. I am a child of fascism, and spent about ten years of my young adulthood on the questions: "How could it happen?

Where were you when the transports were put together? Didn't you smell the gas?'"[7]

Sölle's first book *Christ the Representative* (1967) was her response to the 'death of God' theology then in vogue – at the same time that Metz was engaging with theologies of the secular. Like Moltmann, she saw that the event of Auschwitz necessitated a change in the way we think of God's 'omnipotence'. The theme of the weakness of God is reinforced by perhaps her best-known book in English, *Suffering* (1973). It is worth drawing attention to difficulties she had with Moltmann's treatment of this in *The Crucified God*. She objects to the 'blurring' of the distinction between victim and executioner which slips into Moltmann's presentation, when Jesus believes himself to have 'come to grief over God', the Father. Sölle recognises that this potentially sado-masochistic interpretation (which is to be resisted on feminist grounds as well as more generally) runs counter to the overall thesis of Moltmann's book, of a compassionate God who suffers with us; this is the picture of God which emerges from her own book on this theme.

Political Theology (1974) is an engagement with and critique of the existential theology of Rudolf Bultmann: she distances herself from him in much the same way as Metz had to distance himself from Karl Rahner, because Bultmann overemphasised the individual dimension of Christian life at the expense of the social. It is perhaps in her anxieties and warnings about first-world Christianity, however, where Sölle most closely resembles the later, rather pessimistic Metz, in memorable phrases such as Europe's 'death by bread alone'. In the article on sin mentioned above she writes in a vein strongly reminiscent of Metz's critique of the paralysis and sleepiness of bourgeois society, declaring that: '[s]in – the absence of warmth, love, caring, trust – is the most normal thing in the world':

> When I try to say how I see the world, I can't get away from an image that forces itself on me and won't let go: the Ice Age – this slow advance of cold, a freezing process which we experience and try to forget. Ice Age in the schools, in the factories, in the high-rise silos we live in, in those smallest units formerly known as families. ... in the First

World, more and more people are spiritually retarded from over-nourishment, to sum up in one word the condition we enjoy. We don't just live in an advancing Ice Age; we produce it, maintain it and profit from it. It is absurd that we want to deny the fact of this 'sin'; that is, the domination of freezing over retreating human beings. (Sölle, 1982)

Conclusion

A mischievous academic colleague of mine once set the following exam question: 'Liberation Theology gave a voice to the oppressed; European Political Theology gave a voice to disaffected academic theologians. Discuss.' The reader will have to judge for herself how fair a comment this is. Certainly the gap between Europe and Latin America should not be over-emphasised, as Metz, Moltmann and Sölle were keen to maintain a dialogue with their South American cousins. This mutual exchange has not been without its tensions and real disagreements, but the convergence of basic attitudes is most poignantly symbolised by the bloodstained copy of *El Dios Crucificado*, found at the murder scene of the University of Central America, El Salvador, in November 1989. The book belonged to Jon Sobrino, a prominent liberation theologian; the blood was of one of his murdered Jesuit colleagues.

As for disaffection: there is a certain amount of theological 'grumpiness' around, and Metz in particular has been taken to task for his 'negativity', as we shall see in chapter 13. Once again, it seems, we have to account for a tension between 'Augustinian' and 'Thomist' strains in how the Church relates to society. It is hardly surprising if Metz, Moltmann and Sölle tend towards the former, given the horrendous events that shaped their youth. Assessing their legacy is not easy. Their writings are dated in many respects, which is far from surprising, because they were engaging with other theological styles and questions that have themselves receded from relevance. And if it appears that Sölle's work has had the shortest shelf-life, again this is not surprising, in the light of her sustained and effective engagement with the other 'publics' for theology: the Church and the wider society, as well as the academy.

Then again, there is that 'rolling news' bulletin, with its brutal trivialisation of suffering – those advent calendars!

It may be an appropriate judgement is to follow Jon Sobrino's lead, in claiming for liberation theology the definition of a religious 'classic', and ask whether the same title belongs to the work of this distinctive generation of theologians. Sobrino here follows David Tracy in *The Analogical Imagination*, where the 'classic' describes articulations of the spirit that prove to be of enduring fruitfulness. A definitive judgement on the validity of a 'classic', by its nature, has to be postponed. Nevertheless, provisionally we would be laying claim to:

> something valuable, something 'important'; some disclosure of reality in a moment that must be called one of 'recognition' which surprises, provokes, challenges, shocks and eventually transforms us; an experience that upsets conventional opinions and expands the sense of the possible; indeed a realized experience of that which is essential, that which endures. The presence of classics in every culture is undeniable. Their memory haunts us. Their actual effects in our lives endure and await ever new appropriations, constantly new interpretations. Their existence may be trusted to time, to the generations of capable readers and inquirers who will check our enthusiasms and ensure the emergence of some communal sense of the importance of certain texts, images, persons, events, symbols. (Tracy, 1983:108–9)

Chapter 9

'FROM DESPAIR TO WHERE?'

Habermas and Communicative Theology

Critical Theory Continued: Jürgen Habermas

Edmund Arens begins his book *Christopraxis* (1996) with a quotation from the Gospel of John: 'Those who do what is true come to the light, so that it may be clearly seen that their deeds have been done in God' (John 3:21). These words of Jesus are a reproach to Nicodemus, who fearfully comes to Jesus at night. They might also be taken as a riposte to Hannah Arendt, who compared the activity of the Christian to the furtive secrecy of the criminal.

This verse sums up the approach of the second strand of theology associated with Critical Theory, which understands authentic gospel living in terms of the 'Communicative Action' theory of Jürgen Habermas, 'seeing in his expanded concept of reason a way to rehabilitate Christian values over against instrumental concepts of reason that have colonized most areas of human experience' (Hewitt, 2004:466). A word of clarification is needed here, about precisely *who* is undertaking this dialogue. Arens files the theologians inspired by Habermas under the category 'political' theologians; they are constructing a 'communicative political theology' (1997:232). Marsha Eileen Hewitt designates these interlocutors 'public theologians', rather than political. She gives reasons why she considers 'public theology' to be not only very different from political and liberation theologies, but even a step backwards from them. I propose that we try and sort this out in the next chapter.

Habermas is one of the most important social theorists of the late twentieth century. A figure of comparable stature would be the American philosopher John Rawls, but despite the enormous impact of *A Theory of Justice* (Rawls, 1999 [1971]) there has been surprisingly little direct contact between Rawls and political theology, at least compared to the Habermas discussions.[1] In an article entitled 'Saint John: the Miracle of Secular Reason' Matthew Scherer draws attention to the 'saintliness' of John Rawls, as evidenced both by his 'miraculous' works and by some aspects of Rawl's own life. This is only partly tongue in cheek: Scherer is asking seriously about 'the persistence of political theology within a discourse that disavows it' (341), in a way which, as we shall see, closely matches the theological 'interrogation' of Jürgen Habermas. Scherer concludes that

> admirable appeals to justice may find their root in the ineliminable experiences of personal suffering that they tend to obscure. And that the faith Rawls seeks to inspire in his conception of liberalism is much more closely analogous, in the needs it serves, to modalities of religious faith, which Rawls has been taken to have escaped. In the end, then, it would appear than even an avowedly secular, liberal, democratic politics stands in deep need of its saints, and that this very need can serve as a vital source of moral and political instruction.
>
> (Sherer, 2006:362)

Habermas is regarded as the main heir to the Frankfurt School, carrying on the task they set themselves in the 1930s, namely, the construction of 'a theory of the historical development of the present epoch'. This theory examines the relationships 'between the economic life of society, the psychic development of the individual, and the changes in various sectors of culture in the narrower sense'. As noted in the last chapter, the original intention was to draw on the work of Marx and Freud, though this became more complicated, not least after the Nazi catastrophe. Habermas seeks to carry forward the overall aim of the Frankfurt School by constructing 'an integrated theory of the

subject and of intersubjectivity, a theory of society and of
history' (Arens: 1997:229).

It is not possible to summarise here the scope and detail of
Habermas' work; excellent guides are available. What interests
us specifically is his (ambiguous) engagement with theology. In
keeping with its Marxist and Freudian ancestry, Habermas'
construction of a 'Theory of Communicative Action' adopts a
'methodological atheism': the assertions of theology and religion are only of value in the public sphere if they can be translated into a public language, accessible to everyone. Despite this
challenge, some political theologians see this theory as the best
way to release and consolidate the emancipatory potential of the
Christian tradition. This has not been simply a defensive move:
these same theologians have been able to articulate how the
Theory of Communicative Action is itself flawed, insofar as it
does not take into account the religious dimension of human
hope.

In chapter 4 we considered Hannah Arendt's concept of
political action. Insofar as this action was both interpersonal and
accompanied by speech, it could be said that her vision is a
forerunner of Habermas' work. He posits authentic political
action in terms of communication, and argues that interpersonal
communication is fundamentally oriented to *consensus*. Of
course this communication is distorted and frustrated in all
kinds of ways. For this reason, Habermas invites us to imagine,
as a kind of template for political action, an 'ideal speech
community'; that is, one in which there is equality of access to
the public arena: no one excluded, and no one debarred from
speech, provided each person strives to give reasons for their
case which are publicly comprehensible. Also posited along
with this community setting is unlimited time for discussion,
during which distortions are overcome and, eventually, consensus achieved.

A Theological Response

Helmut Peukert, yet another German theologian, has attempted
to articulate a critical *theology of communicative praxis*, or a
'theology of communicative action' along these lines.[2] His

engagement with contemporary philosophers of science led him to the view that scientific rationality is based upon communicative action, making the insights of Habermas an appropriate way forward for thinking about science and theology together. However, according to Peukert, the deep structure of communicative practical reason, which is characterised by *equality, reciprocity and solidarity*, contains a glaring contradiction. There is a gap between the universalism of the communication ethics he develops and the 'annihilation of the innocent other' in history. Simply put: what is the status of the victims of history? If there is no possibility of solidarity with them, then an ideal communication ethic is a sham. Communicative discourse is in principle unlimited and unrestricted, but it is evident that when perfect solidarity has finally been achieved, these lucky few (Bertolt Brecht's phrase: 'we who come after'):

> are obliged to live with the consciousness that they owe everything to the oppressed, the downtrodden, the victims of the whole process of human emancipation. This generation has inherited everything from past generations and lives on what *they* paid for. ... The happiness of the living consists in the appropriation of the dead. Is happiness at all conceivable under these presuppositions?[3]

This last generation, it seems, must either be blissfully forgetful, or drawn to nightmarish grief and despair. This is, in effect, to go back to the exchange between Walter Benjamin and Max Horkheimer. The response of theology to this crisis is similar to Benjamin's: an insistence on an 'anamnestic solidarity' with the dead in resurrection (*Anamnesis* is the Greek word for remembrance, or literally 'unforgetting').[4] This is summed up in two theses:

> The Judeo-Christian tradition is concerned with the reality experienced in the foundational and limit experiences of communicative action and with the modes of communicative action still possible in response to these experiences; a fundamental theology can and must be developed as a

theory of this communicative action approaching death in
anamnestic solidarity and of the reality experienced and
disclosed in it. (Peukert, 1984:215)

As McCarthy makes clear, Peukert has then to deal with the
'here comes the cavalry' objection: being in a monstrous
situation cannot entail, as if by a syllogism, a happy solution.
Peukert goes no further than identifying 'the worm at the heart
of the apple of progress', but the lines of argument are clear:
'Communicative action in universal solidarity with the innocent
victims of history only makes sense if this end is attainable, and
it is attainable only on the assumption of a Lord of History who
will somehow redeem past history' (36). Arens argues that:

> the insistence on the anamnestic constitution of reason and
> on anamnestic solidarity … indeed sheds light on the vic-
> tims of history and makes clear that modernity has not at
> all put an end to victimization but, on the contrary, has
> enlarged both the numbers and the quality of victimization.
> By claiming universal justice, universal solidarity, and the
> recognition of the others as others …, political theology 'in
> the face of and at the end of modernity'… affirms that the
> universality that the enlightenment had in view must not be
> abandoned but that it must be adequately brought up,
> namely as precisely the taking into account of the uni-
> versality of suffering that has to be addressed, denounced,
> and overcome. (Arens: 1997:237)

Arens himself attempts a reading of biblical and ecclesial
traditions as a communicative praxis ('Christopraxis'), while
Paul Lakeland envisages the Church as an 'ideal speech community.'[5] So there has been no shortage of theological interlocutors, and through a reluctant dialogue with them Habermas has
become more sympathetic to the emancipatory possibilities of
religion. All of which makes for a rich and important exchange
of ideas, the most significant symbol of which has to be the
discussion between Habermas and Cardinal Joseph Ratzinger at
the Catholic Academy of Bavaria in January 2004: an 'unlikely
dialogue'[6] between the foremost 'watchdog' of Catholic

doctrine – subsequently to become Pope Benedict XVI – and the liberal intellectual heir to a tradition of Western Marxism.

Habermas Takes Note of the Theologians

Jürgen Habermas converses with theologians in the collection *Habermas, Modernity and Public Theology*. Here are essays from five theologians: David Tracy, Helmut Peukert, Francis Schüssler Fiorenza, Matthew Lamb and Charles Davis, as well as essays from two non-theologians and Habermas' response, 'Transcendence from Within, Transcendence in this World' (Habermas, 1992:226–50). David Tracy sets the scene,[7] stressing how communicative rationality can and must contribute to the task of helping theology address its public, 'constituted by open conversations, plural discourses and diverse communities' (5). Charles Davis (152–72) sees possibilities in the Theory of Communicative Action for expounding the validity of religious hope, while Helmut Peukert characterises both Enlightenment and Theology as 'unfinished projects' (43–65). Both these two and Matthew Lamb see the challenge of theodicy – solidarity with suffering victims – as central to the discussion. All welcome the framework (superior to those of Marx and Weber) Habermas gives them for thinking about religion in modernity, though with reservations. In particular, Habermas is challenged for his neglect of the positive and emancipatory dimension of religion in the public sphere.

Habermas' reply, though respectful, makes it clear that different understandings of religion are at work (Fiorenza, 1992:15).[8] He admits that he finds this discussion 'difficult': he is more at ease responding to objections from sociologists and philosophers, but is nervous of his lack of expertise in theology. However, given that this theological interest, mainly in Germany and the USA, has now stretched over several decades,[9] he feels that continued silence on his part would be inappropriate.

Habermas begins by recognising common ground on which theologians and philosophers can speak to each other, 'insofar as they share a self-critical assessment of modernity' (226). He recalls the admirable efforts of theologians of the Confessing Church in post-war Germany, and cites with approval the public theology of David Tracy and Francis Schüssler Fiorenza, for whom the churches are 'communities of interpretation in which issues of justice and conceptions of goodness are publicly discussed'. In comparison with other, secular, communities of interpretation

> it could turn out that monotheistic traditions have at their disposal a language whose semantic potential is not yet exhausted, that shows itself to be superior in its power to disclose the world and to form identity, in its capability for renewal, its differentiation, and its range ... where theological argumentation is pushed so far into the neighbourhood of other discourses, the perspectives from within and from without meet without restraint. (229)

So far so very good. Habermas sees how political theology has attempted to break out of the *cordon sanitaire* that would keep theological and social scientific discourses rigorously apart from one another, afraid of mutual contamination. The task is to bring both sides beyond the postures of nihilistic condemnation and dogmatic self-assertion, and into a relation 'where arguments are used'. But he then poses two key questions and a warning:

> If this, however, is the common ground of theology, science, and philosophy, what then still constitutes the distinctiveness of theological discourse? What separates the internal perspective of theology from the external perspective of those who enter into a dialogue with theology? ... the more that theology opens itself in general to the discourses of the human sciences, the greater is the danger that its own status will be lost in the network of alternating takeover attempts. (231)

Habermas takes note of a philosophical tradition which understands itself as critically appropriating or retrieving religious contents within the universe of argumentative discourse: from Hegel, to Ernst Bloch, Walter Benjamin and Critical Theory. The similarity between Adorno's philosophical critique and Metz's theological protest is specifically noted (232). Once again, however: how is philosophy to be differentiated from theology here? The difference (according to Habermas) must be the *methodological atheism* which philosophy must show towards the content of religious experience. Such experiences can only be resources for philosophy insofar as they are incorporated into the 'universe of argumentative discourse that is uncoupled from the event of revelation' (233). Habermas judges that the theologians have not succeeded in this translation: theirs is an 'indirect procedure of apologetic argumentation', which seeks to force the secular opponent into a corner, forcing them to concede theologically defended affirmations. Habermas reasserts his current position on the matter:

> As long as religious language bears within itself inspiring, indeed unrelinquishable semantic contents which elude (for the moment?) the expressive power of a philosophical language and still await translation into a discourse that gives reasons for its positions, philosophy, even in its post-metaphysical form, will neither be able to replace nor repress religion. (237)

However, this does not means that he agrees with Helmut Peukert on the necessity of a theological foundation for a discourse theory of morality and ethics:

> The anamnestically constituted reason, which Metz and Peukert, rightly, continually advocate ... confronts us with the conscientious question about deliverance for the annihilated victims. In this way we become aware of the limits of that transcendence from within which is directed to this world. But this does not enable us to ascertain the countermovement of a compensating transcendence from beyond. That the universal covenant of fellowship would be able to be effective retroactively, toward the past, only in the weak memory of the living generations, and of the anamnestic witnesses handed down falls short of our moral need. But the painful experience of a deficit is still not a sufficient argument for the assumption of an 'absolute freedom which saves in death'. (238)

Peukert, says Habermas, resorts to an experience accessible only in the language of the Christian tradition: specifically, the death on the cross as an anticipation of God's goodness, and the guarantee of a favourable outcome to our unconditional solidarity. Charles Davis similarly adopts an 'apologetic' argumentation when he asserts that '[a] secular hope without religion cannot affirm with certainty ... a future fulfilment'. Habermas does not see that this search for certainty can be justified; he refers us instead to 'a post-Marxist social theory that has become more humble', whose diagnoses are reliably but not infallibly grounded. 'Kant already had answered the question "What may we hope for?" with a *postulate* of practical reason, not with a premodern certainty that could inspire us with *confidence*.' (240) Habermas expresses gratitude to his theological interlocutors, therefore, for their engagement with his theory, but at the heart of his response to them is a firm rejection of 'apologetic figures of thought'.

He wonders whether theology is in danger of losing its distinctiveness: for Habermas, the task of communicating religious traditions in the public sphere can only be a translation from one language to another. Unlike his interlocutors, he does not believe theology is communicative.

Recent Conversations: Secularisation and the Post-Secular

The later writings of Habermas, which we consider below, have a change of emphasis: they are not so much focused on the question of whether theology has something crucial to add to the Theory of Communicative Action: by and large, Habermas' answer still seems to be in the negative. Instead, two specific but related themes come to the fore, each establishing the positive contribution which religion and theology can make — even if this does not quite coincide with what political theologians think that contribution should be. They are:

• a reappraisal of our understanding of the phenomenon of 'secularisation', in the wake of 9/11, and
• a renewed exploration of how religious traditions can and should contribute to the project of 'post-secular' democracy.

To begin with the most pressing and dramatic of these themes. The events of September 11th, 2001, and the debate concerning the violent and fundamentalist 'return of religion', have confirmed Habermas in the need to revisit the phenomenon of *secularisation*. This he did in a speech delivered within a couple of months of 9/11.[10] It is important to stress the difference between what Habermas has to say about these events, and the view of commentators like Richard Dawkins, who insist that the actions of suicide bombers are just the type of atrocities that religious people have always inflicted on others, ever since this 'virus' first infected the human race. For Habermas, on the other hand, '[d]espite its religious imagery, fundamentalism is, as we know, an exclusively modern phenomenon'. Because the process of secularisation (which he calls a 'process of creative destruction'), has taken place inappropriately, and too rapidly, people in traditional societies have come to feel threatened and embattled. There is a further ironic aspect to this, namely the use of apocalyptic language by President Bush promising retribution, and the upsurge of religious practice in the United States, 'as if the blind attacks had struck a religious chord deep within the innermost core of secular society'. What is clear to Habermas is that, thanks to Osama bin Laden, there has been a qualitative change in the relationship between modern secular society and religion. Even in Europe, where for centuries we have been living with 'the Janus head of modernity', there is still ambivalence regarding secularisation. If we are to avoid a 'clash of civilisations', we need to be attentive to this ambivalence.

The models of secularisation previously in use (which speak of a 'replacement' or 'expropriation' of the religious by the secular) will not suffice, because they oppose religion and modernity. Instead, we need a model which can describe what is happening in 'post-secular' societies, a term Habermas starts to use from now on. For this he resorts once again to a 'translation' model, by which religious claims need to be translated into a publicly accessible secular discourse. Communities of believers and the secular state speak to each other by exercising 'democratically enlightened common sense'. This 'common sense' requires of believers that they: renounce violence; engage seriously with the truth claims of other faiths; and recognise the validity of the social sciences and of the secular basis of the modern constitutional state.

The challenge of 'translation' is developed further in the historic conversation between Habermas and Cardinal Ratzinger, though here their topic is a little less dramatic than the paradigm shift imposed by 9/11.[11] These two prominent German scholars address a crucial question: *is the liberal secular state nourished by normative preconditions that it cannot itself guarantee*? This raises the possibility of the state's dependence upon conceptual, ethical or religious traditions; if such a dependence were proved, it would undermine the state's commitment to ideological neutrality in the face of pluralism. In the background here is the issue of European constitutional unity, and whether there is sufficient democratic enthusiasm and commitment to sustain such a project on purely secular grounds.

Habermas breaks the theme down into two aspects: firstly, asking whether political rule is at all open to a secular (non-religious) justification. Even if such a foundation were firmly established, however, there remains the problem of how citizens are to be motivated, since the sources of their solidarity might dry up. This second part of the challenge requires, for Habermas, an understanding of secularisation as a twofold learning process, by which both Enlightenment traditions and religious doctrines learn their respective limits.

Regarding the first point, Habermas holds a Kantian Republican justification of the democratic constitutional state, drawing on a tradition of rational law derived from seventeenth- and eighteenth-century philosophy (rather than earlier classical and theological sources), to be securely founded; nor should Catholic Christianity, at least, have any difficulty with this. The second challenge – how to motivate and enthuse – remains, especially given that the democratic constitutional state demands a very high level of active participation. Citizens are required to actively exercise their communicative and participatory rights, not simply with regard to their own interest, but with respect to the common good. So how does one ensure this high motivational outlay (one cannot prescribe solidarity, or force people to vote)? Political virtues are essential for democracy, and Habermas concedes that these are habits which need to be nurtured from spontaneous and 'prepolitical' sources. This does not imply, yet, that the liberal state is incapable of reproducing motivational preconditions out of its own resources: nevertheless, a cognitive process, without moral discernment and consensus, is not enough:

> Solidarity among the members of a political society, however abstract and legally mediated it may be, emerges only when the principles of justice find their way into the more densely woven network of cultural values. ... A derailing modernisation of society as a whole could very well erode the democratic bond and drain the democratic state of the kind of solidarity upon which it depends, without being able to command it legally. (255)

He even envisages this as reversion to a kind of 'war of all against all', though it is 'rights' rather than 'weapons' that are wielded here. This disintegration is in fact what we have with market economies, which cannot be democratised, and yet increasingly assume control over areas of life previously held together by political or prepolitical forms of communication. Failing democratic operations (especially at the supra-national level, such as attempts at international law) are leading to disillusionment and increased 'civic privatisation'.

Philosophy's Indebtedness to Religion

Habermas prefers not to over-dramatise the situation. The ability of an ambivalent modernity to stabilise itself by drawing on the power of communicative reason alone is, for him, an open, empirical question. In order to succeed, this modernity requires a measure of interaction which includes, but goes well beyond, 'respect' for those persons and for those ways of life which derive integrity from religious conviction. But what about the other direction? Does philosophy learn anything from religious traditions? In a section which reads a bit like 'what have the Christians ever done for us?' Habermas recounts that these traditions 'articulate, subtly spell out, and hermeneutically keep alive over thousands of years' intuitions about fall and redemption; about something which has been lost generally and cannot be recovered, namely:

> sufficiently differentiated possibilities of expression and sensibilities for misspent life, for societal pathologies, for the failure of individual life plans and the deformation to be seen in distorted life contexts. (257)

He is alert to the ways in which the mutual penetration of Christianity and Greek metaphysics brought about a philosophical appropriation of genuinely Christian content, in terms of:

> heavily laden, normative conceptual networks such as: responsibility; autonomy and justification; history and memory; beginning anew, innovation and return; emancipation and fulfilment; externalisation, internalisation and embodiment; individuality and community.

Habermas speaks of the 'secularizing release of religiously-encapsulated potentials of meaning'. Above all, the shining example, as it were, of such a 'saving translation' undertaken by philosophy is the translation of man's likeness to God into the notion of human dignity, in which all partake equally, in which all are respected unconditionally. He mentions Walter Benjamin as one such 'translator', rendering biblical concepts accessible to the general public, beyond the boundaries of a particular religious community.

Given the threats identified earlier, Habermas argues that it is in the state's own interests to have a care for the sources of our endangered solidarity – hence talk of a 'post-secular society'. The term 'post-secular' is more than simply a resigned acknowledgement of religion's *de facto* continued existence in the public sphere: rather, it reflects a normative insight that has consequences for how believers and non-believers interact politically. If both sides can understand secularisation of society as a complementary learning process, each will be able to take seriously the other's contributions to controversial issues.

The liberal state demands a political integration of its citizens, which goes beyond an undemanding alignment of religious ethos with the imposed laws of a secular society. Ethos and laws need to be connected, or 'embedded', 'from within'. This is a costly process for believers. But it is also costly for non-believers, who, beyond the demands of tolerance of their religious fellow-citizens, are expected to acquire 'a self-reflexive handling of the limits of Enlightenment', and perhaps even to participate in efforts to translate relevant contributions from a religious language to a publicly accessible one.

Cardinal Ratzinger responds, finding himself largely in agreement regarding 'post-secular society, the willingness to learn and mutual self-limitation'. He acknowledges those pathologies of religion requiring reason for their purification, but also 'even more threatening' pathologies or *hybris* of reason that in its turn calls for correction, by attending to the great religious traditions of humanity. A fully emancipated reason, which ignores this 'necessary correlativity of reason and faith, of reason and religion, which are appointed to mutually cleanse and heal one another' (268), will be destructive. There is, in short some degree of agreement between the theologian and the social theorist, that religion and faith traditions do have a very important contribution to make to the project of secular democratic society. But they differ on what exactly this contribution is, and the 'concessions' which Habermas makes to belief probably fall short of what Cardinal Ratzinger (and presumably political theologians) would want to hear.

Is Habermas a Suitable Partner for Theology?

There are plausible reasons why some theologians remain sceptical about Habermas as a conversation partner. Just how useful is a system which insists on 'methodological atheism' for the project of political theology? There must also be a concern about whether Habermas' 'translation' model requires the believer to concede too much; a 'devil's pact' which favours the secularist side of the bargain. As Hewitt reminds us (2004:466), there are limits to how far theology can lay open its operations to public discourse, as a Habermasian approach would require:

at least some of theology's axiomatic assumptions are non-negotiable.

In fact, one of the most perceptive thinkers regarding the dangers for theology is Jürgen Habermas himself. We have seen how in 1992 he welcomed the conversation with theology, but asked how this discipline was to preserve its distinctiveness in this dialogue: 'the more that theology opens itself in general to the discourses of the human sciences, the greater is the danger that its own status will be lost in the network of alternating takeover attempts' (1992:231). In the conversation with Cardinal Ratzinger, there is a related concern. He describes the persistent movement towards transcendence in philosophy as the place where dialogue with religious belief begins:

> [R]eason, reflecting upon its most basic foundation, discovers that its origin lies in an Other; and that it must recognise the fateful power of this other if it is not to lose its rational orientation in an impasse of hybrid self-empowerment. (2006:256)

Here, there is a temptation for the theologian. This process of a 'conversion of reason through reason' is to be found in such very different thinkers as Schleiermacher, Kierkegaard, Hegel, Feuerbach, and Marx. There is no initial theological intention, but reason 'becoming aware of its own limits steps beyond itself toward an Other' – whether this 'Other' is a quasi-mystical encompassing cosmic consciousness, an unforeseen historical event, or the messianic salvation of an unalienated society. These are the 'anonymous gods of post-Hegelian society', says Habermas, and they are an easy prey for theology, which can see them as 'pseudonyms' for the trinity of the personal God!

If Habermas is a 'siren voice' for theology, at least he has the good grace to tell us where the rocks are. A fuller appraisal of Habermas' continued importance for political theology is not possible here: Edmund Arens is confident of the fruitfulness of this kind of social theory as a resource, enabling theology to be 'interdisciplinary, competent and critical, including a self-critique of the Judaeo-Christian tradition and praxis' (Arens, 1994:16).

The dialogue has continued;[12] though still with reservations. Nicholas Adams in *Habermas and Theology* (Adams, 2006) argues that Habermas is 'not a serious theological partner in dialogue' (Adams, 2006:13): that influence in either direction has been minimal; and that 'Habermas wants the power without the danger of religious and theological discourse' (13). Eduardo Mendieta challenges each of these points, asserting that religion has always been an indispensable point of reference for Habermas. Mendieta also distances him from a Hegelian view of religion subsumed into philosophy. Contrary to announcing the death of religion (as Hegel does), 'Habermas goes a long way to show how religion continues to be generative for social solidarity (and unrest and enmity) and philosophical creativity.'[13]

At the very least, in the post 9/11 context one can note the fact of Habermas being a rare thing: a secular commentator who is sympathetic to the role of religion in the public sphere. If the dreaded 'clash of civilisations' is to be avoided, and if we are to find a way out of the *Kulturkampf* which is hotting up around us, then the dialogue between Jürgen Habermas and the theologians will continue to be important for the foreseeable future.

Conclusion: 'Ruined Athens' or 'New Jerusalem'?

We have left hanging a question raised in chapter 7, about what, precisely, the signpost 'Auschwitz' points to. The theologians and the philosophers considered in the subsequent two chapters have responded in different ways, in accordance with their varied readings of the crisis and the 'rupture' of thought it entails;

- for George Steiner, 'we must learn to persist in some dispensation of twilight with what dignity and minor virtues we can muster'. We must accept, as our destiny and as precondition of our survival, a condition of homelessness, symbolised by his rich metaphor of the Sabbatarian journey. Only thus can there be that 'modulation of strangers into guests' which will save humanity;
- for the post-war political theologians, those who 'come after',

the task has been to address honestly the 'dialectic of Enlightenment', but still to keep faith with the Enlightenment and its postulates of hope, by taking up the messianic intuitions of its marginal thinkers; and

• for Jürgen Habermas, and the theologians inspired by his communicative action theory, the challenge is to confront secularist accounts of our condition with the necessity of a religious contribution, understood as a 'translation' of religious imperatives into publicly accessible discourse oriented towards emancipation and justice.

Some observations from the late political philosopher Gillian Rose may help us. In a collection entitled *Judaism and Modernity,* she opens with a parable on 'friendship', asking us to imagine that a good friend has let us down badly.[14] There are a number of responses which we can make, the obvious one being to try to speak to the friend, so as to find out the cause of the misunderstanding. This approach may lead to reconciliation, or it may lead to a mutual or unilateral decision to break off this particular friendship. Then there is a second set of more extreme responses: one may redefine one's understanding of friendship, or one may even decide to renounce friendship altogether, and break off with all one's friends.

Most would agree that this second range of possibilities is extreme and inappropriate: and yet Rose asserts that if we substitute the word 'reason' for 'friendship', we have a description of what has happened with a number of post-modern philosophers who have adopted fundamentally anti-rational strategies in the face of the crisis of modern rationality. What they offer is a false choice, between a 'ruined Athens' and a 'New Jerusalem': 'the apparently unnegotiable and expiatory opposition between reason and witness, between knowledge/power and new ethics, between relativising explanation and prayer' (Rose, 1996:30).

What does she mean by all this? The 'ruined Athens' is the wreckage of modernity's hopes and projects, whether for perpetual peace or for a rationally-organised Utopia, and so on. 'New Jerusalem' refers to a number of post-modern philosophical and theological responses – many of which, as it happens, are of Jewish provenance. Rose speaks of 'an exodus from the *imperium* of reason', She is warning against the temptations of fundamentally anti-rational strategies in the face of the crisis of modern rationality: 'Post-modernism in its renunciation of reason, power, and truth identifies itself as a process of endless mourning, lamenting the loss of securities which, on its own argument, were none such'.[15]

If we re-read her parable on friendship, we see how Rose is claiming that these strategies represent the second, 'over the top' response: they are an 'attenuated mourning' for certainties that never were, and also an irresponsible evasion of the *risks* of political community – what she calls the 'third city', the city we all live in and are responsible for.

There is a further dimension to Auschwitz which Rose points out, in her desire to situate it at 'some place on this earth', as Primo Levi puts it. Auschwitz is a 'fourth city': architectural plans make it clear that the Nazis originally intended to develop this site as a garrison town, a permanent settlement which was to form part of the Reich's defences against Germany's great and ancient enemy to the East. In other words, the camp had a geography, a history and a rationale. Rose wants to resist the tendency to situate the evil of the death camps outside of history, a kind of irruption from hell, and therefore from the other side of rational explanation. And if it makes sense to ask rational questions about Auschwitz, it makes sense to ask rational questions about the men who built it. Otherwise, philosophy – and political theology – runs the risk of a disembodied wandering between Athens, Jerusalem and Auschwitz, without ever coming home to the city where all of us must, after all, live our lives.

Part 4

THE GIFT

Chapter 10

THE POLITICAL WORD OF GOD

Political Theology and Scripture

Looking Ahead, Left Behind

Regrettably, I have not yet made the time to read all fifteen of the *Left Behind* novels by Tim LaHaye and Jerry Jenkins. Since 1995, over sixty million copies of these books have been sold,[1] with a multi-media franchise comprising two motion pictures, more than twenty children's books, graphic novels and computer games. The series narrates the end of the world, as foreseen by the writer of the Book of Revelation (especially chapter 20), and by biblical prophecy in general. Assuming that most readers of the present book are in a similar state of deprivation to me, I offer the following summary:

- Israel is restored to the Middle East as a nation;
- the world coalesces into a single government, economy and religion;
- political and social chaos ensues, out of which Russia and Islamic nations launch a sneak attack on Israel;
- after a terrible war, peace is brokered by a European leader who is in fact the Antichrist, and who takes over the world for a seven-year period called the Tribulation;
- the Antichrist (in alliance with the Russians and the Chinese) later enters into battle with Jesus and the heavenly host, on the plains of Armageddon in Israel;
- the Antichrist is chained to a lake of fire for a thousand years, during which time Christ establishes a new kingdom on earth;
- after this millennium, however, Satan is let loose from hell again, a further battle ensues (at Jerusalem), and Satan is

finally defeated; and
- the earth is destroyed and a new earth descends from the heavens.

Though much of the content of this series is directly inspired by the Book of Revelation, there are other New Testament sources: the event known as the 'Rapture', in which true believers are summoned by the returning Jesus, echoes the faithful (both living and dead) being 'caught up' to meet the Lord 'in the air', as described by Paul (1 Thessalonians 4:13–17). Those 'raptured' are the true Christians, transferred immediately to heaven, though many of those 'left behind' are converted to Christ during the period of the Tribulation – including the Jews.

But of course there is also a good deal of interpretation going on here, and the diligent and competent reader of earlier chapters will recognise some key themes. The 'One World Government' precisely echoes the fear of undifferentiation in Carl Schmitt's warning of the dangers of widespread international co-operation. Far from leading to peace and harmony, Schmitt asserted that internationalism is in fact a recipe for chaos and instability. His symbol for this was the League of Nations; in the *Left Behind* novels, it is the United Nations, now located in Babylon (Iraq), which embodies this grave threat. Similarly, the 'One World Religion' is a syncretistic amalgam of world faiths. Though it is led by the Pope and the Catholic Church, its ulterior aim is the extermination of true Christianity. The anxiety to sort good from false believers under the heading of good and bad armies is an example of the Manichaean dualism which Augustine resists by his construction of the 'Two Cities' doctrine. Finally, the motif of the *katēchon* or restraining force appears, in the chaining of Satan for a specified period:

> The angel threw [Satan] into the abyss, locked it and sealed it, so that he could not deceive the nations any more until the thousand years were over. After that he must be set loose for a little while … After the thousand years are over, Satan will be set loose from his prison and he will go out to deceive the nations scattered over the whole world.
>
> (Revelation 20:1–3, 7–8)

And if we are tempted to be *too* smug about the excesses of the *Left Behind* mentality, we should note that even biblical and classical theological traditions are not entirely free of disturbing voyeuristic and resentful elements. The early Church Father, Tertullian, tried to dissuade his readers from attending blood-soaked gladiatorial shows by suggesting they wait for the Final Judgement, when they will be able to enjoy a much better spectacle, namely the torments of the damned!

If there is one indispensable skill for doing political theology, it is probably the ability to handle sacred texts responsibly. At times this seems to be a lost art, not least when Christians, Jews and Muslims draw upon their respective scriptures to make extreme political claims – and even more so when those scriptures are used to justify attitudes of hostility and even actions of violence. We return to the dilemma set out in the first chapter: that the gospel engenders and inspires political engagement, but offers no blueprint for specific political stances or options. It is precisely this gap that political theology is intended to negotiate.

Charles Davis approaches this issue head-on in an essay on the 'Political Use and Misuse of Religious Language' (Davis, 1993:112–28). This was written during a sabbatical in Israel, and the specific claim that occasioned it was the denial of Zionist Israelis that Palestinians can have any political rights in the Holy Land, because this land has been definitively granted by God to the people of Israel as their possession.[2] It is inconceivable that any human political claim could be allowed to override such a gift. Davis notes that, historically, Christianity and Islam have both made similar claims, that is, they have made political assertions on the basis of religious writings. The dilemma is the one mentioned above: on what grounds does the political theologian refuse such blatantly unjust claims, and yet still maintain that the Bible has real political purchase?

Davis begins by analysing the special nature of religious language, in comparison with the political. Broadly speaking, Davis sees religious language as arising from ordinary everyday usage: our calling God 'Father' is a specialised use of a word which signifies an everyday human relationship. Every walk of life can supply metaphors and concepts in this way: our words for God can be drawn from agriculture, warfare, and marital

relations, as well as politics ('God is King'). There is no difficulty about moving from any sphere of human life to speak of
God; the problems arise when we try to move in the opposite
direction, namely from a religious affirmation ('God is King')
to a specific political claim ('This land is ours'). What is happening with the extreme Zionist claim mentioned above is a
misuse of religious language for political purposes, and must be
challenged as such.

We are reminded of the description of the theologian as
'someone who minds their language in the presence of God'.
Attentiveness to language and how it operates, especially religious language, is essential. Davis suggests what an abuse of
such language looks like, but is less precise about a positive
relation between religious and political language. Once again:
what are we to understand as a responsible use of the Bible in
political theological discourse? Before looking to specific
challenges in eschatology, to do with 'violent endings', we will
explore the general landscape under three headings:

- political theology and the Old Testament;
- political theology and the New Testament; and
- political theology and the in-between time.

Political Theology and the Old Testament

The need for a sensitive biblical 'hermeneutic' or guiding principle of understanding begins with the recognition that we are
dealing with the sacred texts of two religious traditions, Judaism
and Christianity. All too often the Church has been insensitive in
the way it has simply 'highjacked' the sacred traditions of Israel.
This is sometimes true even of liberation theology, which has
been criticised for its enthusiastic acceptance of world-trans-
forming historical events, such as the Exodus, but markedly
indifferent towards the Jewish people whose history this is.

In most liberation theologies the Jewish Exodus is used as a
paradigm of revolution, but contemporary Jews are nowhere to
be found in the writings of the theologians. This continues an
age-old Christian tradition of seeing the Jewish people as
bequeathing the 'Old Testament' and Jesus and then disappear-

ing from history, their mission accomplished. The use of the
Jewish story is coupled with our historical invisibility. Thus,
liberation theologians often miss an element crucial to the
Exodus story itself; that it has a history of interpretation by the
people who lived the story and who live today.[3]

Bearing in mind the criticism of Marc Ellis, the question
arises: how does a Christian political theologian deal respect-
fully and responsibly with this people's history? Oliver
O'Donovan[4] offers four precise comments about how the Old
Testament is to be used for political theology: firstly, Israel's
traditions must be respected as history, not just as raw material
to be used to construct a theological artefact. There should be no
ahistorical isolation of one element, such as Jubilee, Exodus etc.
In particular, the Exodus event needs to be stands in a tradition
alongside the conquest of Canaan, federation theology alongside the ideology of monarchy, and so on. Following on from
this, the theologian cannot simply appeal to a 'subversive
counter-history' which exists beneath the surface of the 'official' history of Israel. We need 'to have done with perpetual
unmasking'. Thirdly, and again following on from the first two
points, Israel's history may not be rewritten as a 'Whig' history
of progressive undeception, charting a 'secularising' emergence
of rationality from barbarism. A more subtle understanding is
required of why Israel looked to sacral institutions at one point
in her history, and away from them at another.

Finally, and more positively, Israel's history must be read as a
history of redemption, as 'the story of how certain principles of
social and political life were vindicated by the action of God in
the judgement and restoration of the people'. Christianity, says
O'Donovan, remains indebted to the Israelite tradition for the
full articulation of its political vision. '[A]ny question about
social forms and structures must be referred to a normative
critical standard: do they fulfil that will of God for human
society to which Israel's forms authoritatively point us?'
(O'Donovan, 1996:25).

O'Donovan attempts a recovery of the notion of biblical
'authority' by explicating the phrase 'Yahweh malak' [God
reigns], using three points of reference: *jeshuah*, salvation,
mishpat, judgement, *nahalah*, possession of the land. These are

related to a fourth category, namely the human response to God's reign, which is praise or acknowledgement – though this needs to be strictly understood as independent of Yahweh's ruling actions as such: the effectiveness of his rule does not depend on it being acknowledged, much less effected, by human action (for example in alleged 'enthronement ceremonies').

To examine briefly each of these categories: 'salvation' is usually found to refer to military victories. Yahweh's foremost saving action is winning battles, seen as an expression of his favour and righteousness, and also vindication of a diminished and humbled people (especially in the post-exilic period). God is also seen as the 'judge' of his people, and of the other nations. This very important concept needs to be understood differently from classical, Aristotelian understandings of justice: the biblical notion is of justice as an event or performance, one which has lasting validity. The third category, 'possession', denotes something possessed and handed on through generations, primarily referring to the land which is both a unitary inheritance of the people as a whole, and something which is apportioned locally. As indicated above, praise is the appropriate human response to these actions, though this human acknowledgement is independent of the actions themselves.

O'Donovan is insistent, as we have seen, that we should not isolate one event from the Old Testament and emphasise it to the expense of others. Scholarly opinion does differ on this, however. For many commentators the narrative of the Exodus presents a unique and lasting 'paradigm'; this is most evident in liberation theology. Walter Brueggemann looks at the 'politics of Exodus' in some depth, having first established the three political issues or tensions that shape the history of Israel: centralised authority versus local authority; covenantal relations between the have and have-nots; autonomous small states in the face of pressure from large imperial neighbours (Brueggemann, 2004:9). The Exodus story becomes a paradigm by which all these issues are addressed; at its centre is the confrontation: 'Pharoah versus YHWH', where YHWH is presented not only as the primary, indeed exclusive actor in Israel's political story, but also as an 'anti-Pharoah'. Many of the positive political commitments which Israel undertakes are to be seen in counterpoint to the oppressive system of their neighbours, beginning with Egypt. It is in the memory of the Exodus narrative, enacted as liturgy, that Israel constructs its own political theology, one which includes 'acute social analysis, the legitimacy of protest, Holy Presence as a defining factor, human initiative as indispensable, and an alternative (covenantal) mode of public power entertained as a legitimate practical possibility' (Brueggemann, 2004:14).

He goes on to suggest that two kinds of Old Testament literature perform two political functions: the *Torah* (the first five books of the Bible, from Genesis to Deuteronomy), and the *prophetic literature* – basically, 'the Law and the Prophets'. The *Torah* provides the foundational account, understood as paradigm, which pivots on the Sinai tradition of covenant as Israel's alternative public vision. The writings of the prophets maintain the life and speech of Israel as it seeks to enact or apply the paradigm in the 'real world'. It is in this real world that the three challenges – centralisation of authority, discrepancy between rich and poor, and threat of imperial domination – are to be faced. Inevitably, living out the vision of *Torah* in these circumstances will usually be confrontational.[5]

Political Theology and the New Testament

O'Donovan seeks to recover the notion of 'authority' for political theology, beginning with the affirmation of God's Kingship. In the New Testament, the authority of Jesus is understood as an extension of the mediation of Yahweh's kingship discussed above: he manifests saving works of power, most especially on behalf of the victims of demonic possession; he pronounces judgement on Israel and in favour of those who have been dispossessed; and he enables the people to acquire a fuller, more secure possession of the law. This elicits a faith-response from Israel that amounts to an acknowledgement of his political claims, for example the enthusiasm for the Messianic entry into Jerusalem:

> Jesus proclaimed the coming of the Kingdom, but the apostolic Church did not. It told the story of what happened when the Kingdom came: its conflict with the

established principalities and powers and its vindication at
God's hand through the Resurrection. (120)

Political theology here becomes a matter of Christology, that is,
doctrine of Christ. Two roles meet in Christ: he is the mediator
of God's rule (as the Davidic monarch was), and he is the
representative individual, whom we encounter in Jeremiah and
his exilic imitators. These roles come together in the figure of
the Suffering Servant of Deutero-Isaiah. 'In the Christ-event we
found the elements of God's rule: an act of power, an act of
judgement and the gift of possession. ... in which God's rule
was mediated and his people reconstituted in Christ' (133). The
representative act unfolds in four 'moments': Advent; Passion;
Restoration and Exaltation, which is the drama of the Paschal
event. O'Donovan sees Christ's drama repeated or 'recapitulat-
ed' in the Church, whose life is marked by the same four
moments. The moment of Exaltation is signified in the
Ascension, which is clothed in the imagery of a royal coronation
(144–5). Secular authority now derives from that of Christ: it
has therefore been 'problematised'. Here are to be found some
of those notoriously tricky texts of the New Testament which
have exercised political theologians over the centuries. First and
foremost is the declaration of the disarming of the principalities
(Colossians 2:15); prayers for the secular rulers (1 Timothy 2:
1ff); Romans 13:1–7, which we need to 'read with fresh eyes';
the hint of a Two Kingdoms mentality for aliens in a *diaspora* in
1 Peter 2:13–17; the question of Christians and litigation; and
the Book of Revelation, drawing on the eschatology of the Book
of Daniel.

It is worth noting, alongside this confrontational 'dialectical'
vision unfolding through a number of key 'moments', a not
dissimilar scheme put forward by the Swiss Jesuit theologian,
Raymund Schwager. Drawing on the 'theodrama' of Hans Urs
von Balthasar, and the anthropology of René Girard, Schwager
understands the events of Holy Week as a dramatic theology, in
five 'acts'. These follow dialectically from one another: Jesus'
preaching of the *basileia*, the Kingdom of God (Act I) is met
with indifference and rejection, therefore Jesus pronounces a
message of judgement (Act II). As conflict escalates and hearts

are hardened, the forces ranged against Jesus bring about his death in what looks like a typical 'scapegoating' scenario (Act III); the dramatic 'twist' comes with Act IV (The Resurrection), in which, instead of pouring out his wrath, God vindicates his Son by raising him from the dead, and by offering mercy and new life to his killers. The final Act (the Coming of the Holy Spirit) celebrates the power given to the apostles to step into the streets of Jerusalem and create a new community in the public sphere of this world.

Schwager's theological explication of Girard's mimetic theory has considerable political implications.[6] Once again, as with the Old Testament 'stand-off' between 'Pharoah and YHWH', we have between Act IIIs and IV, a confrontation between two versions of God. Both Jesus and his killers live and act out of religious conviction; both sides appealed to their God for vindication. So the question which hangs over Golgotha, therefore, is: *who was right?* Jesus the Crucified, or the ones who crucified him? God is silent at Golgotha, which makes it look as if Jesus was desperately deluded, and the ones who destroyed him as a blasphemer were in the right. But the Resurrection gives us the definitive answer: God is the God of Jesus Christ, and not the God of the zealous mob. The Resurrection is, so to speak, the Father's 'No' to the death of His Son.

Astonishingly, the first words of the Risen Lord are 'peace be with you'. They are not at all the words of vengeance or condemnation which we might expect (see the parable of the vineyard in Mark 12:1–10, and its crux question: what will the owner of the vineyard do to those tenants who killed his son?). This is what is distinctive, therefore, about the new community which is gathered in Act V. This new gathering here is different from the gathering of a mob which shores up its dubious religious identity over against heretics or outsiders. It gathers, not around an unwilling 'scapegoat' victim, but around the Lamb of God, who gave himself willingly for the lives of others.[7]

Political Theology and the In-between Time

With the interpretation of the Book of Revelation which we find
in the *Left Behind* literature, we are back in the world of the
katēchon, seen here as part of a wider discourse – about inter-
vals, or pregnant pauses. Perhaps there is no finer example than
the wonderful verse in Revelation 8:1: 'When the Lamb broke
open the Seventh Seal, there was silence in heaven for about half
an hour'! Both the Book of Revelation, and the *Left Behind*
literature which it inspires, address the question of the long
interval of time (much longer than half an hour!) between the
Resurrection of Christ and his Second Coming. Through the two
thousand years of the Church's existence, Christians have sometimes speculated feverishly about this 'pregnant pause': how
long it will last, and what we are supposed to do for its duration?

A distinction between *millennialist* or chiliastic and
amillennialist positions allows for a crucial difference between believers whose faith impels them to fill the interval
between Resurrection and Final Judgement with detailed and
extremely violent prophecies; and mainstream Christian thinking which insists on our ignorance of God's future, and therefore
on keeping this space 'empty': the future belongs to God and we
shouldn't try and fill in the details. 'The empty throne waits for
the Messiah. If someone occupies this throne, we can be certain:
this is a perverted or false Messiah.'[8]

The interest generated by the *Left Behind* literature is nothing
new, including even its more lurid imaginings. I leave aside the
specific anxiety about how this literature may or may be influ-
encing policy-makers of the most powerful nation on the planet;
even if we take it lightly, as a kind of harmless variant of science
fiction, the Christian believer is still required to make sense of
its religious themes, in a way that the secularist is not.

The realm of theology which concerns us here, 'eschatology',
is defined by Jenson (2004:406) as: 'Christian discourse about a
final outcome and transformation, an "eschaton", of history.'
Political theologians who have sought to ask seriously *what may
I hope for*? have helped to generate a renewed interest in eschatology, specifically in the different scriptural scenarios of the
end times. These are not easy to harmonise: nevertheless, they

are all evocations of one single occurrence, 'an infinite implosion of love, of a created community pressed and agitated into perfect mutuality by the surrounding life of the triune God' (Jenson, 2004:406). As far as the biblical imagination is concerned, eschatology and politics are the same thing, whether we are looking at God's promise of fulfilment to Israel in the Old Testament, or the advent of the 'Kingdom' in the New. For the early Church, notably with Augustine, 'biblical and classical Christian eschatology can be taken directly as political theory'.

However, after the fine synthesis of Augustine, modernity has been characterised by a tendency to 'de-politicize eschatology and de-eschatologize politics'(413). The principal theological tradition of modernity, running from Friedrich Schleiermacher to Rudolf Bultmann, stresses the religious and existential experience of the individual, in such a way that the *eschaton* is deprived of political meaning. Over time a split emerged between eschatology as the fate of the individual (traditionally taught as the Catholic doctrine of the 'Four Last Things': death, judgement, heaven and hell), and as the collective destiny of the world. The challenge set for contemporary political theology, therefore, has been to repair this split, and especially to recover the lost dimension, to 're-politicize' eschatology.

Eschatology in Moltmann and Metz

Theologians from the Reformed tradition, such as Karl Barth and Jürgen Moltmann, have been prominent in urging the centrality of eschatology to all theology: not as an appendix, and certainly not as something to be annulled by the distorted modern tradition cited above. In *The Theology of Hope* Moltmann asserts that 'the eschatological outlook is characteristic of all Christian proclamation, of every Christian existence and of the whole Church' (1967:16), and emphasises the future as breaking in on the present from above. The God of scripture is above all a God of promises, who has already broken into history from above in the Exodus, and in the Resurrection of Jesus: he will therefore break into history once again.

The account of eschatology which Moltmann gives here is a *dialectical* one, stressing difference and contrast rather than similarity: '[p]resent and future, experience and hope, stand in contradiction to each other' (18). Johann Baptist Metz similarly speaks of a 'non-identity' of present and future – or, to use another piece of jargon, their 'non-contemporaneity'. There will never be a moment in this epoch in which the Kingdom of God has definitively arrived, when we can say that a given regime or government manifests the fullness of God's purposes for humanity.

This oppositional stance is sometimes referred to as the 'eschatological reserve' or 'eschatological proviso'. A term associated with Metz, it means the opposite of the very detailed predictions set out by the theological imagination of the *Left Behind* novels, because our stance towards the future is one of sustained ignorance rather than detailed knowledge:

> [W]hat distinguishes 'Christian eschatology' from the ideologies of the future in the East and the West, is not that it knows more, but that it knows less about that future which mankind is trying to discern, and that it persists in its lack of knowledge. (Metz, 1980:11)

We do not know what the future holds, says Metz, and the task of the Church is to 'institutionalize' this agnosticism towards the future, by establishing itself as 'an instance of critical liberty'. But the stage is not left entirely empty: what we do have are the scriptural hints of God's promised future. Moltmann and Metz draw attention to the form of *promise* through which God addresses humanity. Here the prophecies of Isaiah 65:17–25, and Revelation 21:2–4, holy mountain and Holy City, echo one another. In each of these passages, God pledges a 'new heaven and a new earth', in a future time of justice, peace and joy, expressed in images of conviviality and nuptial union. They act as a judgement on the present world, contesting it and revealing its inadequacy. We are reminded of Bloch and liberation theology's rendition of God's 'name' in Exodus 3:14 as 'I will be who I will be': God's future, understood as promise (and not Evolution or History), is the key to understanding who we are.

This kind of utopian imagination is crucial for exercising the 'anamnestic solidarity' which is the cornerstone of Metz's political theology. Metz takes up the anguished questioning of Walter Benjamin concerning the victims of history. For both these German thinkers, redemption cannot simply look 'forward' to the future generations who will be history's beneficiaries. If it is only some future generation which enjoys the fruit of emancipation (as with orthodox Marxist eschatology), then there is a sense in which this lucky final generation have 'stolen' from their predecessors: 'The monstrous inequity of generational succession is that all our possession becomes a kind of robbery, something we have taken from those who shared it with us but with whom we cannot share in return' (O'Donovan, 1996:288). The impotence of Klee's Angel is unbearable: redemption must also stretch backwards, to embrace those whom death has silenced and shrouded in oblivion.

For Metz, the memory of the passion, death and resurrection of Jesus Christ functions as a 'dangerous memory', because it calls into question the plausibility of present social structures and relations. Politically, it acts as an initial movement of negation with respect to the status quo, and 'shocks us out of ever becoming permanently reconciled to the facts and trends of our technological society' (113).

Here are important questions. For Metz in particular, the *eschaton*, or end-time, brings a negative, critical dimension to political theology. But is this all there is: a stance of critical refusal of the present, simply because it is not the future which God has promised us? A number of critics express their concern that Metz neglects any positive constructive task for political theology. The liberation theologian Juan Luis Segundo is unhappy with the notion of an 'eschatological reserve': it implies an unbridgeable separation between an absolute ideal and the messy, relative choices which we have to make in the present. If God's Kingdom is permanently beyond our reach, then there is nothing to choose between any of the various political systems and options, such as democracy or totalitarian dictatorship. An 'eschatological reserve' would see no difference between them, denying that any particular political system can 'cause' the Kingdom to come into being. This is absurd, and not surprisingly has a paralysing effect on the struggle for social justice: 'But who consecrates his life to an "analogy"? Who dies for an "outline"? Who moves a human mass, a whole people, in the name of an "anticipation"?' (Segundo, 1974:112)

R. R. Reno similarly asserts that 'Metz cannot remain exclusively in the moment of non-identification.' Metz presents us with powerful moral imagination, but one which is unanchored, and limited almost exclusively to negation and critique: 'an endless process of demystification, a perpetual clearing of the stage for the major dramatic action which never begins, or at least never takes place in this theater' (Reno, 1992:296, 303).

It is true that in later writings Metz has been less explicit about the notion of the eschatological reserve, perhaps partly in response to these criticisms. It may also be the case that times have changed: Metz wrote about the 'eschatological proviso' at a time (in the 1960s and 1970s) when there was a lot of political fervour around, and with it, perhaps, a danger of 'messianic' expectations. As we move further into post-modernity, however, far from rampant messianism, Metz notes the pervading mood of a *sleepiness* regarding the project of emancipation – as if we have grown weary with the burden of being subjects, and are happy to sink into a second immaturity, lulled by the gentle waves of evolutionary time. Metz has declared that the crisis which faces Christianity is not the crisis of its central message, but a crisis of the *subject and of the institutions* which are to convey it. He sees in post-modernity a confirmation of his diagnosis of the fragility of the subject, who is simultaneously supported and undermined by that same modernity which brings him or her into being.

The question remains: how do we deal with this long stretch of 'in-between' time, between the first and second comings of Christ? If this is a space for us to imagine and dream, to labour and struggle for God's Kingdom, then our projects and commitments will have a real vitality and purpose. But suppose I fill this space, not with dreams of liberation and solidarity, but with nightmares of resentment, vengeance and cruel vindication – all, still, in the name of the Lord? We may decide, on the other hand, that this is God's space, that we should protect it, and leave the canvas blank for God to paint the genuine future God has promised us. But doesn't this leave us too passive, taking up a purely negative stance which leaves us outside history and outside the world (and proves that Hannah Arendt was right)?

Happy Endings?

There is a further theme to be addressed: as we have noted, scriptural warrant can be found for a whole range of eschato-logical possibilities, from the reconciling vision of the New Jerusalem to the gleeful bloodletting of the *Left Behind* authors. Once again, we meet the problem of violence, which we addressed when trying to define the very nature and origins of the political (Arendt, Schmitt and others). Now it seems that we really have come full-circle, in which case we might want to explore a link between two forms of political imagination, *protology* and *eschatology*. 'In my beginning is my end.'

Just as there is a fashion nowadays for novelists to present us with alternative endings to a novel,[9] European political theo-logians and Latin American liberationists have imagined the end-time differently. From a European 'communicative' per-spective, the utopian character of the Kingdom is prominent; the prophecies of Isaiah 65 and Revelation 21 articulate God's future in terms of: fellowship with God, security, material well-being, conviviality, and a complete absence of death and sad-ness. By contrast, Latin American liberation theology pays more attention to the dramatic character of justice.[10] The end of his-tory is not a 'happy end'; it is a Last Judgement, with Matthew 25:31–46 as its paradigm. In this passage, Jesus speaks of the return of the Son of Man as King, surrounded by angels, and gathering all the nations. The people are divided into righteous and unrighteous, sheep and goats. The fate of each group is decided according to their response to Jesus, who identifies himself with the hungry, the thirsty, the stranger, the naked, the sick and imprisoned. Those who have failed in compassion are sent off to eternal punishment. The judgement meted out in Matthew 25 has less graphic detail than the excesses of the *Left Behind* literature – but it is the same punishment, and just as violently definitive.

The *eschaton* is the location of ultimate justice, but also of ultimate violence. Latin American theologians, speaking from situations of unspeakable oppression and injustice, are readier than their European counterparts to embrace those biblical texts which celebrate the violence of justice. They might well ask, with Duquoc (1986): if we insist on demythologising biblical violence, then what happens to justice? If the history of oppression ends in an excess of pardon, then what is the point of bringing the history of the victims to mind?

The dilemma is that each of these scenarios – the Last Judgement, the universal banquet on the holy mountain – contains violence. In the first case, the wicked are 'sacrificed' to the good. In the second scenario, the demand for justice for the oppressed is overruled by God's bounteous pardon – as with the 'anti-theodicy' in Dostoyevsky's *The Brothers Karamazov*, where Ivan Karamazov, having told his parable of the Grand Inquisitor, explains how he is rejecting God: because he knows that, at the final reconciliation, even the desperate screams of the tortured child will be drowned out again, this time by alleluias.

Whichever of these scenarios we invest in determines the *telos,* or goal, of our political theology. A theology which is ordered towards utopian conviviality will see emancipation in terms of a striving-for-consensus communicative rationality. It will be primarily a correlative exercise, stressing the continuity between our attempts at consensus and the future harmony, though it will also stress the 'non-identity' of the present with this utopian future. For this theology, *covenant is possible.* A theology ordered to a definitive declaration of God's justice, on the lines of Matthew 25, will be a dialectical and prophetic theology, whose primary concern is a denunciation of injustice and indifference. Its realism about the immensity and scope of oppression means that the focus is on *resisting Leviathan* rather than elaborating positive alternatives to it.

Once again, here is a question of emphasis: these two options may seem to be incompatible, as Reno asks (though with a different emphasis in mind): 'How can the Beloved Disciple coexist theologically with a ranting Jeremiah?'[11] We need both, it seems.

Chapter 11

'FRIDAY'S CHILDREN'

Political Theology and the Church

> The silence after he had spoken
> was the silence of a newly baked cake,
> to be savoured by the actual smell of it,
> fresh out of oven.
> As he approached the commemoration of the last supper
> and the metamorphosis of bread and wine
> into body and blood
> the congregation looked awake, alert, apprehensive,
> as if we were in danger from the priest
> or as if he were in danger from us
> or as if we were all in danger together
> as the moment of truth approached.
> There was that sense of the moment of truth approaching.
> There was an air of drama, expectation, butterflies.[1]

Having surveyed the main scriptural themes, we resume our discussion of contemporary political theology from the perspective of the community of God's faithful people. This will involve further reflection upon eschatology, above all upon martyrdom (witness) as a theologico-political discourse.[2] The resonances of such an investigation carry much further than a study of 'Church and State', or some such well-trodden area. As we noted in chapter 1, Rowan Williams has stressed the need for an account of human action that goes beyond simply the successful assertion of will – politics as power, 'raising the spectre of purest fascism' (Creston Davis *et al*, 2005:1). He proposes to counter this spectre with a notion of action as *testimony*, with martyrdom as the most distinctive instance of this for the Christian.

Theology is now understood as 'the discipline that follows what is claimed as the supreme act of testimony, and thus the supremely generative and revisionary act of all human history: the Cross for Christians, the gift of Torah and communal identity for Judaism' (3).

And yet, we have heard warning voices: John Gray and Mark Lilla, on the seductive nature of political messianism; Andrew Shanks (citing Milan Kundera) on the sentimentality of political *kitsch*; Gillian Rose's wariness of post-modernity's false choice between a 'ruined Athens' and a 'New Jerusalem'. What her image implies is a further complication of the 'doctrine of the Two' which oriented our discussion in earlier chapters. The question then was: how do Christians negotiate their 'dual citizenship', belonging as they do to the earthly and heavenly cities? But now we are 'unhoused': the earthly city of Reason has been ransacked, and the heavenly city is as far away as ever. What if, as in George Bernanos' image, the Church is not a community of pilgrims after all, but a platoon of troops, caught behind enemy lines and trying to make it back to the safety of their own front?

Less dramatically, the challenge for the Church can be succinctly stated as coming to terms with the death of Christendom, without acquiescing in the privatisation of the Great Separation. If our context is now 'post-Westphalian', but a return to Christendom is neither possible nor desirable, then what 'doctrine of the Two' is appropriate?

One option is a controversial theological approach called 'Radical Orthodoxy', which understands itself as post-modern, insofar as it rejects as illusory the autonomy of the 'secular' – because the 'secular' is itself a theological construct. All attempts at social theory independent of theology are themselves only disguised or illegitimate theologies. Correcting this misapprehension means a return to pre-modern resources, above all to the 'City of God' theology of Augustine. The programmatic texts are John Milbank's *Theology and Social Theory*, which had a considerable impact on theologians when it appeared in 1990, and the collection of essays entitled *Radical Orthodoxy*. The pugnacious tone (ironic, given that Radical Orthodoxy is at base an appeal to the 'ontological peace' described by Augustine) echoes in the firm slap with which the gauntlet is laid down on page one:

> For several centuries now, secularism has been defining and constructing the world. It is a world in which the theological order is either discredited or turned into a harmless leisuretime activity of private commitment ... And today the logic of secularism is imploding. Speaking with a microphoned and digitally simulated voice, it proclaims – uneasily, or else increasingly unashamedly – its own lack of values and lack of meaning. In its cyberspaces and theme-parks it promotes a materialism which is soulless, aggressive, nonchalant and nihilistic.
>
> (Milbank *et al* (eds), 1999:1)

Hence Radical Orthodoxy's attempt to 'reclaim the world', by resituating its concerns and activities – including politics – within a theological framework. In *Theology and Social Theory* Milbank attempts a 'sceptical demolition of modern, secular social theory, from a perspective with which it is at variance ... Christianity'. The Church has all the social theory it needs within its own scriptural and patristic traditions; modern theology should reject the false humility which sees it being 'positioned' by secular reason, rather than the other way round.

It is true to say that the gauntlet has been picked up by theologians on the whole, rather than social theorists, which may not be so surprising. And these theologians have plenty of reservations – not least the obvious one, of a post-modern project like this slipping into a pre-modern conservatism, despite the best intentions of its authors. Nevertheless, the project cannot be overlooked. To understand where it fits in it may be useful to refer to a description from Charles Davis (1994:i), of three intellectual options open to us at this time: *neo-conservatism*, *post-modernism* and *modernity as an unfinished project*. Each is defined in terms of the stance it takes towards modernity; each has its own theological variant. If

Charles Davis (following Habermas) is correct in the diagnosis of neo-orthodoxy as an understandable but ultimately inconsistent stance, then our choice of a credible intellectual and theological approach lies between the remaining two options.

To return to Gillian Rose's image: do we stay within the ruins of Athens, mending the city walls as best we can, or do we leave its ruined *imperium* in search of the New Jerusalem? In the case of 'Radical Orthodoxy', the exodus from Athens takes the form of a robust view of ecclesiology, the doctrine of the Church, as the only 'true' politics. The Christian community is called to forsake its false humility, and to come out fighting against the distortions of a bankrupt modernity which persistently denies its own disguised theological suppositions.

Though modern and post-modern approaches to political theology diverge, we should recognise what their diagnoses have in common. Theologians in both camps are all too aware of the 'dialectic' of Enlightenment; no one is pretending that all is well with modernity. Beyond this generally agreed diagnosis, however, a gap opens up. Where Johann Baptist Metz seeks to work within modernity, William Cavanaugh sets up a very direct confrontation between ecclesiology and modernity, broadly in line with the challenge voiced by Milbank. For these two theologians, enlightenment modernity is a spent project, not an unfinished one.

Models of the Political Church

It is not possible to do more here than list the following themes and approaches. The theological discipline of 'ecclesiology', or reflection upon the Church, has in recent years been taken with the notion of models or paradigms. This is partly due to the Second Vatican Council, which highlighted several significant images of the Church, such as Mystery, Body of Christ, and above the Church as People of God. It is also due to the success of Avery Dulles' book, *Models of the Church*, a classic of 'comparative ecclesiology'. Dulles suggested five models, though in the later, expanded edition (2000) he added 'Church as a Community of Disciples' as a preliminary paradigm. What follows is a summary of some descriptions put forward by political theologians for thinking about the Church; though Dulles' scheme may be helpful to have in mind, these descriptions do overlap, and are not intended to be 'models' in any formal sense.

i. The Church in continuity with the people of Israel, and with Christ

The political entity Israel is essential to Christian self-understanding. 'The history of salvation is not told separately from the history of politics. In the scriptures the story of salvation takes flesh on a public stage and interacts with pharaohs, kings, and Caesars. Salvation itself is imaged as a coming kingdom and a new city' (Cavanaugh, 2004:393). Oliver O'Donovan is insistent that a total response to the historical and political traditions of Israel is the interpretive key that will enable us to do political theology responsibly:

> The hermeneutic principle that governs a Christian appeal to political categories within the Hebrew Scriptures is, simply, Israel itself. Through this unique political entity God made known his purposes in the world … As the structures of Israel's experience pass by us in their historical sequence (tribe, monarchy, cultural-ethnic enclave, movement of world-renewal), the concepts deployed by Israel's writers in the interpretation of those structures (peace, judgement, possession, worship) allow us to find the sequence of happenings intelligible. And from those concepts we may derive an orientation of political principle through which the legacy of Israel regulates our own political analysis and deliberation. Yhwh's victory lays hold on our intelligence and claims us still.
>
> (O'Donovan, 1996:27, 29)

The other regulatory influence on the Church's political imagination is of course, Jesus Christ: 'In Christ's triumph every aspect of his work was given to the church to share in: his coming, his passion, his restoration and his triumph too.' The sacraments are a series of formed acts and observances, through which 'in acted speech (performance shaped by the interpreting word, word embodied in performance)' the church recapitulates again the saving acts of Christ. O'Donovan suggests four sacramental actions:[3] Baptism, Eucharist, the Lord's Day, and the Laying on of Hands. These accompany the four moments of recapitulation, linked in a single dramatic 'performance': Advent, Passion, Restoration and Exaltation. With this last, it is the laying on of hands is the sign of the Church's empowerment, though later tradition derives three separate sacraments from what O'Donovan sees as one single action.

ii. The Church as an instance of socio-critical freedom and dangerous memory

Johann Baptist Metz sees the Church as exercising a special responsibility for the world to which it belongs. It does not stand apart from or above the world, but neither can it be identified totally with it. In relation to his political theology, he understands three functions for the Church. Firstly, it is an institution of socio-critical liberty: because it is eschatologically oriented (i.e. toward the future end time) it must insist on the 'non-identity' of the present with God's future, in the face of the falsely messianic claims of political regimes or systems. History is subject to God's 'eschatological reserve' or proviso, and the Church as an institution seeks to ensure that the Messiah's throne remains empty until his return. Secondly, the Church is the public form of the 'dangerous memory of Jesus Christ', interrupting the complacency and amnesia of our modern consciousness. The Church is the visible form of the *memoria passionis* of Christ.

However, this memory also serves as a critique of the Church itself, which leads us to a third paradigm for Metz, that of a church of subjects, a Church *of* people rather than *for* people. We have seen how he is concerned with 'subject concepts', and how the fragile identity of the modern subject must be fortified against the forces which seek to undermine it. He sees the ecclesial reforms of the Second Vatican Council (1962–5) as an opportunity for it to become a *Subjektkirche*, a 'Church of subjects', implied in the conciliar image of 'people of God' and its call for active participation of all members of the Church. This finds further explication in another paradigm, the Church as *Basiskirche*, or base church, in accordance with the grass-roots base community model found in Latin America (Molt-mann and Sölle are similarly inspired by Latin America's 'new way of being Church').

iii. The Church as an ideal speech community

This derives from the application of Habermasian action theory to theology, taking up an understanding of language as inherently emancipatory. Language contains a drive for truth understood as 'uncoerced consensus, arrived at through a conversation to which all have equal access.' As we have seen, this has prompted some theologians to give an ecclesiological account of the 'ideal speech situation':

> The discourse of the community is founded in the emanci-patory drive of language, a drive toward an ideal speech situation which is never fully present but whose postulation is a necessary condition for the reality of that imperfect and transitory consensus achieved in the community at any given moment. Although Habermas does not use the term, his vision is an eschatological vision. (Lakeland, 1990:243)

Edmund Arens uses the same method to articulate his own view of the Church as an example of communicative rationality, oriented towards ideal speech (Arens, 1995:1). He suggests that this rationality is expressed as two communicative practices, *witnessing* and *confessing*, which 'represent complementary and at the same time basic communicative actions of faith' (125). These are further differentiated into four kinds of witness (kerygmatic-missionary, diaconal, prophetic, and witness by suffering), and three kinds of confession (in worship, instruc-tional confession and situational confession). The principal dif-ference between the two modes is that witnessing seeks to achieve consensus by persuading, while confession presupposes a consensus already achieved by the community. Witness is undertaken by Christians individually and collectively, 'with the intention of convincing, inviting and winning those recipients for that to which and to whom they bear witness'; confession is undertaken by the community of believers as it 'completes, makes present, repeats, and appropriates an agreement' (144).

iv. The Church as a public agent in civil society

David Tracy articulates a framework for 'public theology' when he proposes, first of all that theology is a public discourse, that is, accessible, and not the private language of a sect, and secondly, that the theologian addresses one or more of three publics, namely the academy, the Church, and society (Tracy, 1981; see also Martinez, 2001).

Broadly understood, public theology follows the tradition of Reinhold Niebuhr and John Courtney Murray in seeking to undergird liberal democracy with Christian values. Their successors come from both left and right of the American political spectrum: the Church is seen as an agent in civil society, seeking its flourishing by articulating Christian values on which to ground market and political processes (Bretherton, 2006:383). The term 'public theology', in other words, covers a range of theological commitments and encounters. According to one lucid description of the programmatic intentions of public theology, it is 'concerned with how the Christian faith addresses matters in society at large … [and] with the "public relevance" of Christian beliefs and doctrines', not just to Christians but to all humanity:

> It should be conceived from a perspective that recognises both the marginal location of the Christian faith in a post-Christendom world, and the value of other disciplines. … Public theology has several audiences which demand different levels of academic rigor: the world, the Church, and the academy …. Public theology also addresses practical questions, often in the secular language of human rights, justice, etc. Public theology is located as one voice among many in the marketplace of ideas. Theology is no longer the only voice in the public domain and it does not have a privileged status. Unlike other types of theology, it does not seek to 'convert', but is concerned with the well-being of society.[4]

Examples of 'critical engagement' would include dialogue with political liberalism, virtue ethics, communitarianism, and so on. Edmund Arens considers four variants of communitarianism (associated with Alasdair MacIntyre, Charles Taylor, Robert Bellah and Michael Waltzer). He finds the last three fruitful for emancipatory political theology: Taylor's politics of recognition, Bellah's idea of communities of remembrance, and Waltzer's prophetic social critique. David Tracy speaks of these exchanges as 'mutually critical correlation'. As stated in the last chapter, the 'communicative' task for the Church and for the theologian is to find the language which will make these points of common interest publicly accessible: a task of 'translation', in other words.

v. The Church as the city on a hill

This is the opposite approach to public theologians, insofar as it proclaims the distinctiveness and separation of the Church from political institutions, rather than a systematic engagement with them. The term can be used to cover varying degrees of mistrust or withdrawal, and in fact it is unlikely that any ecclesial tradition neglects this image of separation entirely: even the Catholic Church of Vatican II, which sought to 'correlate' itself positively with the 'modern world', nevertheless included the idea of 'sign and beacon to humanity' among its key metaphors.

We note here the continued significance of the Radical Reform movement which we encountered in chapter 5, not least with the Anabaptist influence on the Pilgrims who journeyed to America, and their contribution to the ideal of religious liberty and to traditions of prophetic separation. The Mennonite commitment to peace activism makes for a powerful counterwitness. In John Howard Yoder it produced a distinctive theological voice, best known for his 1972 classic *The Politics of Jesus*, and for his mentoring of Stanley Hauerwas. With Yoder, a 'withdrawal' model of church, rejecting 'Constantiniasm' and espousing the radical pacifism of Jesus, predominates.

Hauerwas has 'articulated the most coherent and influential political theology in and for the North American context' (Reno, 2004:302). He does not regard the task of theology to be a grounding of systematic co-operation between church and state, whether by means of a common language or by 'public reason'.

Co-operation should be on an *ad hoc* basis only; a 'discrimi-
nating' or 'tactical' engagement, as opposed to either complete
withdrawal or wholesale involvement. Rather than trying to
seize control of social space, the Church is itself an alternative
or contrast civil society. It is from this position as a dissident or
contrast society that the Church has the critical distance to say
'no', but also to imagine, 'to open new horizons, provide new
languages of description and embody alternative practices'
(Bretherton, 2006:386). Reno gives us another definition of
Hauerwas' ecclesiology, citing his father's occupation as a brick-
layer: 'the church is the fundamental and density-creating form
of God's power in the world', the kiln which gives the soul its
brick-like mass and strength, bricks which can then be used for
building – or as projectiles, if a more confrontational style is
needed! An alternative *polis*, therefore, where virtue and character are nurtured; the aspect of a 'withdrawn' or skirmishing
Church being suggested by his book titles ('resident aliens: life
in the Christian colony', 'wilderness wanderings', 'dispatches
from the front').[5]

A similar conception of the Church as a 'contrast society' is
put forward by Norbert and Gerhard Löhfink, from Germany, to
quite a lot of criticism. With erudite scriptural scholarship they
see the Church as isomorphic with Israel's status as a light to the
nations; a 'city on the hill'. In *Jesus and Community* (1985;
reworked as *Does God Need the Church?* (1999)), Gerhard
Löhfink argues for a normative tradition on community which
can be traced, unbroken as it were, through the scriptures and
early Church; Jesus never intended to found a new religious
body, distinct from Israel, but was intent on a restoration of the
full twelve tribes. Like Walter Brueggemann and the theologians
of liberation, Löhfink is especially impressive on drawing out
political temptations and possibilities from the experiences of
the gathered community, Israel, whose defining events are
Exodus and the bestowal of Torah. Löhfink's own commitment
to the struggle to realise this ideal is shown in his decision to
resign his professorship at the University of Tübingen in order
to work with the Catholic Integrated Community (which had
been founded by young German Christians after the Second
World War).

vi. The Church as an alternative (Eucharistic) performance

The 'post-modern Augustinian' school of Milbank, Cavanaugh and others regards as mistaken the idea that the Church and Christians are required to throw their efforts into upholding the project of modern secularity (as Metz would hold, above). Rather, they should be prepared to resist it and present a 'counter-politics'. The position looks similar to that of Hauerwas, but is perhaps more programmatic than tactical. This is a matter of the Church being more itself, and more distinctively visible: Cavanaugh is very critical of easy assertions of a 'sacramental' correlation between the Church and world, such that 'everything is graced', and can be seen as a sacrament. This optimism does not allow any specific sign to be saturated with meaning, nor does it take account of the fact that it is this 'graced' world which set itself against Christ and murdered him (Cavanaugh, 1998:12–14).

He calls us to a confident and articulate Eucharistic practice, with the link between Eucharist and martyrdom heavily underscored. The great symbols of this Eucharistic visibility are the praxis of the base communities in Latin America; and the action of Archbishop Oscar Romero in February 1977, of cancelling all Sunday masses in the Archdiocese of San Salvador except the funeral mass of Rutilio Grande SJ, who had been shot by government security services. At this moment of great tension and sorrow, Romero 'was drawing on the power of the Eucharist to collapse the spatial barriers separating the rich and poor ... by gathering the faithful in one particular location around the altar, and realising the heavenly universal *Catholica* in one place, at one moment, on earth.'[6]

Public versus Political Theology

There is a terminological issue which we postponed from the previous chapter. Much of the literature tends to link political, liberation and public theologies together (Martinez, 2001). However, Hewitt claims that public theology is quite different from the other two, in fact a regression from them. According to her, public theology has undertaken a role of giving a spiritual or religious critique of modern society, responding to its crises by helping it to develop the ultimate meanings implicit in secular experience. It has chosen the route – in her view, retrograde – of spiritual renewal, rather than historical change or political action:

> Public theology has fallen behind the intent of the former political theology, whose critical method, however limited, rejected attempts to Christianize the world. Public theology intends to substitute Christian theology for history and society as the locus of meaning in the quest for social justice, resulting in a theology that is merely applied to politics and society ... Public theology reverses political theology's acceptance of the 'secularized,' 'religiously emancipated society' (Metz, 1970:37) in an attempt to restore itself implicitly to cultural and political hegemony.
>
> (Hewitt, 2004:467)

It is probably fair to say that 'public theology' in its homeland, the United States, is at least partially fuelled by the perceived anxieties concerning the hegemony of the religious Right. As long as 'fundamentalism' is the high-profile, public face of Christianity, there is an understandable felt need to present an alternative – in which case, any kind of public recognition and 'visibility' may be better than none. Being marginal to national debate in a country which is at war is, no doubt, a further frustration. Nevertheless, Hewitt's strictures must be questionable, at least, given the quality of some of the work being done under the banner of 'public theology', and not just in America. And the obvious retort to Hewitt from an aggrieved public theologian would be that this style of concerned theology at least 'critically engages' with the real world of public debate about policy-making and implementation, in a way that a permanently negative critique cannot hope to do. The debate is a live one.

Time versus Space: Alternative Practices

To complicate matters further, the Radical Orthodoxy strategy differs from both political and public theology. Its proponents would vigorously dispute, point for point, each of the intentions set out by Clive Pearson's description. 'If theology no longer seeks to position, qualify or criticise other discourses, then it is inevitable that these discourses will position theology'; theology most certainly does have a central, not marginal responsibility, which can only be discharged by a Church which is visible and distinctive, in the face of sinister forces and influences that would have it otherwise. So there is a clash between 'public' theologies and a 'Radical Orthodox' approach.

The clear blue water that has appeared between the first two options (political and public theologies) and the third option (Radical Orthodoxy) is explained by Cavanaugh (2006) in terms of a turning away from an Augustinian framework. On his reading of *The City of God* the Augustinian version of the 'doctrine of the Two' is a temporal, eschatological one: the two cities (signifying two loves) will co-exist, intermingled, until the end of time, when the Lord will sort out who's who, like the farmer sorting out wheat from chaff. The word *saeculum*, from which our word 'secular' derives, initially means 'age' or 'epoch'. It is this temporal perspective that Radical Orthodoxy is trying to recapture; John Milbank has explicitly christened the radically orthodox way as 'post-modern critical Augustinianism'.

'With the waning of the Augustinian view and the rediscovery of Aristotle and Roman law in the eleventh and twelfth centuries, however, there begins the process of turning the temporal into a space, one that will eventually be seen as standing outside the church' (Cavanaugh, 2006:343). From now on, the problem of the 'doctrine of the Two' is about two powers or jurisdictions, jostling each other for elbow-room, within a single territory that came to be known as 'Christendom'. Political and public theologies are still operating within its presuppositions: these are, so to speak, 'land reclamation projects', which recapture secular space for theology: either by means of sacramental optimism ('all is graced'); or by 'correlating' the gospel with society's unacknowledged spiritual yearnings; or by acquiescence in an amicable division of space – which is what happened after Augustine, a recognition of 'two realms' or 'two planes', secular and religious.

William Cavanaugh's critique of John Courtney Murray

draws out the political implications in terms of contemporary American attitudes towards the Iraq war (2006:320). He urges instead a temporal, not a spatial reading of the doctrine of the Two, in accordance with his eschatological reading of Augustine. It is not the case that there are two jurisdictions, fighting for territorial rights within the same single public space: Church and State are not two parts of a whole. 'For Augustine, neither city is a space with clearly defined boundaries, but both are sets of practices or dramatic performances ... the task of the church is to interrupt the violent tragedy of the earthly city with the comedy of redemption' (315). These two performances happen simultaneously: which is why it should and must be possible for the Church to create an alternative public performance, a drama of reconciliation not war, rather than simply be expected to suspend its own performance by ceding precedence to that of the State.

It should be acknowledged that these are large claims, and far from uncontroverted. Chris Insole offers a response to Cavanaugh (Insole, 2006, 2005) in which he agrees in large part with Cavanaugh's re-telling of the narrative of early modernity, before the Great Separation (see chapter 4), but takes him to task for misrepresenting the liberal ideal in a number of ways. Insole is also sceptical of the appeal, in both Cavanaugh and Hauerwas, to notions of 'practice' or 'performance', as a kind of panacea: 'Human salvation is not achieved by being in community. No matter how virtuous the intentions, practices, performances and efforts of that community, imperfectability and sin will show through' (Insole, 2006:329).

The urgency of the search for 'alternative performances and practices' is of course heightened in a state of metaphorical war on terror and literal war in Iraq. These have, unsurprisingly, dominated contemporary discourse on the 'theologico-political'. Since 2002, the journal *Political Theology* has included several articles on Just War theory and the theological case for and against a pre-emptive strike, issues of citizenship and discipleship in the US, and the thinly veiled theology of George W. Bush. One of the ironies we can point to is that two voices on opposite sides of the debate regarding the justice of the war in Iraq – William T. Cavanaugh and Jean Bethke

Elshtain – are both inspired by Augustine.[7] No one said this subject was straightforward.

Political Agency: 'Look Busy!'

Perhaps we can spell out a bit more what these 'practices and performances' are. The joke on the bumper sticker reads: 'Jesus Is Coming: Look Busy!' What, exactly, are we supposed to be *doing*? We have a number of options, to compare and contrast with the high ideal of political 'action' championed by Hannah Arendt (chapter 3). The vision she articulates, of political activity as free, open and un-coerced communication, is extensively developed in Critical Theory's articulation of a 'communicative rationality'. As we have seen in chapter 9, Jürgen Habermas defines emancipation in terms of an 'ideal communicative action' which includes everyone. This in turn is subjected to a theological critique by political theologians (Peukert, Metz) who insist that such a notion only makes sense in terms of Christian eschatology. Put simply, in order to posit an ideal speech situation, you have to posit a resurrection from the dead – otherwise the dead are excluded from the conversation.

While we wait for this to happen, our own political strivings in the 'interval' will be a model and anticipation of this future conversation. The Church, in particular, must be an example of communicative rationality, even if it too often falls short of this ideal. As we have seen, Edmund Arens reflects upon 'the structures, the dimensions, and the theological quality of Christian praxis'. He distinguishes between two basic ecclesial concepts – *witnessing* and *confessing* – which 'represent complementary and at the same time basic communicative actions of faith' (125). In bearing witness, Christians individually and collectively 'point to Jesus Christ by vouching for the truth of their testimony with their own existence ... with the intention of convincing, inviting and winning those recipients for that to which and to whom they bear witness.' Confession, on the other hand, is 'that action, oriented by memory, in which the community of believers completes, makes present, repeats, and appropriates an agreement. To confess means to achieve consensus'. (144).

'Witness by suffering' and 'situational confession' are ob-
viously connected. It is here that the discourse of *martyrdom* as
a political category comes to the fore, because it straddles these
two basic activities. And martyrdom is, after all, one model of
political holiness, perhaps even its definitive expression. In
Metz's later work, as we have seen, the challenge is to give an
account of the subject other than the narcoleptic bourgeois subject, whose 'freedom' consists in being immune to suffering as
far as possible. Taking discipleship of Jesus Christ seriously, by
contrast, means a readiness to 'suffer the suffering of others',
especially where the choice is an exclusive one, between one
kind of subject or the other. Metz describes this as an *active*,
rather than passive acceptance of suffering: it can be translated
as a 'suffering unto God' (*Leiden an Gott*).

For Jürgen Moltmann, martyrdom is 'the fellowship of
Christ's sufferings': the Church is *ecclesia martyrium*, and takes
its bearings from those whose witness is linked to the testimony
of Christ in this special way. A Christianity that has forgotten its
martyrs has been politically assimilated, because it has forgotten
the crucified Christ as well:[8]

> [T]he martyrs anticipate in their own bodies the sufferings
> of the end-time, which come upon the whole creation; and
> dying, they witness to the creation which is new. Anyone
> who participates in 'Christ's sufferings' participates in the
> end-time sufferings of the world. (204)

They are witnesses to the coming truth against the ruling lie:
William Cavanaugh aligns martyrdom with a new configuration
of the problematic of Church and State: '[M]artyrdom disciplines the community and helps it to claim its identity', such
that in the Eucharist it re-enacts Christ's conflict with the forces
of disorder. 'The body of the martyr is thus the battleground for
a larger contest of rival imaginations, that of the state and that of
the church' (Cavanaugh, 1998, 64–5).

But if confession-martyrdom is a speech-act, what is the content of this communication? Jean-Luc Marion, at the close of
God without Being, addresses the paradox that Christian speech
is necessarily 'tongue-tied': the believer can never simply take

upon herself the utterance 'Jesus is Lord'. How can the speaker ever be legitimated and qualified to say such a thing? The answer, as Nicholas Lash reminds us, is that the primary witness is not the martyr herself, but 'God's self-witness, the "martyrdom" of God' (Lash, 1981). Only understood in this way can predication (utterance) and performance (action) be perfectly legitimate. And both of these, taken together, are the statement and enactment of a claim to sovereignty: a political claim.

The confession of faith passes through the one who speaks, but it comes from much further away and it goes much farther. It passes right through him: coming from the mystery, 'hidden before the centuries,' of adoption of men in the Son (Ephesians 1:4–5), it aims at the recapitulatory lordship of the Son over the universe (Ephesians 1:10).[9]

Where does this leave us, with respect to Hannah Arendt's judgement that Christianity is incompatible with politics as free, un-coerced speech-action? If we recall, her ideal is one of *natality*: 'With word and deed we insert ourselves into the human world, and this insertion is like a second birth'. But the Christian is excluded, because his or her good deeds are 'silent', hidden from public view like crimes. The only way of being 'worldly', and 'political', of genuinely initiating something new, is denied to the Christian, who is unable to take this risk of self-disclosure.

Is she right? Two words of riposte may be offered. Firstly, what Edmund Arens and others have done is to elaborate a theology of communicative action which, I believe, acknowledges the complexity of Christian communicative action and yet, contrary to Arendt, enables that action to overcome paralysis and incoherence, and to be both valid and effective. Arens' typology of confession and witness allows the Church to say different things to different people in different situations: sometimes aiming at confrontation or prophetic challenge, at other times articulating a consensus. Theology, 'the discipline that follows what is claimed as the supreme act of testimony' (Williams) can therefore help us construct accounts of human action which are honest, which go beyond overt or disguised assertions of the will to power.

Secondly, it is, in a sense, all down to posture. A striking image used by Ernst Bloch is that of the 'upright gait', which he explores in a 1971 essay entitled 'Upright Carriage, Concrete Utopia'. Marxist analysis and action coincide with Christian theology in the realisation that standing straight is, miraculously, possible.[10] But there is another aspect to this image. B. D. Shaw suggests a distinction between the classical and Christian versions of heroism, summed up in the Greek word *hypomenē*, meaning 'the capacity to undergo (suffering)'. The term has implications of horizontality – a vanquished soldier on the battlefield, or a woman in labour – and as such was depreciated, by comparison with the 'vertical' ideal of the victorious warrior, or a man standing up to deliver a speech in the *agora*. According to Shaw, it is one of the great cultural achievements of Christianity that through the terrible tribulations of its martyrs, it should have brought about a new appreciation of this virtue, the patient and hopeful endurance of suffering (Shaw, 1996). W. H. Auden, once again:

> Let us honor if we can
> the vertical man
> though we value none
> but the horizontal one.

The Christian response, which political theology seeks to articulate, is clear: let us honour and value both.

EPILOGUE

Before bringing proceedings to a close, we need to highlight a puzzling and acute dilemma, which really requires a much more extended treatment than is possible in this work. I refer to the marked and disturbing imbalance between the attention given by political theologians and critical theorists to the *Shoah* and the Nazi catastrophe, and the thinness of the theological reflection upon the experience of countries which until 1989 were under Soviet control, the 'Second World'.

There can be no 'taking leave of Auschwitz' for theology. Yet there is a curious neglect of those societies and churches which, for decades longer than Germany under National Socialism, bore the brunt of a brutally atheistic and dehumanising Leviathan, at a cost of millions of lives, once the expense of Stalinist purges and engineered famines is reckoned. Much of the venom of these regimes was aimed directly at the churches, and at individual Christians. And yet, where one would expect a theological critique, on a par with post-war European political theology, or the Latin American liberationists, there is very little. It seems, to return to the list of models of the church in the last chapter, that we need to add a seventh: the silent Church, which, distressingly, remains silent still.

The feeling is strong that this horrendous slice of history, the 'darkness at noon', has yet to be brought to theological light; one cannot help wondering about the culpability of Western political theologians for the continued neglect. To give just two examples, from the resources we have been working with, the splendid *Blackwell Companion* (Scott and Cavanaugh, 2004) testifies to the centrality of the German wartime experience, with chapters on Schmitt, Barth, Bonhoeffer, Moltmann and Metz. The editors find room for chapters on political theologies in Asia, on Gustavo Gutiérrez, and on southern feminist theologies; but there is nothing on (post)communist societies. The same is true of the thirty-four essays in *Political Theologies* (de Vries and Sullivan, 2006), a collection which is largely given over to the challenge of Islam and secular society, pluralism and democracy, all for the most part concerns of western societies.

The evidence seems to suggest that 'political theology' is an activity exclusive to Middle European or American theologians, who manage to have worthwhile conversations with partners in the South, but not to the East. The 'Silent Church' remains silent. When we factor in the mistrust engendered by political theology's reliance on traditions of quirky Marxism, it may be that a major task presents itself, of finding a new, common starting-point for political theologies across the region.

András Maté-Tóth (from Hungary), reflecting on 'a possible theology of (in) the Second World' (Tóth, 2000:27), sets out the resources: biblical images of imprisonment, Egyptian or Babylonian captivity (depending on the severity of the repression), and a variety of theological approaches (neo-scholasticism, traditionalism, underground), but with renewal hampered by an uneven and fraught engagement with 'theological modernity'; post-1989, the filling of many new skins with old wine.

Probably three broad avenues may be discerned. Firstly, in keeping with the anamnestic solidarity so emphasised by Metz and others, the painful task of truth recovery must be undertaken, and the same dilemmas faced as in other compromised societies, such as Guatemala and El Salvador, Chile and Argentina, South Africa, Northern Ireland and so on, of how the exigencies of justice, truth, reconciliation, the enhancement of democracy and human rights (the imperative 'never again') must be balanced and negotiated. As with all these other cases, the role of Christians and the Christian tradition in articulating transcendent values cannot be neglected. Paramount, however, must be an embrace and empowerment of the victims, and a receiving of their testimonies as the basis for theological reflection.[1]

Secondly, the churches, required to reflect anew upon their changed status and yet, in too many cases, already required to express repentance, for collusion and compromise under totalitarianism, and for a lack of imagination post-1989, when the temptation to restorationism was more powerful than the call to creative and constructive witness. If the model of the catacomb church, and the discourse of martyrdom, are valid here – and of course they are – then so too is the painful example of the *traditores*: those who complied with Diocletian's edict in 303, requiring the 'handing over' of Christian books to be burned.

Thirdly, the implications of what Tóth calls 'a Chernobyl of souls', after the eradication, over decades and across populations, of the classic concepts of person and conscience, and the disorientation caused by the collapse of the system that was to replace them. As ever, theology draws on the philosophers: Vaclav Havel's analysis of 'post-totalitarianism' is open to theological explication. Citizens like the greengrocer in Havel's parable, living in a post-totalitarian dictatorship (where all idealism has been dissipated and only the brutality remains), have the choice of continuing to live in the lie – pretending the emperor isn't naked – or deciding to living in Truth.[2] Another remarkable witness is Petre Tutea (1902–91), an Orthodox intellectual whose life in prison and under house arrest in Romania, together with experiences of torture and 're-education' are recorded by Alexandru Popescu (Popescu, 2004). As the title of the book implies, Tutea's version of 'living in truth' is the choice the individual makes between 'sacrifice' and 'moral suicide'.

It is understandable that the exigencies of a post-9/11 world should grab most of the headlines, and whatever theological energy is around. Even so, I would suggest that the comparative neglect of the themes, persons and histories we have been discussing represents an impoverishment, both for political theology, and for the inchoate contextual theology of and in the Second World.

Return of God, Return to God

For eschatology and for political theology, there must be a 'return to fundamentals': the doctrine of God.[3] The impossible challenge for the political theologian, as for any believer, is: how do we 'mind our language' in the presence of the returning God;

how do we ensure that our speech about God has integrity? Rowan Williams alerts us to the ways in which 'invulnerable' theological pronouncements may simply represent 'the retreat from conversation implicit in the concealment of purpose ... [which] is manifestly a *political* matter' (2000:4). We need to be so careful.

It is one thing to wager and anticipate the end – with joyful hope, or under protest like Ivan Karamazov – our 'being pressed and agitated into perfect mutuality by the surrounding life of the triune God'. But: precisely *who does the pressing and the agitating*? The cry of *Yahweh malek*, patiently explicated by the political theologian, cannot mean the same as the *Allahu Akbar* of the so-called suicide bomber.

I am no further than this, in addressing the more dramatic manifestations of the persistence of the 'theologico-political'. With a huge, frenzied literature on this subject, I make no apologies for not adding to it. Suffice to say that, tempting as it may be to put the Islamist bomber on the other side of history and rationality, along with the Nazi monsters, this will not do.[4] For what it is worth – this will come as no surprise – I am more impressed by arguments which root fundamentalist terrorism in modern (nineteenth-century) complexities of resentment and romantic nihilism, rather than an atavistic and perennial instinct to destroy people in the name of God. The idea of 'terror' as a doctrine or strategy derives from the 1880s, as does the apotheosis of the terrorist as 'noble, terrible, irresistibly fascinating, uniting the two sublimities of human grandeur, the martyr and the hero' (Rapoport, 2002:4). For René Girard and others, our indispensable guide is Fyodor Dostoyevsky, author of *The Devils* and *Notes from Underground*. On their account, Islamist terrorism is neither 'medieval', nor even Islamic, but an 'exacerbated desire for convergence', what Girard calls 'mimetic rivalry on a planetary scale'.[5]

I began this book reading a free newspaper on the London tube. Of all the cities we have been considering: earthly and heavenly, Athens and Jerusalem, Babel, Auschwitz, it is the denizens of my adopted city, London, who may help us to keep some perspective. In the wake of the bombings of July 2005 (perpetrated, as it happens, by young men from 'some place on this earth' – my native city, Leeds) the admirable 'we can take it' sentiment ran something like this: 'Hitler tried to break us in the Blitz – in the 70s and 80s it was the turn of the IRA – now the Arabs have had a go, so now they can — off too!' The parallels are illuminating. There was no compromise with Hitlerism, of course, and the evil of National Socialism was comprehensively defeated: this was, after all, 'our finest hour'. But a political settlement with militant Irish republicanism *was* reached, and bitter enemies now co-operate in the same power-sharing administration.[6]

What will be the final verdict upon Islamist 'terror': will it be extinguished by its crusading enemies, or will there be some kind of accommodation with them? If the latter, does anyone doubt that this will be a 'theologico-political' accommodation?

But if the suicide bomber is wrong, so is the *Left Behind* Christian, and for much the same reasons. As Robert Jenson reminds us, our disparate eschatological imaginings are all evocations of one single occurrence, 'an infinite implosion of love, of a created community pressed and agitated into perfect mutuality by the surrounding life of the triune God.' The eschatological reality which we have called the 'kingdom of God' has traditionally been considered alongside another description: fulfilment as 'deification', or the 'vision of God'. These two yearnings correspond, roughly, to Western and Eastern Christian viewpoints. If both are true, then 'somehow entry into the kingdom of God must be entry into the triune life of God, and vice versa' (414).

God's self, as Trinity, displays a perfect polity; Jesus the Son brings the Church, the redeemed community, with him into the *polis*. This is the wager: that God 'will be who I will be', that God will 'keep faith' with us.

NOTES

1. In *The New Atheists* (DLT, London, 2007), Tina Beattie surveys the virulent critiques of religion that have been offered recently by Richard Dawkins, Christopher Hitchens, Sam Harris, Daniel Dennett, Polly Toynbee and Ian McEwan. Beattie notes with irony that no one has done more than writers like Richard Dawkins to keep God 'alive', thanks to their strident and best-selling condemnations of religious belief. She goes on to regret the intolerant and discourteous tone of the current 'Religion versus Science' debate.
2. Mark Lilla, *The Stillborn God: Religion, Politics and the Modern West* (A. Knopf, NY, 2007).
3. John Gray, *Black Mass: Apocalyptic Religion and the Death of Utopia* (Allen Lane, Penguin, London, 2007).
4. See 'On the Miscarriage of All Philosophical Trials in Theodicy'; Kant, 1992 [1791].

1: What Is Political Theology?
1. Scott and Cavanaugh, eds, 2004.
2. One version of this separation is given the name 'Erastianism' (after the Swiss theologian Thomas Erastus, 1524–1583), which denotes the view that the state is supreme in church matters.
3. Words from http//www.cyberhymnal.org/htm/a/l/allthing.htm, which helpfully points out that 'most hymnals omit this verse'!
4. O'Donovan, 1996. See also Bartholomew *et al* (eds.), 2002, *A Royal Priesthood: A Dialogue with Oliver O'Donovan*, for the results of a Scripture and Hermeneutics consultation around the ethical and political issues arising from O'Donovan's book.
5. Hent de Vries and Lawrence E. Sullivan (eds), 2006: Introduction, 1–88.
6. De Vries, 2006:2. The 'Westphalian doctrine' refers to the decision by the Treaty of Westphalia 1648, at the close of the Thirty Years War, to allow the religious allegiance of a state to be determined by its ruler: *'cuius regio eius religio'*.
7. De Vries lists: Varro's distinction between political, mythical and cosmological theologies; Ernst Kantorowitz's study of medieval political theology (Kantorowiz, 1997[1957]); Spinoza's *Tractatus Theologico–Politicus* (1670), and the twentieth-century usage of Carl Schmitt.
8. De Vries, Hent, 2005, *Minimal Theologies: Critiques of Secular*

Reason in Adorno and Levinas. Johns Hopkins UP.

9. Creston Davis, John Milbank, Slavoj Zizek (eds), *Theology and the Political* (Duke University Press, London, 2005). This volume collects the papers from the 'Ontologies in Practice' conference, University of Virginia, September 2002.

2: Witness Against the Beast

1. I have lifted the title of this chapter from E. P. Thompson's fine study of William Blake, a fiery prophetic 'witness' against the Leviathan and Behemoth politics of his own day (Thompson, 1993).

2. For the work of René Girard, see Kirwan, 2004; Fleming, 2004.

3. The same mechanism – violence channelled outwards in order to preserve civil peace – is wonderfully conveyed by the speech of King Henry IV, at the beginning of Shakespeare's *Henry IV Pt I*. (I. 1. 1–27). The king is exhausted with putting down rebellions; he longs to bring an end to the 'civil butchery', and unite the country behind a single military (and religious!) project, namely a Crusade, marching 'all one way' in 'mutual well-beseeming ranks' to the Holy Land. 'The edge of war, like an ill-sheathed knife, no more shall cut his master.'

4. Livy, *History of Rome*, I:24–26; Augustine, *City of God*, Bk III.14. For a discussion of these passages, see Atkins, 2001: 25–6.

5. 'Tragedy and Revolution' in Creston Davis *et al* (eds), 2005, *Theology and the Political*, 7–21. (Eagleton , 2005).

6. W. H. Auden, 'Vespers' from *Horae Canonicae* (Auden, 1991: 637–39).

7. Martin Luther, *Temporal Authority: to what extent it should be obeyed* (1523); see Lull (ed.), 436–7.

8. It may be worth pointing out that some commentators follow Schmitt himself in translating this as 'friend–enemy', since the term 'foe' can have connotations of 'demonising' the other, which is not Schmitt's intention.

9. For discussions of the theological background, see Palaver 1996, 2007, and Hollerich, 2004.

10. The German words for 'order' and 'location' are *Ordnung* and *Ortung*.

11. Hannah Arendt makes a similar connection: 'The word *polis* originally connected something like a 'ring wall,' and it seems the Latin *urbs* also expressed the notion of a 'circle' and was derived from the same root as *orbis*. We find the same connection in our word 'town,' which originally, like the German *Zaun*, meant a surrounding fence.' (Arendt, 1958: 64).

12. This vision looks similar to the 'Clash of Civilisations' concept advanced by Samuel Huntington in 1992, which has been hugely influential in shaping attitudes towards the relationship between Islam and the West in particular.

3: 'Love of the World'

1. Bernauer, 1987, 7–8.
2. This objection might be read alongside Shanks, 1991, whose introduction to *Hegel's Political Theology* draws on Milan Kundera's understanding of ideological 'kitsch'; see chapter 8.
3. Steiner, 1992:104–7.
4. Or, to take an extreme but very topical example: Andrea Brady draws attention to the ways in which the immense grief after the 9/11 atrocity was used to shape US self-identity ('a sensible Leviathan responding instinctively to pain'), not least in framing its military response in terms of an apocalyptic 'war on terror': Brady, 2002.
5. See Forrester, 1988, chapter 1: 'Piety and Politics in the Ancient World': especially 5–14.
6. Procopé, in Burns (ed.), 1988:32.
7. See chapters 5 and 6 by Markus, in Burns (ed.), 1988:83–91 and 92–122.
8. See in particular two essays in Bernauer (ed.) 1987: 'The Faith of Hannah Arendt' (Bernauer, 1987:1–28), and 'Enspirited Words and Deeds: Christian Metaphors Implicit in Arendt's Concept of Personal Action' (Roach, 1987:59–80).
9. See Benjamin (2002 vol. 4) for the text of the essay 'On the Concept of History' which includes this fragment.
10. For an overview, see *Theology and Critical Theory* (Ward, 2000), and the contributors to *Theology and the Political: the New Debate* (Davis, C. *et al*, 2005).
11. The title of another book by Zizek, *The Puppet and the Dwarf: the Perverse Core of Christianity* (Zizek, 2003), indicates his indebtedness to Benjamin's parable. See also *On Belief* (Zizek, 2001).

4: 'The Doctrine of the Two'

1. 'Letter to Emperor Anastasius', in O'Donovan and O'Donovan (eds), 1999:179.
2. I summarise here from Steven Ozment's *The Age of Reform* (Ozment, 1980), ch. 4: 'The Ecclesiopolitical Tradition', 135–81.
3. For a modern version of Augustine's jest about the pirate and the emperor, see Cavanaugh, 1995:413–14; Cavanaugh takes up Tilly's analogy between the modern State's monopoly on violence, and the gangster running a 'protection racket'!
4. *Scripta super libros sententiarum* II, Dist.44, quaest.3: see Dyson (ed), 2002:278. We have already noted that this interpretation of 'Render to Caesar the things that are Caesar's' is highly problematic!

5: 'A Stormy Pilgrimage'

1. In *To The Christian Nobility of the German Nation* (1520). Luther's most important work in this area is *Temporal Authority, to what extent it should be obeyed* (1523); the text can be found in Lull (ed.),

2005:429–59, and Höpfl (ed.), 1991:1–46.

2. Bloch, 1969 [1921]. For a commentary on Bloch's reading of Thomas Müntzer, see Roberts, 1990:13–19.

3. Bloch, 1969:229.

4. William T. Cavanaugh, '"A fire strong enough to consume the house:" the Wars of Religion and the Rise of the State', *Modern Theology* 11.4 (October 1995), 397–416. This essay forms a prelude to the critique of the nation–state which he offers in *Torture and Eucharist* (1998), and to the liturgical and ecclesiological emphasis of this key book and subsequent writings.

5. For an extended and sympathetic examination of O'Donovan's account of Christendom, see Greene, 2002:314–40; also O'Donovan's response in the same volume (341–3).

6: 'Stillborn Gods'

1. Lefort, 2006:231–55.

2. G. W. F. Hegel, from the *Philosophy of Mind*, cited in Lefort, 2006:149.

3. Kant, 1992 [1791].

4. For a recent reappraisal of Kant's religious writings, see Firestone, C. L. and S. R. Palmquist (eds), 2006, especially Galbraith's essay, 179–89, on Kant and theodicy.

5. This edition of Kant translates: 'Nature the contriver of things' (Lucretius).

6. Milan Kundera, *The Unbearable Lightness of Being*. Faber and Faber, London, 1984; Shanks, 1991:1–4.

7. Shanks, 1991:184–8; V. Havel, *Living in Truth*. Faber and Faber, London, 1987.

8. Sölle, 1967 and 1975; Moltmann, 1974.

7: Theology in a Land of Screams

1. The photograph appears in an article in the *Guardian* newspaper, 17 January 2004, 9; the article reports that the image was being posted on www.evidenceincamera.co.uk.

2. Primo Levi, *If this is a Man*. Abacus, 1979 [1958]:23.

3. Rubenstein, 1966; Rubenstein and Roth, 1987; Cohen, 1981 and 1984.

4. Ellis, 1986 and 1997.

5. For one theologian's attempt to sort out some of the political-theological complexities, see Davis, 1994.

6. Extensive historical surveys of the Churches under National Socialism are to be found in Burleigh, 2000, and Scholder, 1985, 1988.

7. For commentary on the Barmen texts, see Ahlers, 1986; for more extended commentary on Barth's political theology, see Wilmer, 2004, and Hunsinger, 1976.

8. Barth and Rosenzweig are the authors of two ground-breaking works, of theology, the *Epistle to the Romans* (second edition, 1922) and *The Star of Redemption* (1921) respectively.

9. Steiner, 1989:231; see also Nicholas Lash's reflection upon Steiner's image of the Saturday, in Lash, 1990:109-19.

10. Steiner, 1996:344.

8: 'We Who Come After'

1. The chapter title echoes a poem by Bertolt Brecht, written in 1938: 'To Those Born After':

> Hatred of oppression still distorts the features,
> Anger at injustice still makes voices raised and ugly.
> Oh we, who wished to lay for the foundations for peace and
>   friendliness,
> Could never be friendly ourselves.

2. The text of the *Theses* to be found in Benjamin, 1973 [1955], also Benjamin, 2002, vol. 4.

3. For reasons of space, I will refer to just two very important books by Moltmann, *The Theology of Hope* (1964) and *The Crucified God* (1974), though his output and his significance go well beyond these two works.

4. For a more extended discussion of Metz's roots in Germany, and therefore 'Mitteleuropa', see Martinez, 2001: 24-38.

5. Roberts, 1990:16. For Bloch's reception by theologians, see Tom Moylan, 'Bloch against Bloch: the Theological Reception of *Das Prinzip Hoffnung* and the Liberation of the Utopian Function' (Moylan, 1997), though Moylan argues that in fact Bloch had a profounder influence over prominent liberation theologians such as Gustavo Gutiérrez than Moltmann and Metz.

6. The title of a tribute to Sölle, on her death in 2003.

7. *Sin Is When Life Freezes: a meditation on I John 1:8*; the article first appeared in *The Christian Century*, May 12, 1982.

9: 'From Despair to Where?'

1. See Freeman (ed.), 2003, for an overall view of Rawls; for attention to the religious and theological implications of Rawls' work, see Dombrowski (2001) and Scherer (2006).

2. Peukert, 1986 [1984].

3. Peukert, 1984:209–10.

4. See discussion in McCarthy, 1986 and 1991.

5. See Arens (1996), and Lakeland (1990).

6. de Vries (ed.), 2006:49; for the texts of the conversation, see Habermas, 2006:251-60, and Pope Benedict, 2006:261-8.

7. *Habermas Modernity and Public Theology* eds D. S. Brown and Francis Schüssler Fiorenza. Crossroad, NY, 1992 . 'Theology, Critical Social Theory and the Public Realm', 19-42

8. See Browning and Fiorenza (eds), 1992:226-53.

9. Habermas cites R. S. Siebert and the 'impressive' bibliography compiled by Edmund Arens (ed), 1989:9-38.

10. Habermas, 2001.

11. See Habermas, 2006:251-60; also in Mendieta, (ed.), 2005:339-48.

12. Habermas has contributed to *Liberation Theology, Postmodernity and the Americas* (REF), and in the essays collected by Eduardo Mendieta: *Jürgen Habermas, Religion and Rationality: Essays on Reason, God, and Modernity*. Polity Press, Cambridge, 2002. 'Religion in the Public Sphere', European Journal of Philosophy 14.1 (2006):1-25.

13. Mendieta, 2007:7; Mendieta's review of Adams finds the book worthwhile, but with severe misgivings about some of the overall judgements, as indicated above.

14. Rose, 1993:1.

15. Rose, 1996:1.

10: The Political Word of God

1. Titles include: *Tribulation Force: the Continuing Drama of Those Left Behind* (1996), *Soul Harvest: the World Takes Sides* (1998) and *Armageddon: the Cosmic Battle of the Ages* (2003). Summaries of the books can be found at http://www.leftbehind.com.

2. To emphasise how some things never change: when President Bush visited Israel in January 2008, with the intention of regenerating a peace process between Israel and Palestine, he was greeted with Zionist placards, urging 'Bush, read your Bible!'

3. Ellis, 1986:74.

4. O'Donovan, 1996; for critical engagement with O'Donovan's *The Desire of the Nations*, including his use of scripture, see essays in Bartholomew *et al* (eds), 2002.

5. See Brueggemann's *The Prophetic Imagination* for a fuller treatment of political theology as an 'alternative imagining' to imperial theology.

6. Schwager's chapter on Christology (Schwager, 2004) is a summary version of the case he sets out in *Jesus and the Drama of Salvation*.

7. With this combination of insights from Girard and Balthasar, a distinctive vein of political theology is opened up, which is explored by the dramatic theology research group at the University of Innsbruck. For background, see Schwager (1998 and 2004), Fleming (2004), and Kirwan (2004), as well as Girard and Palaver references.

8. Agnes Heller, cited at Manemann, 2005:52.

9. See Paul Fiddes' study of eschatology in literature and theology (Fiddes, 2000) for a discussion of this annoying 'post-modern' literary device.

10. Duquoc 1986, and 1996; Kirwan, 2006.

11. Reno, 1992:304.

11: 'Friday's Children'

1. Paul Durcan, 'The Death of the Ayatollah Khomeini', in *Daddy Daddy*. Bladestaff Press, 1990: 46.
2. The title of this chapter alludes to a poem by W. H. Auden on Dietrich Bonhoeffer, called 'Friday's Child'. It is a reflection upon Christian martyrdom; according to the nursery rhyme, of course, Friday's child is 'loving and giving'.
3. O'Donovan, 1996:174 ff.
4. Clive Pearson's definition of public theology can be found at: http://www.csu.edu.au/faculty/arts/theology/pact/pdf/What_is_Public _Theology.pdf
5. For overviews of Hauerwas, consult Reno, 2004, and *The Hauerwas Reader* (Berkman and Cartwright (eds), 2001). For key ecclesiological writings, see Hauerwas 1983 and 1995.
6. Cavanaugh, 1999:196.
7. See Elshtain 2004, and 2005 for her work on Augustine; she is also the author of *Just War against Terror: The Burden of American Power in a Violent World* (Elstain, 2003).
8. Moltmann, 1989:196-204.
9. Marion, 1991:196.
10. See Bloch, 1971:168-73; Gustavo Gutiérrez reminds us that, for the Christian, humans can only stand upright if the centre of gravity is outside ourselves (Gutiérrez, 1988:205).

Epilogue

1. See testimonies, from the Czech experience, of Jan Sokol and Oto Mádr in *Concilium* 2000/3, 'Religion During and After Communism' (Tomka and Zulehner (eds), 2000).
2. The parable of the greengrocer has been wonderfully brought to life in the highly acclaimed German film by Florian Henckel, *The Lives of Others (Das Leben der Anderen)*, in which Gerd Weisler, an interrogator for the Stasi, is finally alerted to the utter cynicism of the system he is upholding. Now 'post-totalitarian', he decides, at great personal risk, to subvert a surveillance operation in which he is involved.
3. Jenson, 2004:406.
4. *Paradise Now* (2005), a collaboration of Arab and Jewish film-makers, drew hostile responses (including accusations of 'pro-Nazism') for daring to portray two would-be suicide bombers and to examine their motives. Parallels with Arendt's commitment to understanding Adolf Eichmann come to mind.
5. See Girard, 2001; Jürgensmeyer (ed.), 1992 and 2000; McKenna, 2002; Rapoport (2002) and Regensburger (ed) 2002, for articles arguing this case.

BIBLIOGRAPHY

Adams, Nicholas, 2004, 'Jürgen Moltmann' in Scott and Cavanaugh (eds), 2004, pp. 227–40.

Adorno, Theodor, and Horkheimer, Max, 1972 (1944), *Dialectic of Enlightenment*. Verso, London and NY.

Ahlers, Rolf, 1986, *The Barmen Theological Declaration of 1934: the Archaeology of a Confessional Text*. Edwin Mellen Press, Lewiston.

Alison, James, 1996, *Raising Abel: The Recovery of the Eschatological Imagination*. Crossroads, NY.

Arendt, Hannah, 1951, *The Origins of Totalitarianism*. Harcourt, NY.
1958, *The Human Condition*. University of Chicago Press.
1963, *Eichmann in Jerusalem: a Report on the Banality of Evil*. Faber and Faber, London.

Arens, Edmund, 1995 [1992], *Christopraxis: A Theology of Action*. Fortress Press, Minneapolis.
1997, 'Interruptions: Critical Theory and Political Theology between Modernity and Postmodernity', in Batstone *et al* (eds), 1997, pp. 222–42.

Ashley, J. M., 1998, *Interruptions: Mysticism, Politics and Theology in the Work of J. B. Metz*. University of Notre Dame.
1998, 'Introduction: Reading Metz' in Metz, 1998, *A Passion for God: The Mystical Political Dimension of Christianity*, pp. 7–21.
2004, 'Johann Baptist Metz' in Scott and Cavanaugh (eds), 2004, pp. 241–55.

Atkins, Margaret, 2001, '"God Resists the Proud" Augustine on the Writing of History', *The Month*, January 2001, 23–9.

Auden, W. H., 1991 [1976], *Collected Poems*, Faber and Faber, London.

Augustine of Hippo. *The City of God*. Translation by R. W. Dyson, Cambridge University Press.

Bartholomew, Craig, Chaplin, Jonathan and Song, Robert and Wolters, Al (eds), 2002, *A Royal Priesthood? A Dialogue with Oliver O'Donovan*. Paternoster Press, Cumbria.

Barth, Karl, 1965, *The German Church Conflict*. Lutterworth Press, London.

Batstone, D, Mendieta, E. *et al* (eds), 1997, *Liberation Theology, Postmodernity and the Americas*. Routledge, NY and London.

Baum, Gregory, 1984, 'The Holocaust and Political Theology', *Concilium* 174, 1984, 34–42.
1987, *Theology and Society*. Paulist Press, Mahwah, NJ.

1995, *Essays in Critical Theory*. Sheed and Ward, London.

1996, *The Church for Others: Protestant Theology in Communist East Germany*. W. B. Eerdmans, Grand Rapids, Mich.

Bauerschmidt, Frederick, 2004, 'Aquinas' in Scott and Cavanaugh (eds), 2004, pp. 48–61.

Bell, Daniel Jr., 2001, *Liberation Theology after the End of History: the Refusal to Cease Suffering*. Routledge, London.

Benedict XVI, Pope, 2006, 'Prepolitical Moral Foundations of a Free Republic', in de Vries and Sullivan (eds), 2006, pp. 261–8.

Benjamin, Walter, 1973 [1955], *Illuminations*. Fontana Press, London.

2002, *Selected Writings* (vols 1–4), ed. by Michael W. Jennings *et al*, Belknap Press of Harvard University Press, Cambridge and London.

Bernauer, J. W. (ed.), 1987, *Amor Mundi: Explorations in the Faith and Thought of Hannah Arendt*. Martinus Nijhoff, Boston.

1978, 'The Faith of Hannah Arendt: *Amor Mundi* and its Critique–Assimilation of Religious Experience' in Bernauer (ed.), 1987, pp. 1–28.

Bernstein, Richard J., 2002, *Radical Evil: A Philosophical Investigation*. Polity Press, Cambridge.

Bloch, Ernst, 1969 [1921], *Thomas Müntzer als Theologe der Revolution*. Suhrkamp, Frankfurt.

1971, *On Karl Marx*. Herder and Herder, NY.

1985 [1954–59], *The Principle of Hope*. Blackwell, Oxford. (Three volumes)

Boyle, 1987, 'Elusive Neighborliness: Hannah Arendt's Interpretation of Saint Augustine', in Bernauer (ed.), 1987, pp. 155–134.

Bradstock, Andrew, 2004, 'The Reformation' in Scott and Cavanaugh (eds), 2004, pp. 62–75.

Brady, Andrea, 2002, 'Grief work in a war economy', *Philosophy* 114 (July/August 2002), 7–12.

Bretherton, Luke, 2006, 'A New Establishment? Theological Politics and the Emerging Shape of Church–State Relations', *Political Theology* 7.3 (2006), 371–92.

Brown, Peter, 'The Political Ideas of St Augustine's *De Civitate Dei*' in B. Smalley (ed), *Trends in Medieval Political Thought*, Oxford University Press, 1965.

Browning, D. S., and Fiorenza, F. (eds), 1992, *Habermas, Modernity and Public Theology*. Crossroad, NY.

Brueggemann, Walter, 1978, *The Prophetic Imagination*. Fortress Press, Philadephia.

1993, *The Bible and Postmodern Imagination: Texts under Negotiation*. SCM Press, London.

2004, 'Scripture: Old Testament' in Scott and Cavanaugh (eds), 2004, pp. 7–20.

Burleigh, Michael, 2000, *The Third Reich: A New History*. Macmillan, London.

2005, *Earthly Powers: Religion and Politics in Europe from the Enlightenment to the Great War*. Harper, NY and London.

2006, *Sacred Causes: Religion and Politics from the European Dictators to Al Qaeda*. Harper, NY and London.

Burns, J. H. (ed.), 1988, *The Cambridge History of Medieval Political Thought* c.350–c.1450. Cambridge University Press.

Calvin, John, [1996] *On Civil Government* in Wooton (ed.), 1996, pp. 100–121.

[1991] *Institutes of the Christian Religion* in Höpfl, H. (ed.), 1991.

Cavanaugh, William T., 1995, '"A Fire Strong Enough To Consume the House": The Wars of Religion and the Rise of the State', *Modern Theology* 11.4, October 1995, 397–420.

1998, *Torture and Eucharist*. Blackwell, Oxford.

1999, 'The World in a Wafer: A Geography of the Eucharist as Resistance to Globalization', *Modern Theology*, 15.2 (1999), 181–98.

2002, *Theopolitical Imagination: Discovering the Liturgy as a Political Act in an Age of Global Consumerism*. T. & T. Clark, Edinburgh.

2004, 'Church' in Scott and Cavanaugh (eds), 2004, pp. 393–406.

2006, 'From One City to Two: Christian Reimagining of Political Space', *Political Theology* 7/3 (July 2006), 299–321.

Chadwick, Henry, 1988, 'Christian Doctrine' in Burns, J. (ed.), 1988, pp. 11–20.

Chopp, Rebecca, 1986, *The Praxis of Suffering*. Orbis, NY.

Cohn-Sherbok, Dan, 1987, *On Earth as it is in Heaven: Jews, Christians and Liberation Theology*. Maryknoll, Orbis, NY.

1989, *Holocaust Theology*. Lamp Press, London.

1996, *God and the Holocaust*. Gracewing, Leominster, Herefordshire.

1997, *The Crucified Jew: Twenty Centuries of Christian Anti-Semitism*. W. B. Eerdmans, Grand Rapids, Mich.

2002 (ed.), *Holocaust Theology: a Reader*. New York University Press, NY.

Cohen, Arthur, 1981, *The Tremendum: A Theological Interpretation of the Holocaust*. Crossroad, NY.

1984, 'In our Terrible Age: the *Tremendum* of the Jews', *Concilium*, 1984, 11–16.

Davis, Charles, 1978, *Theology and Political Society*. Cambridge University Press.

1993, *Religion and the Making of Society: Essays in Social Theology*. Cambridge University Press.

Davis, Creston, Milbank, John, Zizek Slavoj (eds), *Theology and the Political*. Duke University Press, London, 2005.

Detienne, Marcel, 2006, 'The Gods of Politics in Early Greek Cities', in de Vries and Sullivan (eds), 2006, pp. 91–101.

Dombrowski, Daniel A., 2001, *Rawls and Religion: the Case for Political Liberalism*. State University of New York Press, Albany.

Duquoc, Christian, 1986, 'The Forgiveness of God', *Concilium* 184 (1986), 35–44.

1996, 'Théologies Politiques et Eschatologie', *Recherche des Sciences Religieuses* 84/1 (1996), 67–86.

Ellis, Marc and Maduro, Otto (eds), 1989, *The Future of Liberation Theology: Essays in Honour of Gustavo Gutiérrez*. Orbis, NY.

Elshtain, Jean Bethke, 1995, *Augustine and the Limits of Politics*. University of Notre Dame Press, Indiana.

2003, *Just War Against Terror*. Basic Books, NY.

2004, 'Augustine', in Scott and Cavanaugh (eds), 2004, pp. 35–47.

Fiddes, Paul, 2000, *The Promised End: Eschatology in Theology and Literature*. Blackwell, Oxford.

Field, Lester L., 1998, *Liberty, Dominion and the Two Swords: On the Origins of Western Political Theology, 180–398*. University of Notre Dame Press, IN.

Figgis, J. N., 1931, *Studies of Political Thought from Gerson to Grotius*. Cambridge University Press.

Fiorenza, Elisabeth Schüssler and Tracy, David, (eds) 1984, 'The Holocaust as Interruption', *Concilium*, 174.

Firestone, C. L. and S. R. Palmquist (eds), 2006, *Kant and the New Philosophy of Religion*. Indiana University Press.

Fleming, Chris, 2004, *René Girard: Violence and Mimesis*. Polity Press, Cambridge.

Forrester, Duncan, 1988, *Theology and Politics*. Blackwell, Oxford.

Fox, Robin L., 1986, *Pagans and Christians*. Viking, London.

Freeman, Samuel (ed.), 2003, *The Cambridge Companion to Rawls*. Cambridge University Press, 2003.

Frend, W. H. C., 1965, *Martyrdom and Persecution in the Early Church: a Study of as Conflict from the Maccabees to Donatus*. Oxford University Press.

Galbraith, Elizabeth, 2006, 'Kant and "A Theodicy of Protest"', in Firestone, C. L. and S. R. Palmquist (eds), pp. 179–189.

Girard, René, 1977 [1972], *Violence and the Sacred*. Johns Hopkins University Press, Baltimore; Athlone, London.

and Mark Ansbach, 1992, 'Response' in Juergensmeyer, 1992, 141–48.

1996, *The Girard Reader*, ed. James Williams. Crossroad, NY.

2001, 'What we are witnessing is mimetic rivalry on a planetary scale', *Le Monde* (06/11/01): http://www.media.euro.apple.com/ en/livepage/

Gottwald, Norman (ed.), 1983, *The Bible and Liberation*. Orbis, NY.

Greene, Colin J. D., 2002, 'Revising Christendom: a Crisis of Legitimization' in Bartholomew *et al* (eds), pp. 314–40.

Gunton, Colin E., 1988, *The Actuality of Atonement; a Study of Metaphor, Rationalty and the Christian Tradition*. T. & T, Clark, Edinburgh.

Habermas, Jurgen, 2002, *Religion and Rationality: Essays on Reason, God, and Modernity* (edited by Eduardo Mendieta). MIT Press, Ma.

2006, 'On the Relations between the Secular Liberal State and Religion', in de Vries ands Sullivan (eds), 2006, pp. 251–60.

Hauerwas, Stanley, 1983, *The Peaceable Kingdom: a Primer in Christian ethics*. University of Notre Dame Press, Notre Dame.

1991, *After Christendom*. Abingdon Press, Nashville.

1994, *Dispatches from the Front: Theological Engagements with the Secular*. Duke University Press, Durham, NC.

2001, *The Hauerwas Reader*. Berkman John, and Michael Cartwright, Michael (eds), Duke University Press, Durham, NC.

Hauerwas, Stanley, and Rowe, Gilbert T., 1995, *In Good Company: the Church as Polis*. University of Notre Dame Press, Notre Dame, IN.

Havel, Vaclav, 1989, *Living in Truth*. Faber, London.

Hewitt, Marsha Aileen, 2004, 'Critical Theory' in Scott and Cavanaugh (eds), 2004, pp. 455–70.

Hobbes, Thomas, 1996 [1651] *Leviathan*. Oxford University Press.

Hollerich, Michael, 2006, 'Carl Schmitt' in Scott and Cavanaugh (eds), 2004, 107–22.

Höpfl, Harro (ed.), 1991, *Luther and Calvin on Secular Authority*. Cambridge University Press.

Hunsinger, George (ed. and tr.), 1976, *Karl Barth and Radical Politics*. Westminster Press, Philadelphia.

Insole, Christopher J., 2004/5, *The Politics of Human Frailty: a Theological Defence of Political Liberalism*. SCM Press, London, Notre Dame Press, IN.

2006, 'Discerning the Theopolitical: a Response to Cavanaugh's Reimagining of Political Space', *Political Theology* 7/3 (July 2006), 323–35.

Janz, Denis R., 1998, *World Christianity and Marxism*. Oxford University Press.

Jenson, Robert W., 'Eschatology' in Scott and Cavanaugh (eds), 2004, pp. 407–20.

Juergensmeyer, Mark (ed.), 1992, *Violence and the Sacred in the Modern World*. Cass, London.

2001, *Terror in the Mind of God*. University of California Press.

Kant, Immanuel, 1996 [1795], *Towards Perpetual Peace: a Philosophical Project*, tr. M. J. Gregor; Practical Philosophy/Immanuel Kant. University Press, Cambridge.

1992 [1791], 'On the miscarriage of all philosophical trials in theodicy', in *Works of Emmanuel Kant: Religion and Rational Theology*; Cambridge University Press, pp. 19-37.

Kantorowitz, Ernst H., 1997 [1957], *The King's Two Bodies: a Study in Medieval Political Thought*; pref. by W.C. Jordan. Princeton University Press.

Kaufman, Peter I., 1990, *Redeeming Politics*. Princeton University Press.

Kirwan, Michael, 2004, *Discovering Girard*. Darton, Longman and Todd, London.

2006, 'Learning to Say No: Does the Eschatological Reserve Have a Future?' *Political Theology* 7/3 (July 2006), 393–409.

Lakeland, Paul, 1990, *Theology and Critical Theory: the Discourse of the Church*. Abingdon Press, Nashville.

Lash, Nicholas, 1981, 'What might martyrdom mean?' in Horbury W. and McNeil B., eds, *Suffering and Martyrdom in the New Testament*. Cambridge University Press, pp. 183–98.

    1990, 'Friday, Saturday, Sunday', *New Blackfriars*, 71.936 (March 1990), 109–19.

LeFort, Claude, 2006, 'The Permanence of the Theologico-Political?' in de Vries and Sullivan (eds), 2006, pp. 148–87.

Lilla, Mark, 2007, *The Stillborn God: Religion, Politics, and the Modern West*. Knopf Publishing Group.

Löhfink, Gerhard, 1985. *Jesus and community: the Social Dimension of Christian Faith*; translated by John P. Galvin. SPCK, London.

1999, *Does God need the church?: Toward a Theology of the People of God*. Liturgical Press, Collegeville, Min.

Luther, Martin, [1991]. 'On Secular Authority' (1523) in Höpfl, H., 1991; also:

    [2005]. 'Temporal Authority: to what extent it should be obeyed' (1523) in *Basic Theological Writings*, ed. Timothy F. Lull (second edition). Fortress Press, Augsburg, pp. 429–59.

Markus, Robert A., 1971, *Saeculum: History and Society in the Theology of St. Augustine*. Cambridge University Press.

1988, 'Introduction: the West' and 'The Latin Fathers', in Burns, J. H. (ed.), 1988, pp. 83–122.

1989, 'Refusing to Bless the State: prophetic church and secular state', *New Blackfriars* 70: 1989, 372–79.

Marion, Jean-Luc, 1982, *God without Being*. University Press, Chicago.

Martinez, Gaspar, 2001, *Confronting the Mystery of God: Political, Liberation and Public Theologies*. Continuum, NY.

Máté-Tóth, András, 'A Theology of the Second World? Observations and Challenges', *Concilium* 2000.3: 27–35.

McCarthy, Thomas, 1991, 'Critical Theory and Political Theology: The Postulates of Communicative Reason', in *Ideals and Illusion: On Reconstruction and Deconstruction in Contemporary Critical Theory*. MIT, pp. 200–215.

McGrath, Alistair E., 1988, *Reformation Thought: an Introduction*. Blackwell, Oxford.

McKenna, Andrew, 2002, 'Scandal, Resentment, Idolatry: the Underground Psychology of Terrorism'. *Anthropoetics* 8: 1 (Spring/Summer 2002), posted 01/06/02:

    http://www.anthropoetics.ucla.edu/apo801/resent.htm

Metz, Johann Baptist, 1969, *Theology of the World*. Herder and Herder, NY.

1980, *Faith in History and Society: Toward a Practical Fundamental*

Theology. Burns and Oates, London.

1981, *The Emergent Church: the Future of Christianity in a Post-Bourgeois World*. SCM, London.

1984, 'Facing the Jews: Christian Theology after Auschwitz' in Fiorenza and Tracy (eds), *Concilium*, 174, 26–33.

1998, *A Passion for God: The Mystical Political Dimension of Christianity*, tr. J. Matthew Ashley, Paulist Press.

1999, *Love's Strategy: The Political Theology of Johann Baptist Metz*. Ed., with an introduction by John K. Downey. Harrisburg, PA: Trinity Press International.

Milbank, John, 1990, *Theology and Social Theory: Beyond Secular Reason*. Blackwell, Oxford.

1991, '"Postmodern Critical Augustinianism": a short summa in forty-two responses to unasked questions', *Modern Theology* 7:3, April 1991, 225–37.

1999, Milbank, John; Pickstock; Catherine, Ward, Graham (eds), *Radical Orthodoxy*. Routledge, London.

Moltmann, Jürgen, 1967, *Theology of Hope*. SCM, London.

1974, *The Crucified God*. SCM, London.

1975, *The Experiment Hope*. Fortress Press, Philadephia.

1984, *On Human Dignity: Political Theology and Ethics*. Fortress Press, Philadelphia.

1990, *The Way of Jesus Christ*. SCM, London.

1994, 'Covenant or Leviathan? Political Theology for Modern Times', *Scottish Journal of Theology* 47 (1994)

Moylan, Tom, 1997, 'Bloch against Bloch: the Theological Reception of *Das Prinzip Hoffnung* and the Liberation of the Utopian Function', in Jamie Owen Daniel & Tom Moylan (eds), *Not yet: Reconsidering Ernst Bloch*. Verso, London, 1997, pp. 96–121.

Neiman, Susan, 2002, *Evil in Modern Thought: an Alternative History of Philosophy*. Princeton University Press.

Nicholls, D., 1989, *Deity and Domination: Images of God and the State in the Nineteenth and Twentieth Centuries*. Routledge, London.

O'Donovan, Oliver, 1996, *The Desire of the Nations*. Cambridge University Press.

2002, 'Response to Colin Greene' in Bartholomew *et al* (eds), 2002, pp. 341–3.

2004, *Bonds of Imperfection: Christian Politics Past and Present*. Eerdmans, Cambridge.

O'Donovan, Oliver, and O'Donovan, Joan Lockwood, 1999. *From Irenaeus to Grotius: a Sourcebook in Christian Political Thought 1000–1625*. Eerdmans, Cambridge.

Ozment, Steven, 1980, *The Age of Reform: 1250–1550: An Intellectual and Religious History of the Late Medieval and Reformation Europe*. Yale University Press, New Haven and London.

Palaver, Wolfgang, 1995, 'Foundational Violence and Hannah Arendt's

Political Philosophy', *Paragrana* 4 (1995) 2, 166–76.

1996, 'Schmitt on *Nomos* and Space', *Telos* 106 (Winter 1996), 105–27.

1999, 'Biblisches Ethos und Politik' in *Theologische Ethik heute. Antworten für eine humane Zukunft. Hans Halter zum 60. Geburtstag*, eds Bondolfi, Alberto/Münk, Hans J. NZN Buchverlag, Zurich, pp. 353–70.

2007, 'Carl Schmitt's "Apocalyptic" Resistance against Global Civil War', in: Hamerton-Kelly, Robert (ed.), *Politics & Apocalypse*. Michigan State University Press, East Lancing, Michigan, pp. 69–94.

Petrella, Ivan, 2006, *The Future of Liberation Theology*. SCM, London

Peukert, Helmut, 1984, *Science, Action and Fundamental Theology: Towards a Theology of Communicative Action*. MIT, Cambridge.

1992, 'Enlightenment and Theology as Unfinished Projects', in Browning and Fiorenza (eds), 1992.

Pinnock, Sarah (ed.), 2003, *The Theology of Dorothy Soelle*. Trinity Press.

Plant, Raymond, 2001, *Politics, Theology and History*. Cambridge University Press.

Popescu, Alexandru, 2004, *Petre Tutea: Between Sacrifice and Suicide*. Ashgate, Aldershot.

Ramet, Sabrina Petra (ed.), 1990, *Catholicism and Politics in Communist Societies*. Duke University Press Durham, NC and London.

1992, *Protestantism and Politics in Eastern Europe and Russia: the Communist and Postcommunist eras*. Duke University Press, Durham, NC and London.

Rasmussen, A., 1995, *The Church as Polis: From Political Theology to Theological Politics as Exemplified by Jürgen Moltmann and Stanley Hauerwas*. University of Notre Dame Press, Indiana.

Rawls, John, 1999 [1971], *A Theory of Justice* (second edition), Oxford University Press.

Reardon, Bernard, 1985, *Religion in the Age of Romanticism*. Cambridge University Press.

Regensburger, Dietmar (ed.), 2002, Colloquium on Violence and Religion (COV&R), critical commentaries and articles on *Terrorism, Mimetic Rivalry and War* at: http://theol.uibk.ac.at/cover/war_against_terrorism.html

Reno, R. R., 1992, 'Christology in Political and Liberation Theology', *The Thomist* 56 (1992), 291–322.

2004, 'Stanley Hauerwas', in Scott and Cavanaugh (eds), 2004: 302–16.

Roach, Timothy, 1987, 'Enspirited Words and Deeds' in Bernauer (ed.), 1987, pp. 59–81.

Rose, Gillian, 1981, *Hegel contra Sociology*. Athlone, London.

1992, *The Broken Middle: Out of our Ancient Society*, Blackwell, Oxford.

1993, *Judaism and Modernity*. Blackwell, Oxford.

1996, *Mourning Becomes the Law*. Blackwell, Oxford.

Roberts, Richard H.,1990, *Hope and its Hieroglyph: A Critical Decipherment of Ernst Bloch's Principle of Hope*. Scholar's Press,

Atlanta, GA.

Rouner, L. S. (ed.), 1986, *Civil Religion and Political Society*. University of Notre Dame Press, Indiana.

Rowland, Christopher, 1988, *Radical Christianity*. Polity Press, Cambridge.

(ed.), 1998, *The Cambridge Companion to Liberation Theology*. Cambridge University Press.

2004, 'Scripture: New Testament', in Scott and Cavanaugh (eds) 2004, pp. 21–34.

Rubenstein, Richard, 1966, *After Auschwitz*. Bobbs Merrill.

Rubenstein, Richard, and Roth, J, 1987, *Approaches to Auschwitz*. SCM Press, London.

de Ste Croix, G.E.M., 1963, 'Why were the Early Christians Persecuted?, *Past and Present* (26), 6–38.

Scherer, Matthew, 2006, 'Saint John: The Miracle of Secular Reason', in de Vries and Sullivan (eds), 2006, 341–62.

Schillebeeckx, Edward, 1974, *The Understanding of Faith: Interpretation and Criticism*. Seabury, NY.

Schmitt, Carl, 2005 [1934], *Political Theology: Four Chapters on the Concept of Sovereignty*. University Press, Chicago.

Scholder, Klaus, 1985,1988, *The Churches and the Third Reich* (2 vols). SCM, London.

Schwager, Raymund, 1987 [1978], *Must There be Scapegoats?: Violence and Redemption in the Bible*. Harper & Row, San Francisco.

1992, [1990], *Jesus and the Drama of Salvation*. Crossroad, NY.

Scott, Peter, and Cavanaugh William T. (eds), 2004, *The Blackwell Companion to Political Theology*. Blackwell, Oxford.

Segundo, Juan Luis, 1974, 'Capitalism – Socialism: A Theological Crux', *Concilium* 96 (1974), 105–23.

Shanks, Andrew, 1991, *Hegel's Political Theology*. Cambridge University Press.

Shaw, B. D., 1996, 'Body/Power/Identity: Passions of the Martyrs', *Journal of Early Christian Studies* 4:3, 269–312.

Sölle, Dorothee, 1967, *Christ the Representative*. SCM, London.

1975, *Suffering*, Darton, Longman and Todd, London.

Steiner, George, 1989, 1985, *Antigones*. Clarendon Press, Oxford.

1989, *Real Presences: Is There Anything in What We Say?* Faber and Faber, London.

1992, *Heidegger*. Fontana, London.

1996, *No Passion Spent: Essays 1978–1996*, Faber and Faber, London.

1999 [1974], *Nostalgia for the Absolute*, House of Anansi Press, Canada.

Stephenson, John R., 1981, 'The Two Governments and the Two Kingdoms in Luther's Thought', *Scottish Journal of Theology*, 34: 321–37.

Stark, Rodney, 2004, *For the Glory of God: How Monotheism Led to*

Reformations, Science, Witch-Hunts, and the End of Slavery. Princeton University Press.

Thompson, E. P., 1993, *Witness Against the Beast, William Blake and the Moral Law*. Cambridge CP; The New Press, New York. 1993

Tomka, Miklós, and Zulehner, Paul M. (eds) 2000, 'Religion During and After Communism. *Concilium* 2000.3.

Tracy, David, 1981, *The Analogical Imagination*. Crossroad, NY.

1994, 'The Return of God in Contemporary Theology', in *On Naming the Present: God, Hermeneutics and Church*. Orbis NY, pp. 36–46.

Ulmen, Gary, 1996, 'Schmitt as a Scapegoat: Reply to Palaver', *Telos*, 106 (Winter 1996), 128–38.

Volf, Miroslav, 1996, *Exclusion and Embrace: A Theological Exploration of Identity, Otherness and Reconciliation*. Abingdon Press, Nashville.

de Vries, Hent, and Sullivan, Lawrence E. (eds), 2006, *Political Theologies: Public Religions in a Post-Secular World*. Fordham University Press.

Ward, Graham, 2000, *Theology and Contemporary Critical Theory* (second edition). Macmillan, London.

Williams, Rowan, 1987, 'Politics and the Soul: A Reading of the City of God', *Milltown Studies* 19/20, 55–72.

2000, 'Theological Integrity' in *On Christian Theology*. Blackwell, Oxford, pp. 3–15.

Willmer, Haddon, 2004, 'Karl Barth' in Scott and Cavanaugh (eds), 2004, pp. 123–35.

Wooton, David (ed.), 1996, *Modern Political Thought: Readings from Machiavelli to Nietzsche*. Hackett Publishing, IN.

Yoder, John H., 1994, *The Politics of Jesus* (second edition). Eerdmans, Grand Rapids.

Zamoyski, Adam, 1999, *Holy Madness: Romantics, Patriots and Revolutionaries 1776–1871*. Phoenix Press, London.

Zizek, Slavoj, 2000, *The Fragile Absolute, or Why the Christian Legacy is worth Fighting For*. Verso, London.

2001, *On Belief*, London: Routledge, NY.

2003, *The Puppet and the Dwarf*. Routledge, NY.

INDEX